KEEP MORE OF WHAT YOU EARN

ASSET PROTECTION EXPLAINED

Legal Planning Strategies to Safeguard What You've Built

NGOZI E. BOLIN, ESQ.

For permission contact the publisher at Pantraxxa.com.

Cover by Jim Olen.

Legal Disclaimer

Important Notice to Readers

THIS BOOK IS PROVIDED FOR INFORMATIONAL AND EDUCATIONAL PURPOSES ONLY AND IS NOT INTENDED TO CONSTITUTE LEGAL ADVICE.

No Attorney-Client Relationship

The information contained in this book does not create an attorney-client relationship between the author, publisher, and any reader or user of this material. Reading this book, accessing its content, or using any information contained herein does not establish any professional relationship or create any duties or obligations on the part of the author or publisher to any reader.

Not a Substitute for Professional Legal Counsel

The content of this book is general in nature and may not apply to your specific situation. Legal matters are highly fact-specific and jurisdiction-dependent. Laws, regulations, court decisions, and legal interpretations change frequently and vary significantly between jurisdictions. Nothing in this book should be used as a substitute for competent legal advice from a licensed attorney in your jurisdiction who is familiar with the specific facts of your case.

YOU SHOULD ALWAYS CONSULT WITH A QUALIFIED ATTORNEY BEFORE MAKING ANY LEGAL DECISIONS OR TAKING ANY ACTION BASED ON INFORMATION CONTAINED IN THIS BOOK.

Accuracy and Currency of Information

While every effort has been made to ensure the accuracy of the information contained in this book at the time of publication, the author and publisher make no representations or warranties regarding the completeness, accuracy, reliability, or currency of the information provided. Laws and legal precedents change constantly, and what may have been accurate at the time of writing may no longer be current or applicable.

The information in this book reflects the law as understood by the author as of the publication date. Legal developments occurring after the publication date are not reflected in this material.

Jurisdictional Limitations

Laws vary significantly among different countries, states, provinces, and localities. The information in this book may be based primarily on the laws of specific jurisdictions and may not be applicable in your location. Local laws should always be consulted, and local legal counsel should be retained for matters involving specific jurisdictions.

Limitation of Liability

TO THE FULLEST EXTENT PERMITTED BY LAW, THE AUTHOR, PUBLISHER, EDITORS, CONTRIBUTORS, AND DISTRIBUTORS OF THIS BOOK DISCLAIM ALL LIABILITY FOR ANY LOSS, DAMAGE, OR INJURY ARISING FROM THE USE OF OR RELIANCE ON THE INFORMATION CONTAINED HEREIN, WHETHER SUCH LIABILITY ARISES IN CONTRACT, TORT, STRICT LIABILITY, OR OTHERWISE.

This limitation applies to all damages or injuries, including but not limited to:

- Direct, indirect, incidental, and consequential damages
- Lost profits or business opportunities
- Legal fees and costs

- Punitive or exemplary damages
- Any other economic or non-economic losses

No Warranties

THIS BOOK IS PROVIDED "AS IS" WITHOUT WARRANTY OF ANY KIND, EXPRESS OR IMPLIED, INCLUDING BUT NOT LIMITED TO WARRANTIES OF MERCHANTABILITY, FITNESS FOR A PARTICULAR PURPOSE, OR NON-INFRINGEMENT.

Individual Circumstances

Every legal situation is unique. The examples, case studies, and scenarios presented in this book are for illustrative purposes only and may not reflect the full complexity of actual legal situations. The outcomes described may not be achievable in your circumstances, and past results do not guarantee future outcomes.

Updates and Revisions

The author and publisher are under no obligation to update or revise the content of this book to reflect changes in the law or legal practice. Readers are encouraged to verify all information with current legal sources and qualified legal professionals.

Third-Party Content and References

Any references to third-party materials, websites, organizations, or publications are provided for informational purposes only and do not constitute an endorsement of such materials or entities. The author and publisher are not responsible for the content, accuracy, or availability of third-party materials.

Compliance with Professional Rules

Readers who are legal professionals should ensure that their use of any information in this book complies with applicable professional conduct rules, ethical requirements, and licensing obligations in their jurisdiction.

Intellectual Property Notice

This book is protected by copyright and other intellectual property laws. The information provided is for personal, educational, and non-commercial use only. Any commercial use, reproduction, or distribution requires express written permission from the copyright holder.

Severability

If any portion of this disclaimer is held to be invalid or unenforceable, the remaining portions shall remain in full force and effect.

BY READING AND USING THIS BOOK, YOU ACKNOWLEDGE THAT YOU HAVE READ, UNDERSTOOD, AND AGREE TO BE BOUND BY THE TERMS OF THIS DISCLAIMER.

IF YOU DO NOT AGREE WITH THESE TERMS, DO NOT USE THIS BOOK.

Contents

Introduction

Why Asset Protection Matters to You

Most people don't think about asset protection until it's too late.

Maybe it's a car accident where someone gets seriously injured. A customer who slips and falls at your business. A partner who sues after a deal goes bad. A divorce that turns hostile. A tenant who gets hurt on your rental property. A complaint filed against your professional license. Or a market downturn that leaves you owing more than you expected to creditors you never saw coming.

When these moments arrive, the conversation changes instantly. It's no longer "How do I protect what I have?" It becomes "Why didn't I do something about this sooner?"

This book exists to help you answer that question *before* it's asked.

Asset protection isn't about being paranoid, hiding money, or trying to cheat anyone. It's about understanding how liability actually works in America today and using completely legal, ethical strategies to reduce unnecessary financial risk. Think about it like this: You buy car insurance before an accident happens. You install smoke detectors before there's a fire. You get a prenup before marriage problems arise. Asset protection is the same kind of forward-thinking risk management: preparing for problems you genuinely hope never occur.

Yet most Americans remain confused about asset protection, and it's not their fault. The topic is often:

- Wrapped in legal jargon that's impossible to understand
- Marketed aggressively by companies making unrealistic promises
- Dismissed as "only for rich people"
- Confused with illegal activities like tax evasion or hiding money
- Oversimplified into thinking one LLC or trust will magically protect everything

This book cuts through all of that confusion.

Why This Book Was Written

Let's be direct: The modern American legal and financial system has become increasingly hostile to anyone trying to build and keep personal wealth.

Lawsuits are everywhere. Medical malpractice claims, car accidents, slip-and-falls, business disputes, employment claims, contract disagreements, the list goes on. Damage awards are higher than ever. And here's what most people don't realize: liability can arise from completely ordinary, everyday activities:

- Owning a rental property
- Running a small business
- Serving on a nonprofit board
- Practicing as a doctor, lawyer, accountant, or consultant
- Getting into a car accident
- Having a swimming pool in your backyard
- Posting something online that someone finds offensive

At the same time, your wealth has never been easier to find, freeze, and take. Bank accounts are electronically traceable. Property records are public. Court orders can lock down assets in hours. Once a creditor or plaintiff has a judgment against you, the tools they have to collect are powerful and sophisticated.

Yet almost nobody teaches regular people how asset protection actually works.

Law schools focus on abstract theory that doesn't help real families. Financial advisors often avoid the subject entirely because they're not trained in it or worried about liability. Online information swings wildly between oversimplified blog posts ("Just get an LLC!") and aggressive marketing from companies promising "bulletproof" or "lawsuit-proof" solutions that don't actually exist in the real world.

The result? Most people either do nothing at all, or they do the wrong things at the wrong time, usually after it's already too late.

This book is designed to be completely different.

What You'll Learn in This Book

This is a plain-English guide written specifically for everyday consumers: business owners, professionals, real estate investors, and families who want to understand:

✓ **What asset protection really is** (and what it definitely isn't)
✓ **Which tools and strategies are legitimate** and which are scams or myths
✓ **What actually works, what doesn't, and most importantly, why**
✓ **How U.S. domestic strategies compare to offshore options**
✓ **How to think clearly and strategically about risk** instead of reacting emotionally when you're scared
✓ **How timing affects everything** (and why acting now is crucial)
✓ **Real-world examples** of what works and what fails in court

You don't need a law degree to read this book. You don't need to be wealthy. You don't need any special background in finance or legal structures.

You only need to care about protecting what you've worked hard to build.

Let's Clear Something Up Right Now: Asset Protection Is NOT About Hiding Money

Before we go any further, we need to address the elephant in the room.

Asset protection is NOT:

Tax evasion or avoiding taxes you legally owe
Hiding money from the IRS, your spouse, or the courts
Lying to banks, creditors, or judges
Transferring assets after you've already been sued

Using fake names, nominees, or shell companies to conceal ownership
"Getting away with something" illegal or unethical

Those actions are crimes. They're also stupid. When discovered (and they almost always are) the consequences are catastrophic: criminal charges, contempt of court, asset seizure, massive fines, even prison time.

True asset protection works completely within the law. It relies on transparency, proper documentation, and full compliance with tax and reporting requirements. And here's the key: **it's most effective when you implement it *before* any problems arise.**

Courts have extremely broad powers to reverse last-minute asset transfers, pierce through structures set up in bad faith, and punish people who try to cheat the system. This book will not teach you how to hide assets or break the law because those strategies almost always fail spectacularly.

Instead, this book will teach you **how the legal system actually works** so you can use it properly and effectively.

The Core Idea: It's About Risk, Not How Rich You Are

Here's one of the biggest misconceptions people have about asset protection:

Most people think asset protection is about **how much money you have.**

That's wrong.

Asset protection is actually about **how much risk you carry.**

Think about these examples:

A **surgeon** with a net worth of $500,000 may face far more legal exposure than a retired investor with $5 million in index funds.

A **small business owner** with employees, customers, and commercial property may be more vulnerable to lawsuits than a software engineer earning the same income working for someone else.

A **landlord** with a single rental property faces more potential liability than someone with a diversified stock portfolio worth twice as much.

Your exposure to lawsuits doesn't come from your wealth. It comes from your activities.

The goal of asset protection is to **align your legal structure with your risk profile**, not your ego, not your net worth, but your actual, real-world risk exposure.

Throughout this book, we'll keep returning to this simple but powerful concept:

You don't protect assets from the world. You isolate risk from assets.

Once you truly understand that distinction, everything else starts to make sense.

Domestic vs. Offshore: Let's Talk About It Without the Hype or Fear

Few topics in asset protection generate more confusion (and more emotional reactions) than offshore planning.

Some people immediately dismiss anything "offshore" as shady, illegal, or un-American. Others believe offshore structures make your assets completely untouchable and solve all problems.

Both views are wrong.

Here's the reality: **Offshore asset protection exists because different countries have different legal systems.** Some countries make it easier for creditors and plaintiffs to sue you and take your assets. Others place much higher burdens on claimants, making it harder and more expensive for them to pursue you.

Understanding these differences isn't unpatriotic. It's not sneaky. It's **pragmatic.**

Think about it: Corporations choose where to incorporate based on legal advantages all the time. Banks operate in multiple jurisdictions. Governments compete for business by offering favorable laws. This is standard international commerce and finance.

That said, offshore strategies are not right for everyone. They involve:

- Higher setup and maintenance costs
- Stricter compliance and reporting requirements
- More complexity

- Potential tax implications that must be carefully managed

This book will present offshore planning **objectively** (no hype, no scare tactics) so you can make an informed decision about whether it makes sense for your specific situation or not.

What This Book Will Do (and What It Won't)

This Book WILL:

✓ Explain asset protection concepts in clear, everyday language
✓ Compare the most common tools and structures honestly
✓ Show you the strengths, weaknesses, and limitations of each strategy
✓ Help you think strategically about your personal risk exposure
✓ Prepare you to have intelligent, informed conversations with attorneys and advisors
✓ Give you real-world examples and case studies
✓ Help you avoid common mistakes and scams

This Book Will NOT:

✗ Give you personalized legal advice (every situation is different)
✗ Replace the need for a qualified attorney or tax professional
✗ Promise guaranteed outcomes (no strategy is 100% bulletproof)
✗ Encourage aggressive, abusive, or legally questionable tactics
✗ Tell you exactly what to do without knowing your circumstances

Think of this book as a detailed map, not turn-by-turn directions to your exact address. The goal is to give you deep understanding so you can make informed decisions, not to replace professional guidance tailored to your specific life.

The Most Important Lesson: Timing Beats Complexity Every Time

If you take away only one thing from this entire book, let it be this:

Timing matters more than strategy.

A simple structure (even something basic like a properly set up LLC) implemented early, before any problems arise, will almost always provide more protection than the most sophisticated, expensive, complex plan created after trouble appears.

Why?

Because courts look closely at **intent.** They ask questions like:

- When did you set this up?
- What was happening in your life at that time?
- Were you already being sued or threatened?
- Were you trying to hide assets from a specific creditor?

Creditors look for shortcuts, ways to argue that you set up a structure in "bad faith" just to defraud them. Judges are extremely skeptical of last-minute maneuvers, especially when someone gets sued on Tuesday and transfers all their assets on Wednesday.

The law calls this a "fraudulent transfer," and courts will reverse it.

But if you set up proper protection today, years before any lawsuit or claim, courts will generally respect your planning. You're simply being prudent and responsible.

By reading this book now (before a lawsuit, before a claim, before a crisis) you're already ahead of 95% of people.

Who This Book Is For

This book is written specifically for:

Business Owners and Entrepreneurs
If you operate any kind of business (from a solo consulting practice to a growing company with employees) you face liability every single day. Customer disputes, employee claims, contract disagreements, vendor issues, regulatory problems... the list is endless.

Real Estate Investors
Own rental properties? Flip houses? Develop land? You face premises liability, tenant lawsuits, contractor disputes, and more. Real estate is one of the highest-risk activities for personal liability.

Professionals with Liability Exposure
Doctors, lawyers, accountants, consultants, architects, engineers, therapists, financial advisors: if you can be sued for malpractice or professional errors, you need to understand asset protection.

Executives and Board Members
Serving on corporate boards or in executive roles? You can be personally sued for business decisions. Director and officer insurance helps, but it doesn't cover everything.

High-Income Earners
The more you make, the bigger target you are. Even if you have low liability exposure, your earning power itself is an asset that needs protection.

Families Building Generational Wealth
Want to pass assets to your children and grandchildren? Proper planning protects wealth not just from your creditors, but from your heirs' future creditors, divorces, and poor decisions.

Anyone Who Wants Peace of Mind Instead of Panic
You've worked hard for what you have. You don't want one bad event (one lawsuit, one accident, one business failure) to wipe out everything you've built.

You Don't Need to Implement Everything in This Book

Here's something important to understand: **Most people reading this book shouldn't implement every strategy discussed.**

Asset protection isn't one-size-fits-all. The goal is not "maximum protection at all costs." The goal is **appropriate protection for your life as it actually exists.**

A young professional just starting out needs different planning than a business owner with 50 employees. A real estate investor with 20 rental properties needs different structures than someone with one vacation home. A surgeon faces different risks than a software developer.

This book will help you understand:

- Which strategies make sense for you
- Which are overkill
- Which are worth the cost and complexity
- Which can wait until later

Good asset protection is proportional. It matches the level of protection to the level of risk.

A Final Word Before We Begin

Asset protection is not about fear. It's about clarity.

When your financial and legal affairs are structured properly:

✓ You worry less about lawsuits and claims
✓ You make better business and investment decisions
✓ You can take calculated risks without exposing everything you own
✓ You sleep better knowing one bad event won't undo years or decades of hard work
✓ You have peace of mind that your family is protected

That peace of mind isn't reserved for the ultra-wealthy or financially sophisticated. It's available to anyone willing to learn how the system actually works and plan accordingly.

That's what this book is about. Not scare tactics. Not false promises. Not get-rich-quick schemes or magical solutions.

Just honest, practical, clear information that empowers you to make smart decisions about protecting what matters most.

Let's begin.

PART I: What Asset Protection Really Is

1

Why Asset Protection Matters

Asset protection is not about expecting the worst. It is about recognizing reality.

Modern America is an environment where legal and financial risk is not reserved for the reckless, the unethical, or the ultra-wealthy. It is part of ordinary life. You can do everything "right" and still find yourself facing a lawsuit, a creditor claim, or a financial exposure you never anticipated. When that happens, the structures you put in place (or failed to put in place) often determine whether the damage is limited or devastating.

This chapter explains why asset protection matters, who is most exposed, and how avoidable losses occur every day, not because people were irresponsible, but because they misunderstood risk.

The Reality of Lawsuits, Creditors, and Financial Risk in Modern America

The United States has one of the most active legal systems in the world. Litigation is common, damages can be high, and liability often extends further than people expect.

You do not need to commit wrongdoing to be sued. You only need to be perceived as having responsibility, or assets.

Where Lawsuits Come From

Lawsuits arise from situations most of us encounter in everyday life:

Business disputes: Disagreements with partners, vendors, or competitors can escalate quickly into formal legal action.

Customer or client injuries: If someone gets hurt on your property or while using your services, you may be held responsible regardless of fault.

Employment claims: Allegations of wrongful termination, discrimination, or workplace injury can result in substantial judgments.

Professional errors or allegations: Even if you followed proper procedures, the perception of a mistake can lead to costly litigation.

Tenant and property-related incidents: Rental properties come with risks ranging from slip-and-fall accidents to disputes over security deposits.

Auto accidents: A single car accident can result in claims that exceed your insurance coverage, especially if serious injuries are involved.

Contract disagreements: Business deals that go wrong often end up in court, with one party seeking damages from the other.

Personal guarantees: When you personally guarantee a business loan or lease, you put your personal assets on the line.

Divorce and family disputes: Marital dissolution can expose assets to division or claims you never anticipated.

Many of these risks come not from intentional conduct, but from ordinary participation in economic life. You do not have to be careless or unethical to face financial exposure. You simply have to be involved in activities that carry inherent risk.

The Transparency of Modern Wealth

At the same time, modern financial systems make wealth easier to identify and access than ever before. Bank accounts, brokerage accounts, real estate records, and business ownership are increasingly transparent. Public databases, social media, and financial disclosure requirements mean that determining who has assets and where those assets are located is simpler than it has ever been.

Once a judgment is obtained, creditors have powerful tools to locate, freeze, and seize assets quickly. Wage garnishments, bank levies, liens on real estate, and seizure of business interests are all legally available remedies. In many states, creditors can even force the sale of your primary residence or retirement accounts under certain circumstances.

The result is a simple truth: If you have assets and any form of legal exposure, you are a potential target.

Asset protection exists because ignoring this reality does not make it disappear.

Who Is Most Exposed?

While anyone can face financial risk, some groups are consistently more exposed than others. Importantly, exposure is driven by activity, not morality or intelligence. Being at risk does not mean you have done anything wrong. It means you are engaged in activities that create liability exposure.

Business Owners and Entrepreneurs

Business owners face risk from multiple directions at once:

Customers: Product liability, service failures, and customer injuries can all result in claims against your business and potentially against you personally.

Vendors: Disputes over payment terms, quality of goods, or contract performance can lead to litigation.

Employees: Workplace injuries, discrimination claims, wage disputes, and wrongful termination allegations are common sources of business litigation.

Partners: Disagreements between co-owners can result in costly legal battles that threaten the business and personal assets.

Regulators: Compliance failures, licensing issues, and regulatory investigations can result in fines, penalties, and civil actions.

Lenders: Defaulting on business debt, especially when personal guarantees are involved, can put personal assets at risk.

Even small businesses can face large claims, particularly in industries involving physical locations, services, or public interaction. A food service business, a gym, a daycare center, or a construction company all carry heightened liability exposure simply due to the nature of their operations.

Personal guarantees, co-mingled finances, or poorly structured entities often turn business problems into personal financial disasters. Many entrepreneurs assume that "having an LLC" is enough. In reality, the way that LLC is used matters far more than the fact that it exists. If you treat your LLC like a personal piggy bank, fail to maintain corporate formalities, or personally guarantee every obligation, the legal separation between you and your business may disappear when you need it most.

Professionals With Licensing or Fiduciary Duties

Doctors, dentists, lawyers, accountants, architects, engineers, and financial professionals operate under heightened standards of care. These professions require specialized knowledge, and with that comes increased responsibility. Allegations (whether justified or not) can result in lawsuits, licensing issues, and personal exposure.

A single malpractice claim can upend a career. Even if you are ultimately vindicated, the cost of defense, the stress of litigation, and the potential damage to your reputation can be substantial. Professional liability insurance is essential, but it is not unlimited. Verdicts can exceed policy limits, and policies do not cover every type of claim. Some claims, such as those involving intentional misconduct or criminal behavior, may not be covered at all.

Asset protection planning addresses what happens after insurance is exhausted or when insurance does not apply. It creates a secondary layer of protection that ensures a single professional mistake does not wipe out a lifetime of savings.

Real Estate Investors and Landlords

Real estate creates predictable risk. Properties involve physical structures, tenants, contractors, and the general public. Each of these creates potential liability:

Slip-and-fall claims: A visitor or tenant injured on your property may sue for medical expenses, lost wages, and pain and suffering.

Tenant injuries: Defective appliances, structural failures, or hazardous conditions can result in serious injury claims.

Mold, habitability, and disclosure disputes: Failure to maintain livable conditions or disclose known defects can lead to lawsuits and penalties.

Contractor issues: Disputes over construction work, mechanic's liens, and contractor negligence can all create liability.

Environmental claims: Contamination, lead paint, asbestos, and other environmental hazards can result in costly remediation and legal action.

Owning property directly in your personal name is one of the most common (and avoidable) mistakes. A single incident at one property can expose not only that property, but everything else you own. If you own five rental properties in your personal name and a tenant is injured at one of them, all five properties (plus your bank accounts, retirement savings, and other assets) may be at risk in the resulting lawsuit.

High-Income Earners and Visible Wealth Holders

You do not need to be wealthy to be targeted. You need to appear collectible.

High-income professionals, executives, and individuals with visible assets often attract claims simply because there is something to pursue. In legal circles, this is sometimes referred to as the "deep pockets" effect. Plaintiffs and their attorneys are more likely to pursue claims aggressively when they believe there are assets available to satisfy a judgment.

In many cases, the presence of assets changes the behavior of plaintiffs and attorneys alike. A case that might be settled quickly for a modest sum when the defendant appears to have limited resources may be pursued more aggressively when the defendant is perceived as wealthy. This is not always fair, but it is a reality of the legal system.

Visible wealth, such as luxury homes, expensive cars, or public business ownership, can also attract unwanted attention. Social media posts, public records, and professional profiles can all signal to potential claimants that you are a worthwhile target.

Real-World Examples of Avoidable Losses

Asset protection failures rarely come from dramatic mistakes. They come from small, common assumptions that go unexamined. These examples illustrate how ordinary people, doing ordinary things, can suffer extraordinary losses simply because they did not plan ahead.

Example 1: The "Simple" Rental Property

A couple purchases a rental property in their personal names. They view it as a straightforward investment. They have landlord insurance, they maintain the property reasonably well, and they screen their tenants. Everything seems fine.

Then a tenant is injured due to a maintenance issue. Perhaps a stair railing gives way, or a water heater malfunctions. The injury is serious. The tenant requires surgery and extensive rehabilitation. The tenant's attorney files a lawsuit seeking damages for medical expenses, lost wages, pain and suffering, and punitive damages.

The lawsuit exceeds the couple's insurance limits. The insurance company pays the policy maximum, but a substantial judgment remains. Because the property was owned personally, the claim reaches beyond the rental property itself:

Bank accounts: The couple's checking and savings accounts are frozen and eventually seized to satisfy part of the judgment.

Investment accounts: Brokerage accounts, mutual funds, and retirement savings become targets for collection.

Other real estate: The couple's primary residence and a second rental property are now at risk. Liens are placed on both properties.

Future income: Wage garnishments are put in place, reducing the couple's take-home pay for years.

The loss was not caused by malice or recklessness. The couple did not intentionally harm anyone. They simply owned the property in a way that exposed everything they had to a single incident. If the rental property had been owned by a properly structured LLC, the couple's personal assets would have been protected. The claim would have been limited to the assets of the LLC (primarily the rental property itself) rather than reaching into their personal wealth.

Example 2: The Successful Small Business Owner

A business owner operates a thriving retail store through an LLC. On paper, the business is properly structured. The LLC was formed with the state, an operating agreement was signed, and the business has its own tax identification number.

But in practice, the owner:

Uses a single bank account: Business income and personal expenses flow through the same account. The separation between business and personal finances is blurred.

Signs personal guarantees routinely: Every lease, loan, and major vendor agreement includes a personal guarantee. The owner views this as normal and necessary to get favorable terms.

Treats company money as personal money: The owner withdraws cash from the business whenever needed, without formal documentation or regard for proper distributions.

When a dispute arises with a customer, a lawsuit is filed. During the legal process, the opposing attorney examines the business structure and discovers the lack of separation between the owner and the business. The attorney argues that the LLC is a sham, that the owner has treated it as a mere extension of personal finances, and that the corporate veil should be pierced.

The court agrees. It determines that the separation between owner and business is illusory. Personal assets become fair game. The judgment is entered not just against the LLC, but against the owner personally. The business bank account, the owner's personal savings, the family home, and investment accounts are all now exposed.

The LLC existed, but it did not protect. The business owner assumed that simply forming an LLC was enough. In reality, the way the LLC was used mattered far more than the fact that it existed. Proper maintenance, financial separation, and adherence to corporate formalities are not optional. They are essential to ensuring that the legal protection the LLC is supposed to provide actually holds up when challenged.

Example 3: The Professional Who "Had Insurance"

A licensed professional (a physician, attorney, or accountant) carries malpractice insurance and assumes that coverage is sufficient. The professional has never been sued, has a good reputation, and operates carefully and ethically.

Then a claim arises. Perhaps a patient has an unexpected outcome, a client suffers a financial loss, or a regulatory issue leads to allegations of professional negligence. The professional's insurance company provides a defense, but the case goes to trial. The jury returns a verdict in favor of the plaintiff.

The verdict is significant. It exceeds the professional's malpractice insurance policy limits by a substantial margin. The insurance company pays the policy maximum, but the excess judgment (the amount beyond the policy limits) becomes the personal responsibility of the professional.

The excess judgment follows the individual personally for years, impacting savings, investments, and retirement planning. Wage garnishments reduce take-home pay. Liens are placed on real estate. Retirement accounts may be seized depending on state law. The professional, who believed that insurance was enough, now faces financial devastation.

Insurance is critical. It is the first line of defense. But it is not asset protection by itself. Insurance has limits. It does not cover every type of claim. And when a judgment exceeds policy limits, the shortfall becomes a personal liability. Asset protection planning addresses what happens when insurance is not enough.

These examples are not rare. They happen every day. In most cases, the individuals involved believed they were protected until they were not. They made reasonable assumptions, followed what seemed like common sense, and still suffered significant losses. The difference between protection and exposure often comes down to structure, planning, and foresight.

Asset Protection vs. Fear-Based Planning

One of the greatest obstacles to effective asset protection is fear. Fear can be paralyzing, and it can also lead to poor decisions.

Fear-based planning sounds like:

"I need to hide everything." This mindset leads to secrecy, concealment, and strategies that may cross ethical or legal lines.

"The system is out to get me." This belief fosters distrust, paranoia, and overly aggressive tactics that often backfire.

"I need something bulletproof." This desire for absolute protection leads to unrealistic expectations and schemes that promise more than they can deliver.

"I'll deal with this if something happens." This procrastination leads to inaction until it is too late to implement effective protection.

Fear leads to bad decisions. It can result in:

Overly aggressive structures: Strategies that are too complex, too risky, or too disconnected from legitimate purposes. These often fail under scrutiny.

Illegal or unethical behavior: Fraudulent transfers, concealment of assets, lying to creditors, or other conduct that can result in criminal charges and civil penalties.

Poor timing: Implementing asset protection only after a claim has arisen, when transfers can be easily challenged and reversed.

Paralysis and inaction: Becoming so overwhelmed by fear that no planning occurs at all, leaving you completely exposed.

True asset protection is not reactive. It is not driven by panic or worst-case fantasies. It is driven by probability, proportionality, and planning.

Good asset protection asks:

What risks do I realistically face? Not every risk is equally likely. Understanding your specific exposure (whether from business operations, professional practice, real estate holdings, or other activities) allows you to plan appropriately.

Which assets are exposed to those risks? Not all assets are equally vulnerable. Some assets (like retirement accounts in certain states) may already be protected by law. Others (like real estate owned personally) may be completely exposed.

What level of protection is appropriate, not excessive? Effective planning is proportional. You do not need a $50,000 offshore trust if your total assets are $200,000. You do not need ten separate LLCs if you own two rental properties. The goal is protection that fits your situation.

How can I reduce risk without losing control of my life? Asset protection should not make your life more complicated than necessary. The best strategies are those that provide meaningful protection while allowing you to live, work, and manage your assets normally.

The goal is not to eliminate all risk. That is impossible. The goal is to prevent a single event from becoming a total loss. It is about limiting damage, preserving options, and ensuring that one mistake, one accident, or one lawsuit does not wipe out everything you have worked for.

Protection Is About Structure, Not Secrecy

Perhaps the most important distinction to understand is this: Asset protection works because of legal structure, not concealment.

Courts respect well-designed structures that are:

Created in advance: Asset protection planning done before a claim arises is far more likely to be upheld. Last-minute transfers after a lawsuit has been filed are viewed with suspicion and can be reversed as fraudulent conveyances.

Properly maintained: Structures like LLCs and trusts must be maintained according to legal requirements. This includes filing annual reports, holding meetings, keeping separate finances, and following formalities. A structure that exists on paper but is ignored in practice provides no real protection.

Transparent and compliant: Asset protection does not require secrecy. In fact, secrecy often raises red flags. The best structures are those that are fully disclosed, comply with tax and reporting requirements, and are defensible in court.

Supported by legitimate business or planning purposes: Structures created for legitimate reasons (such as liability protection, estate planning, business operations, or investment management) are far more likely to be respected than those created solely to frustrate creditors.

Courts do not respect last-minute transfers, fake ownership, or schemes designed to frustrate justice. If you transfer assets to a family member to avoid a creditor, if you create a sham entity with no real purpose, or if you conceal assets through deception, courts have the power to unwind those transactions and hold you accountable.

The people who benefit most from asset protection are not the most aggressive. They are the most deliberate. They plan ahead. They implement structures that are legally sound, ethically defensible, and practically effective. They understand that protection comes from doing things correctly, not from outsmarting the system.

The Cost of Doing Nothing

Choosing not to plan is still a decision, and it is often the most expensive one.

Without asset protection:

You bear risks personally that could be isolated. Every business venture, every rental property, and every professional engagement exposes your personal wealth. Risks that could be contained within a specific entity or structure instead reach everything you own.

You rely entirely on insurance and hope. Insurance is essential, but it has limits. Policies have coverage caps, exclusions, and conditions. If a claim exceeds your coverage or falls outside your policy, you are on your own.

You negotiate disputes from a position of weakness. When your personal assets are fully exposed, you have less leverage in settlement negotiations. Plaintiffs and their attorneys know that you have everything to lose, and they negotiate accordingly.

You expose future earnings to past mistakes. A judgment obtained today can follow you for years, garnishing wages, seizing income, and limiting your financial options long into the future.

Asset protection does not guarantee victory in a dispute. What it does is change the stakes, the leverage, and the outcome. It means that a claim against one asset does not automatically reach all assets. It means that you have options in settlement negotiations. It means that a lawsuit, while serious, does not have to be catastrophic.

The cost of doing nothing is measured not just in dollars, but in stress, lost opportunities, and the burden of living with unnecessary risk. The peace of mind that comes from knowing you have taken reasonable steps to protect what you have built is itself a valuable benefit.

Looking Ahead

The chapters that follow will explain how asset protection actually works, inside the United States and beyond. You will learn what tools exist, when they are appropriate, and where their limits lie. You will understand the difference between strategies that work and those that do not. You will see how to build protection that is effective, ethical, and sustainable.

As you read, keep one principle in mind: Asset protection is not about distrusting the world. It is about respecting risk and planning accordingly.

The world is not out to get you, but neither is it perfectly safe. Lawsuits happen. Accidents occur. Disputes arise. These are facts of life, not signs of moral failure. Recognizing this reality and planning for it is not pessimistic. It is prudent.

In the next chapter, we will clarify what asset protection truly is, and just as importantly, what it is not. Understanding the boundaries and limitations of asset protection is just as important as understanding its benefits. Only with a clear, realistic view can you make informed decisions about how to protect what matters most.

2

What Asset Protection Is (and Is Not)

Before discussing tools, structures, or strategies, it is essential to get one thing right: what asset protection actually means.

Most mistakes in asset protection come not from bad intentions, but from bad definitions. People hear the term and imagine secrecy, shell companies, or assets hidden beyond the reach of the law. Others assume it is something only the wealthy use, or that it operates in legal gray areas best avoided.

None of that is true when asset protection is done correctly.

This chapter sets clear boundaries. It explains what asset protection is, what it is not, and why understanding that distinction matters more than any specific strategy.

Asset Protection, Defined in Plain English

Asset protection is the lawful organization of your assets and activities to reduce unnecessary exposure to risk.

That is all it is, and it is enough.

Think of it this way: you lock your car doors, you have homeowners insurance, you keep your business finances separate from your personal accounts. These are all forms of asset protection. The strategies we discuss in this book are simply more sophisticated versions of the same principle: reducing your exposure to preventable loss.

More specifically, asset protection:

- Separates assets from liabilities
- Limits how far a legal claim can reach
- Uses recognized legal structures
- Is implemented before problems arise

It does not make assets immune to the law. It does not eliminate responsibility. What it does is prevent one claim, one lawsuit, or one mistake from cascading into total financial loss.

A Simple Example

Imagine you own a rental property and operate a small consulting business. Without asset protection, a lawsuit from either activity could potentially reach everything you own: your home, your savings, your business, and your rental property.

With proper asset protection, these risks are compartmentalized. A lawsuit from a tenant stays with the rental property entity. A professional liability claim stays with the business entity. Your personal assets remain separate from both.

This is not about hiding assets or dodging legitimate obligations. It is about making sure that one problem in one area of your life does not destroy everything you have built.

A useful way to think about asset protection is this: you are not trying to make assets untouchable. You are trying to keep problems contained.

When done correctly, asset protection works quietly in the background. It is boring, predictable, and rarely tested. That is exactly what you want.

Legal Asset Protection vs. Illegal Concealment

The line between protection and concealment is not subtle, and courts are very good at spotting when it has been crossed.

Understanding this distinction is critical. Cross this line, even unknowingly, and you can turn a manageable problem into a catastrophic one.

Legal Asset Protection

Legal asset protection:

- Is transparent and properly documented
- Uses structures recognized by law
- Has legitimate purposes beyond avoiding creditors
- Is established before any claim or dispute exists
- Complies with reporting and disclosure requirements

Examples include:

- Operating businesses through properly maintained entities
- Holding assets in structures appropriate to their risk
- Using insurance as a first line of defense
- Diversifying assets across lawful jurisdictions

These strategies are widely used by individuals, corporations, institutions, and governments alike. There is nothing secretive or questionable about them. They are standard practice in business and finance.

What Proper Documentation Looks Like

When we say "transparent and properly documented," we mean:

- Written operating agreements or trust documents
- Separate bank accounts for each entity
- Regular financial statements
- Minutes of meetings (for corporations)
- Clear paper trails for all transfers
- Accurate tax returns filed on time

- Honest disclosure on financial statements and court documents

This level of documentation may seem tedious, but it serves a critical purpose. It demonstrates that your asset protection plan was created for legitimate business and planning reasons, not to dodge specific creditors or obligations.

Illegal or Improper Concealment

Illegal concealment typically involves:

- Moving assets after a lawsuit or debt arises
- Hiding ownership through nominees or false documents
- Lying on financial disclosures
- Transferring assets for little or no value to avoid creditors
- Failing to report assets or accounts when required

These actions are not asset protection. They are invitations to penalties, including court sanctions, contempt findings, and in extreme cases, criminal charges.

A Real-World Distinction

Consider two scenarios:

Scenario A: Five years ago, Sarah formed an LLC to hold her rental properties. She maintains separate accounts, files separate tax returns, and keeps detailed records. When a tenant sues over a slip-and-fall, the lawsuit can only reach the assets inside the LLC, not Sarah's personal home or savings.

Scenario B: Tom receives a demand letter from a former business partner claiming he is owed money. The next week, Tom transfers his rental property to his brother for one dollar, hoping to put it beyond the partner's reach.

In Scenario A, Sarah's planning is respected. In Scenario B, Tom has likely committed a fraudulent transfer, and a court will almost certainly reverse it. Tom may face additional penalties for trying to hide assets.

The key difference is intent and timing. Asset protection is planned. Concealment is reactive.

Why Timing Matters More Than Complexity

One of the most counterintuitive truths in asset protection is that simple structures put in place early are often more effective than complex ones created late.

Courts look closely at when something was done and why.

A modest, well-maintained structure established years before a problem arises is usually respected. An elaborate web of entities created after a demand letter arrives is usually unraveled.

Why Courts Care About Timing

Timing matters because:

- Courts infer intent from proximity to claims
- Laws exist specifically to unwind last-minute transfers
- Judges have broad discretion in equity
- You cannot out-engineer bad timing.

This is why asset protection is most effective when it is treated like insurance or estate planning: something you do during calm periods, not emergencies.

The Insurance Analogy

Think of it this way: you cannot buy fire insurance while your house is burning. Similarly, you cannot establish meaningful asset protection once a lawsuit has been filed or a claim has been made.

Insurance companies understand that people who try to buy coverage after a loss has occurred are not managing risk. They are trying to transfer a loss that has already happened. Courts view last-minute asset transfers the same way.

What "Early" Means in Practice

How early is early enough?

While the law varies by jurisdiction, a general rule of thumb is that asset protection structures should be established:

- Before any specific claim or dispute arises

- At least one to four years before any problem (depending on local fraudulent transfer laws)
- As part of routine business planning or life transitions

If you are establishing entities at the same time you are launching a business, getting married, buying real estate, or receiving an inheritance, your timing will appear legitimate. If you are establishing entities the week after you receive a lawsuit, your timing will appear suspicious.

The safest approach is to treat asset protection as an ongoing part of your financial life, not a one-time emergency response.

Fraudulent Transfers, Explained Simply

The term "fraudulent transfer" sounds dramatic, but the concept is straightforward.

A fraudulent transfer occurs when someone moves assets to prevent a creditor from reaching them.

Importantly, fraud does not require lying or criminal intent. In many cases, a transfer can be deemed fraudulent simply because of when it occurred and what it accomplished.

What Courts Look For

Courts typically examine factors such as:

- Was there an existing or foreseeable claim?
- Was the transfer for less than fair value?
- Did the person remain in control of the asset?
- Did the transfer leave the person insolvent?
- Was the transfer made to a family member or insider?
- Was there unusual secrecy around the transaction?

If the answer to several of these questions is yes, the transfer may be undone, sometimes years later.

Common Fraudulent Transfer Situations

This applies to:

- Gifts to family members
- Transfers to trusts
- Moving assets between entities
- Selling assets at steep discounts
- Transferring property to a spouse during divorce proceedings

An Example That Looks Bad

Let's say you own a business that is being sued for $500,000. You know the lawsuit has merit and you will probably lose. You transfer your vacation home to your sister for one dollar. You tell yourself it is a gift, and gifts are legal.

Here is what a court will see:

- An existing claim (the lawsuit)
- A transfer for no real consideration (one dollar for a property worth hundreds of thousands)
- A transfer to a family member (raising suspicion)
- A transfer that makes you unable to pay the judgment (you are now insolvent)

This transfer will almost certainly be reversed. You may also face penalties for attempting it.

The Right Way to Make Transfers

The lesson is not "never transfer assets." The lesson is: transfer assets for legitimate reasons, at appropriate times, and with proper planning.

Legitimate transfers include:

- Selling property at fair market value
- Funding trusts as part of estate planning, well before any claims arise
- Gifting assets in amounts that do not render you insolvent
- Transferring business interests for proper business reasons with

documentation

The common thread is that these transfers serve a purpose beyond defeating creditors, they happen at appropriate times, and they are properly documented.

Common Myths and Misinformation

Asset protection is surrounded by persistent myths that cause real harm. These myths lead people to make expensive mistakes, trust unscrupulous advisors, or avoid legitimate planning out of unnecessary fear.

Let's address the most common ones directly.

Myth 1: "An LLC Protects Everything I Own"

This is perhaps the most dangerous oversimplification in asset protection.

An LLC can protect personal assets from business liabilities, but it does not automatically protect assets inside the LLC, and it does nothing if misused or improperly maintained.

Here is what an LLC actually does: if you operate a business through an LLC and the business gets sued, the lawsuit generally cannot reach your personal assets like your home or personal bank accounts. This is called the "liability shield."

But the shield only works in one direction. If you personally get sued (for a car accident, a personal debt, or any non-business matter), the assets inside your LLC may still be vulnerable. The exact level of protection depends on whether you have a single-member or multi-member LLC and the laws of your state.

What Makes the Shield Fail

Entity protection depends on:

- Proper capitalization (the business must have enough money to operate)
- Separate accounts (business money stays in business accounts)
- Clean records (minutes, resolutions, proper documentation)
- Respecting formal boundaries (treating the LLC as a separate entity)

If you commingle funds, use the LLC account as a personal piggy bank, or ignore corporate formalities, a court may decide the LLC is just a shell and "pierce the veil," allowing creditors to reach your personal assets anyway.

The entity is a tool, not a force field. It only works when used correctly.

Myth 2: "If I Move Assets Offshore, They're Safe"

This myth is fueled by movies, sensational news stories, and unscrupulous promoters who promise easy solutions to complex problems.

Offshore planning can be a legitimate and powerful tool, but it is not magical, and it is definitely not a way to hide assets from legitimate obligations.

The Reality of Offshore Planning

Assets must still be:

- Lawfully transferred (not moved after a claim arises)
- Properly reported (U.S. citizens must report foreign accounts)
- Managed through legitimate structures (real trusts, real entities, not shams)

Moving money offshore after a problem arises can be worse than doing nothing at all. Courts take a very dim view of people who move assets overseas to avoid judgments, and federal law gives courts significant power to reach foreign assets.

Additionally, failure to report foreign accounts can result in severe penalties under laws like the Foreign Account Tax Compliance Act (FATCA) and the requirement to file an FBAR (Foreign Bank Account Report). These penalties can exceed the value of the unreported account

When Offshore Planning Makes Sense

Legitimate offshore planning might make sense if:

- You have international business interests
- You are diversifying against domestic economic or political risk
- You need to operate in multiple currencies
- You have family or business ties in multiple countries

Even then, offshore planning must be done transparently, with proper reporting, and well before any legal problems arise.

Myth 3: "Asset Protection Is Only for the Wealthy"

This myth keeps many people who need asset protection from seeking it.

Asset protection is about risk exposure, not net worth.

Someone with a modest balance sheet but high liability exposure (a contractor, a landlord, a professional in a high-risk field) may need asset protection far more than someone with substantial assets and low risk (a retiree living off a pension and Social Security).

Who Really Needs Asset Protection

Consider these scenarios:

A nurse practitioner with $200,000 in savings faces millions in potential professional liability

A landlord with two rental properties worth $400,000 each faces slip-and-fall risks, discrimination claims, and tenant disputes

A small business owner with $100,000 in inventory and equipment faces contract disputes, employee claims, and customer lawsuits

In each case, the person's exposure far exceeds their net worth. Without proper planning, one lawsuit could wipe them out. With proper planning, their downside is limited.

Asset protection is not a luxury for the wealthy. It is a practical necessity for anyone with something to lose and exposure to liability.

Myth 4: "I'll Fix This If Something Happens"

This is the most expensive myth of all.

Once a claim arises, your options shrink dramatically. What was once legal and effective may become ineffective or even illegal overnight.

Why Waiting Is So Costly

After a lawsuit is filed:

- Most asset transfers will be considered fraudulent

- Courts can freeze your accounts and assets
- You lose the ability to plan proactively
- Your options are limited to expensive, reactive measures

The time to fix your roof is when the sun is shining, not when it is raining. The time to establish asset protection is when things are going well, not when you are facing a lawsuit.

The Planning Window

Think of asset protection as having a planning window that closes when problems begin.

Open window: No claims, no disputes, no foreseeable problems. This is when planning is most effective and most options are available.

Closing window: A dispute is brewing but no formal claim has been made. Some planning may still be possible, but options are limited and timing will be scrutinized.

Closed window: A lawsuit has been filed or a claim has been made. Almost all transfers will be considered fraudulent. Your options are now limited to defense strategies, not asset protection.

Asset protection rewards preparation, not improvisation.

Myth 5: "More Complexity Means More Protection"

Some people believe that if a little asset protection is good, a lot must be better. They create elaborate structures with multiple entities, trusts, and jurisdictions, thinking complexity itself provides protection.

It does not.

Complexity without purpose often signals fear, not strategy.

Why Excessive Complexity Fails

Overly complex structures:

- Increase costs (more entities mean more filing fees, tax returns, and professional fees)
- Increase maintenance risk (the more moving parts, the more can go wrong)

- Attract scrutiny (courts and creditors wonder what you are hiding)
- Fail more often in court (judges are skeptical of structures that seem designed solely to frustrate creditors)

The Right Level of Complexity

Effective asset protection is proportional, not maximal.

The right structure for you depends on:

- The nature and level of your risks
- The types of assets you own
- Your business activities
- Your family situation
- Your budget for setup and maintenance

For many people, one or two well-structured entities, good insurance coverage, and clean financial practices provide more real protection than a dozen entities that are poorly maintained or impossible to explain.

Start with the simplest structure that meets your needs. You can always add complexity later if your situation genuinely requires it.

Clarity Before Action

Understanding what asset protection is and what it is not is not an academic exercise. It is the foundation for every decision that follows.

When you respect timing, legality, and simplicity:

- Courts are more likely to respect your structures
- Creditors face real obstacles
- Disputes resolve faster and at lower cost
- You retain flexibility and peace of mind

Asset protection done right is not dramatic. It does not involve secret accounts, hidden assets, or exotic jurisdictions. It involves boring, well-documented structures established at the right time for the right reasons.

It is about being prepared, not being clever. It is about playing the long game, not looking for shortcuts.

In the next chapter, we will examine the core principles that make asset protection work, regardless of the tools used or the jurisdiction involved. These principles form the foundation of every effective strategy, whether you are protecting a small business, a rental property, or a professional practice.

PART II: Asset Protection Inside the United States

3

Insurance: Your First Line of Defense

Asset protection does not begin with trusts, entities, or complex legal structures. It begins with insurance.

Insurance is often misunderstood in asset protection discussions. Some people assume that insurance alone is enough. Others dismiss it as irrelevant once "real" asset protection planning begins. Both views are wrong.

Insurance is not a substitute for asset protection, but it is an essential part of it. In fact, insurance is usually the first line of defense, absorbing risk before it ever reaches your assets.

This chapter explains how insurance fits into an asset protection strategy, what types of coverage matter most, and where insurance commonly fails.

Why Insurance Is Asset Protection (But Not a Substitute for It)

At its core, asset protection is about who pays when something goes wrong.

Insurance shifts that burden from you to an insurer, up to a defined limit and under defined conditions. When insurance responds as intended, claims are resolved without touching your personal or business assets at all.

That is asset protection in its simplest form.

However, insurance has limits:

- **Policy caps**: Every insurance policy has a maximum amount it will pay out. Once you hit that ceiling, you're responsible for anything beyond it.
- **Deductibles**: You pay the first portion of any claim out of pocket before insurance kicks in.
- **Exclusions**: These are specific situations or types of damage that your policy won't cover at all, no matter what.
- **Coverage disputes**: Sometimes insurance companies disagree about whether a claim should be covered, leaving you in limbo or facing legal battles with your own insurer.
- **Claims that fall outside policy definitions**: If your situation doesn't fit neatly into the policy's language, you may find yourself without coverage even though you thought you were protected.

Once those limits are reached, asset protection planning determines what happens next.

A useful way to think about insurance is this: **Insurance pays claims. Asset protection preserves what insurance does not.**

Strong asset protection planning assumes insurance will fail eventually, not because insurers are bad actors, but because no policy covers everything. There will always be gaps, and planning for those gaps is what separates those who are truly protected from those who only think they are.

Umbrella Liability Policies

For individuals and families, umbrella liability insurance is often the most cost-effective protection available.

What an Umbrella Policy Does

An umbrella policy provides additional liability coverage above your underlying policies, such as:

- Auto insurance
- Homeowners insurance
- Rental property insurance
- It typically covers:
- Personal injury claims (like defamation or false imprisonment)
- Property damage that exceeds your standard policy limits
- Certain lawsuits not fully covered by base policies

Umbrella coverage is designed for severity, not frequency. It steps in when damages exceed standard limits. Think of it as a safety net that catches you when things get really bad.

Why Umbrella Policies Matter

Umbrella policies offer several advantages:

- **High coverage limits for relatively low cost**: You can often get $1 million to $5 million in additional coverage for just a few hundred dollars per year.
- **Broad protection across multiple risk areas**: One umbrella policy can cover liability from your car, your home, your rental properties, and more.
- **Defense costs often included**: Legal fees add up quickly. Many umbrella policies cover these costs in addition to the policy limits.

For people with assets or high income, umbrella coverage is not optional. It is foundational.

A common mistake is carrying high net worth, multiple properties, teen drivers, and public-facing lifestyles with only minimal liability limits. That gap is an open invitation to personal exposure.

Here's a real-world example: Imagine you have a net worth of $2 million but only $500,000 in auto liability coverage. If you cause a serious accident and the injured party wins a $1.5 million judgment, your insurance pays the first $500,000. You're personally on the hook for the remaining $1 million.

An umbrella policy would have covered that gap for less than the cost of a monthly streaming subscription.

What Umbrella Policies Do Not Cover

Umbrella policies do not cover everything. Common exclusions include:

- **Business activities** (unless specifically endorsed or added to your policy)
- **Professional services** (like medical advice, legal counsel, or consulting work)
- **Intentional acts** (if you deliberately harm someone or damage property)
- **Certain contractual liabilities** (obligations you agree to in contracts)

This is where many people develop a false sense of security. They assume their umbrella policy protects them from everything, when in reality significant gaps remain.

Professional Liability Coverage

For professionals, general liability insurance is rarely enough.

Professional liability insurance, often called errors and omissions (E&O) or malpractice insurance, covers claims arising from:

- Advice you provide
- Services you render
- Alleged mistakes or omissions in your professional work
  - These claims often involve:
  - High damages (sometimes millions of dollars)
  - Expert testimony and complex legal proceedings
  - Long litigation timelines that can drag on for years

Even unfounded claims can be financially devastating without coverage. The cost of defending yourself against a baseless lawsuit can easily reach six figures.

Limits Matter More Than People Realize

Many professionals carry coverage that reflects:

- Minimum licensing requirements from their state or professional board
- Cost considerations (choosing cheaper policies to save money)
- Historical norms (keeping the same coverage limits they've always had)
- But claims do not respect minimums.

A verdict or settlement that exceeds policy limits exposes personal assets immediately. Asset protection planning assumes this possibility and plans accordingly.

If you're a physician with $1 million in malpractice coverage but face a $3 million judgment, your insurance covers the first million. The remaining $2 million comes directly from your personal assets: your home, your savings, your retirement accounts. Everything you've worked for becomes fair game.

Tail Coverage and Gaps in Time

One overlooked risk is timing.

Claims may arise:

- After retirement
- After changing firms or jobs
- After closing a business

Without tail coverage (insurance that covers claims made after your policy ends for work done during the policy period) or proper continuity, professionals may find themselves personally exposed for past work they assumed was insured.

This is especially dangerous because many types of professional liability claims can be filed years after the work was performed. You might retire thinking you're safe, only to face a claim five years later with no coverage.

Common Coverage Gaps

Insurance failures rarely occur because people had no insurance at all. They occur because of gaps.

Some of the most common include:

Underinsured Risk:

- Low liability limits relative to net worth or income
- Umbrella limits that have not kept pace with asset growth

Many people bought their insurance coverage years ago and never updated it as their wealth grew. They're driving around with the financial equivalent of outdated brakes.

Business Activities Excluded From Personal Policies:

- Side businesses
- Consulting work
- Short-term rentals (like Airbnb)
- Online activities (e-commerce, content creation)

People often assume these are "minor" activities until they generate major claims. That weekend Airbnb rental seems harmless until a guest is injured and sues for $2 million.

Contractual Assumptions of Liability

- Indemnification clauses (agreeing to cover someone else's liability)
- Personal guarantees on business loans or leases
- Poorly reviewed contracts you signed without understanding the implications

Insurance may not cover liabilities you voluntarily assume. When you sign a contract agreeing to take responsibility for certain risks, you may be stepping outside the protection of your insurance policy without realizing it.

Entity-Level Coverage Mismatches

- Policies in the wrong name (personal policy when you need business coverage, or vice versa)
- Assets owned by entities not listed on policies
- Management activities not insured

- This mismatch can void coverage precisely when it is needed most. Imagine owning rental property through an LLC but keeping the insurance policy in your personal name. When a claim arises, the insurance company may deny coverage entirely because of this mismatch.

Insurance and Asset Protection Must Work Together

The strongest asset protection plans treat insurance and legal structure as partners, not substitutes.

Insurance reduces the number of claims that ever reach your assets. Asset protection planning determines how much damage remains if insurance fails.

When both are aligned:

- Claims resolve faster (insurers handle negotiations)
- Settlement leverage improves (creditors know they can't easily reach protected assets)
- Personal exposure shrinks dramatically (you're protected from multiple angles)

When they are misaligned, insurance can create complacency, and complacency is expensive. Having insurance without proper asset protection planning is like having a good front door lock but leaving your windows wide open.

Regular Review Is Non-Negotiable

Insurance is not "set and forget."

Life changes that require review include:

- Buying or selling property
- Starting or exiting a business
- Marriage or divorce
- Significant increases in net worth or income
- Changes in professional practice (new services, new locations, new partners)

Asset protection planning should include periodic insurance audits to ensure coverage matches reality. At minimum, review your insurance annually. Major life changes should trigger immediate review.

Think of it this way: your insurance coverage should grow and change with your life. The coverage that made sense when you were starting out is almost certainly inadequate now.

Looking Ahead

Insurance absorbs risk. Legal structures contain it.

In the next chapter, we will examine business entities as asset protection tools: how they work, where they fail, and why simply "having an LLC" is rarely enough.

4

Business Entities as Shields

Business entities are among the most widely used and most misunderstood asset protection tools in America.

Many people form an LLC or corporation believing they have created a protective barrier between themselves and risk. Sometimes they have. Often, they haven't. The difference lies not in the paperwork filed with the state, but in how liability flows, how the entity is used, and whether the structure is respected in practice.

This chapter explains how business entities function as liability shields, where they succeed, where they fail, and why state law plays a critical role in determining their effectiveness.

How Liability Flows in Lawsuits

To understand how entities protect assets, you must first understand how liability moves.

In general, personal liability can reach everything you own personally, while business liability should stop at the business if structured correctly.

Without an entity, liability flows freely. If you operate as a sole proprietor, there is no legal separation between you and the activity. A business problem becomes a personal problem instantly.

Entities exist to interrupt that flow.

When properly structured, claims arising from business activities stay inside the business. Personal assets are insulated from business risks. Creditors are limited to entity-level remedies.

But this protection is conditional. It depends on compliance, capitalization, and conduct.

LLCs Explained for Non-Lawyers

The limited liability company (LLC) is the most popular entity for asset protection, and for good reason.

What an LLC Does Well

An LLC separates business liabilities from personal assets. It is flexible in management and taxation. It requires fewer formalities than corporations. And it works well for closely held businesses and real estate.

In simple terms, an LLC creates a legal "container" around risk. If something goes wrong with the business, the risk stays contained within that legal structure. Your personal home, savings, and other assets remain protected from business creditors.

What an LLC Does Not Do

An LLC does not protect you from your own personal negligence. It does not automatically protect assets owned inside the LLC. It does not override poor behavior or sloppy practices. And it does not replace insurance.

If you personally cause harm, sign personal guarantees, or ignore the separation between yourself and the LLC, the protection erodes quickly.

For example, if you are a contractor and you personally injure someone on a job site through your own careless actions, the LLC will not shield your personal assets. The law recognizes that people must be accountable for their own wrongful conduct, regardless of what entity they operate through.

Single-Member vs. Multi-Member LLCs

From an asset protection perspective, this distinction matters significantly.

Single-member LLCs often receive weaker protection in many states. When you are the sole owner, courts and creditors may view the LLC with more skepticism. Some states allow creditors greater access to single-member LLC assets than they would to multi-member LLCs.

Multi-member LLCs are more likely to restrict creditor remedies. When multiple people have ownership interests, courts are more reluctant to disrupt the entity or grant creditors excessive control, because doing so could harm the rights of the other innocent owners.

State law determines how strong that protection is, which is why jurisdiction matters. Some states explicitly protect single-member LLCs with the same vigor as multi-member LLCs. Others do not.

Corporations: S-Corps vs. C-Corps

Corporations offer limited liability similar to LLCs, but with more formal structure.

S-Corporations

S-Corporations provide pass-through taxation, meaning the business itself doesn't pay federal income tax. Instead, profits and losses pass through to the owners' personal tax returns. S-Corps have ownership restrictions: they can have no more than 100 shareholders, and shareholders must be U.S. citizens or residents. They are common for operating businesses.

C-Corporations

C-Corporations are separate tax-paying entities. The corporation pays taxes on its income, and shareholders pay taxes again on dividends they receive (often called "double taxation"). C-Corps have no ownership restrictions and can have unlimited shareholders of any type. They are common for larger or growth-focused companies, especially those planning to raise capital from investors or go public.

What Matters Most for Protection

From an asset protection standpoint, the difference between S-corporations and C-corporations is usually less important than proper capitalization, observance of formalities, and separation of business and personal affairs.

A well-run corporation protects better than a poorly run LLC. The form of entity matters less than how you treat it in practice.

Piercing the Corporate Veil

"Piercing the corporate veil" is the legal doctrine courts use to ignore an entity and hold owners personally liable.

This does not happen randomly. Courts look for patterns of abuse or disregard. When they find those patterns, they essentially declare that the entity is a sham and should not be respected.

Common veil-piercing triggers include commingling personal and business funds, undercapitalizing the entity, ignoring governance requirements, using the entity for personal expenses, and treating the entity as an alter ego (essentially an extension of yourself rather than a separate legal being).

The message is simple: if you do not respect the entity, courts will not either.

Examples of What Not to Do

Commingling is one of the fastest ways to lose protection. If you use the business bank account to pay for your personal groceries, or if you deposit personal money into the business account to cover expenses, you blur the line between you and the entity. Courts interpret this as evidence that the entity is not truly separate from you.

Undercapitalization means starting a business with insufficient funds to reasonably operate or cover potential liabilities. If you form an LLC with $100 in the bank to operate a construction company with significant liability risks, a court might decide you never intended the entity to function independently. You were simply trying to dodge responsibility.

Ignoring governance requirements means skipping annual meetings, failing to keep minutes, not maintaining proper records, or disregarding your own operating agreement or bylaws. These formalities exist to prove the entity is real and separate. When you ignore them, you signal the entity is just paperwork.

Formality Is a Feature, Not a Bug

Many people view entity formalities as unnecessary hassle. In reality, formalities are evidence.

They demonstrate separate existence, legitimate business purpose, and good faith operation. Asset protection depends on proof, not intent alone.

When a creditor challenges your entity, you will need to show the court that you treated it as a real, independent business. Your evidence will be things like:

- Separate bank accounts consistently maintained
- Written operating agreements or bylaws that were actually followed
- Meeting minutes documenting major decisions
- Clear separation between personal and business transactions
- Proper capitalization and financial records

These are not mere technicalities. They are the proof that your entity deserves legal respect.

Charging Orders and Why State Law Matters

Charging orders are one of the least understood and most powerful asset protection concepts.

What Is a Charging Order?

A charging order is a creditor's remedy against an owner's interest in an entity. Instead of taking the assets inside the entity, the creditor is limited to receiving distributions, if and when they are made.

The creditor cannot force distributions. They cannot seize entity assets. They cannot participate in management.

This can dramatically reduce the value of a claim.

Here's why this matters: Imagine you own an LLC that holds rental properties worth $500,000. You personally lose a lawsuit and owe $200,000. Without a charging order limitation, the creditor might try to seize the properties or force a sale. With a charging order limitation, the creditor can only wait and hope you decide to take distributions from the LLC. If you don't take distributions (perhaps reinvesting rental income back into property improvements), the creditor gets nothing.

This creates a powerful negotiating position. The creditor has a legal right to money, but no practical way to collect it. Many creditors will settle for much less than the full judgment amount when faced with this reality.

The Tax Consequence That Strengthens Protection

In many states, there's an additional benefit: if the entity is taxed as a partnership, the creditor with a charging order may be responsible for paying taxes on their share of the entity's income, even if they receive no actual money. This is called "phantom income."

Imagine the LLC earns $50,000 in a year but distributes nothing. The creditor might owe taxes on their portion of that $50,000, even though they received zero dollars. This creates strong incentive for creditors to negotiate a settlement rather than hold a charging order indefinitely.

Why State Law Is Critical

Not all states treat charging orders equally.

Some states make charging orders the exclusive remedy and extend protection to single-member LLCs. In these states, a creditor's only option is to wait for distributions. They cannot foreclose on your ownership interest. They cannot force a sale of the LLC itself. The charging order is their only avenue, and it's a limited one.

Others allow foreclosure on ownership interests and permit broader creditor access. In these states, a creditor might be able to take your ownership interest in the LLC outright, step into your shoes, and potentially force liquidation of the assets.

This difference is why asset protection planning often involves choosing jurisdiction intentionally, not simply forming an entity where you live.

For example, some states like Wyoming, Nevada, and Delaware have particularly strong charging order protections. If you live in a state with weaker protections, you might consider forming your LLC in a more protective state (though this requires careful legal analysis because you may still need to register to do business in your home state, which can reduce the benefit).

Entities Are Tools, Not Magic Wands

Business entities are powerful when used correctly and dangerous when misunderstood.

They require discipline, proper setup, ongoing maintenance, and alignment with insurance and other protections.

Discipline means consistently treating the entity as separate from yourself. Every transaction should be documented. Every expense should be properly categorized. Personal funds should never mix with business funds.

Proper setup means starting with solid legal documents: a well-drafted operating agreement or bylaws, proper initial capitalization, clear ownership structure, and registration in the right jurisdiction.

Ongoing maintenance means annual filings, updated records, regular meetings (even if brief and informal for small entities), and periodic review of your structure as your circumstances change.

Alignment with other protections means understanding that entities work best as part of a comprehensive plan. An LLC should complement your insurance coverage, not replace it. Your entity structure should fit with your estate plan. Everything should work together as a coordinated defense.

When these conditions are met, entities are among the most effective asset protection tools available. When they are ignored, entities become paper shields that fail under pressure.

Looking Ahead

In the next chapter, we will focus on real estate ownership and asset protection, where entity planning is especially important, and where mistakes are among the most costly and common.

Understanding how entities work is foundational. Using them correctly is what makes asset protection real.

Key Takeaways:

Business entities can provide powerful liability protection, but only when properly established and maintained. LLCs and corporations create legal separation between business activities and personal assets, preventing business creditors from reaching your personal wealth. However, this protection requires respect for formalities, proper capitalization, and consistent separation of business and personal affairs. Charging orders, particularly in favorable jurisdictions, offer additional protection by limiting creditors to receiving distributions rather than seizing assets. Entities are tools that require discipline and ongoing attention, not magical shields that work automatically. When used correctly as part of a comprehensive protection strategy, they are among the most effective defenses available to protect what you've built.

5

Protecting Real Estate Assets

Real estate is one of the most powerful wealth-building tools available, and it's also one of the most legally exposed.

Unlike stocks or bonds, real estate is immobile, visible, and directly connected to people's physical safety. When something goes wrong, claims are often personal, emotional, and expensive. For that reason, real estate ownership demands deliberate asset protection planning.

This chapter explains how real estate creates risk, how ownership structure affects exposure, and how common mistakes turn valuable properties into liability magnets.

Understanding Why Real Estate Is Different

Real estate carries unique vulnerabilities that other investments don't share.

Physical Presence Creates Exposure

A rental property sits on a street. People walk on its sidewalks, climb its stairs, breathe its air, and live under its roof. Every surface, every system, and every condition creates potential liability. If a tenant slips on ice, a child is injured by peeling paint, or a visitor falls through a rotted deck, the property owner becomes a defendant.

This is fundamentally different from owning shares of stock. A stock certificate doesn't injure anyone. A bond doesn't leak carbon monoxide. But real property does interact with the physical world, and that interaction produces legal risk.

Emotional Stakes Are High

Real estate claims often involve homes, families, and personal safety. Juries hear stories about children with lead poisoning, elderly tenants who fell down unsafe stairs, or families displaced by uninhabitable conditions. These narratives are powerful. They generate sympathy and anger. And they produce verdicts that can exceed policy limits by millions of dollars.

Even when a property owner has done nothing wrong, the emotional weight of a real estate lawsuit is heavier than most other civil disputes. Courts and juries view housing as a basic need, and landlords as those who profit from that need. Fair or not, this perception shapes outcomes.

Claims Are Persistent

Real estate liability doesn't expire when a tenant moves out. Latent defects, environmental hazards, and building code violations can surface years later. Mold discovered long after a lease ends can still generate a claim. Asbestos exposure doesn't manifest immediately. Lead paint injuries may not be diagnosed until a child is older.

This means property owners face ongoing exposure, sometimes for years after they've sold a property or a tenant has vacated. The statute of limitations provides some boundary, but real estate claims have long tails.

Holding Property Personally vs. in Entities

One of the most consequential decisions a property owner makes is how title is held.

Personal Ownership: Simple but Exposed

Holding property in your personal name is simple, but simplicity comes at a cost.

When property is owned personally, any claim related to the property is a personal claim. If a tenant sues over a slip and fall, the lawsuit names you individually. If a contractor files a lien, it attaches to you personally. If a judgment is entered, it reaches all of your personal assets, not just the property that caused the problem.

This means one property can jeopardize everything else you own. Your primary residence, your bank accounts, your retirement savings (to the extent they aren't protected by statute), and your other real estate holdings are all accessible to that single judgment creditor. One bad outcome on one property creates exposure across your entire financial life.

This exposure exists even if you have insurance. Insurance reduces risk, but it does not eliminate it. Policies have limits. They contain exclusions. Claims can exceed coverage. And sometimes insurance companies deny claims or go bankrupt. Personal ownership means that when insurance fails, you personally absorb the loss.

When Personal Ownership Makes Sense

Personal ownership is most defensible only in limited circumstances:

Primary Residences with Strong Homestead Protection

If you live in a state with robust homestead exemptions and the property is your primary residence, personal ownership may be acceptable. The homestead laws provide statutory protection that can shield equity from creditors. However, this only applies to your home, not to rental properties or vacation homes.

Minimal Third-Party Exposure

If the property has almost no risk of third-party claims (for example, vacant land in a remote area with no public access), personal ownership carries less risk. But even vacant land can generate liability if someone trespasses and gets injured, so "minimal" risk is not "no" risk.

Adequate Insurance in Place

If you maintain high-limit liability insurance and umbrella coverage, personal ownership becomes slightly more defensible. But this is still not ideal. Insurance should be one layer of protection, not the only layer.

For income-producing or tenant-occupied property, personal ownership is usually an avoidable risk. There is almost no scenario where holding rental property personally is the best choice from an asset protection standpoint.

Entity Ownership: Creating Legal Separation

Placing property in a properly structured entity creates liability isolation. The most common entity for this purpose is a limited liability company (LLC), though other structures exist.

When done correctly, claims arising from the property stay with the entity. If a tenant sues over an injury at the property, the lawsuit targets the LLC, not you personally. The plaintiff can reach the assets inside the LLC (primarily the property itself), but your personal assets remain insulated.

Other personal assets are shielded because the legal claim is against the entity, not against you as an individual. Your home, your personal bank accounts, your other properties, and your investment accounts are not part of the lawsuit. This compartmentalization is the core benefit of entity ownership.

What Entity Ownership Does Not Do

Entity ownership does not eliminate liability. It doesn't mean you can ignore maintenance, violate building codes, or disregard tenant rights. The LLC can still be sued. The property can still be taken to satisfy a judgment. But the lawsuit stops at the entity's walls.

Entity ownership also does not protect against personal guarantees, intentional misconduct, or claims where you are personally negligent. If you personally commit fraud, no entity structure will shield you. If you sign a personal guarantee on a loan, you've voluntarily bypassed the entity protection. And if you fail to maintain the entity properly (commingling funds, ignoring formalities, undercapitalizing), courts may disregard the entity in a process called "piercing the corporate veil."

Entity ownership is a tool, not a magic shield. It works when used correctly and maintained diligently. It fails when abused or neglected.

The Mechanics of Proper Entity Use

To preserve liability protection, entity ownership requires discipline:

Separate Finances

The entity must have its own bank account. Rent checks go into the entity account. Expenses are paid from the entity account. Personal funds and entity funds never mix. Commingling destroys the legal separation that makes the entity valuable.

Proper Documentation

Contracts should be signed in the entity's name, not your personal name. Leases should identify the LLC as the landlord. Invoices should be addressed to the entity. Every interaction with the property should reflect that the entity, not you personally, is the owner.

Adequate Capitalization

The entity should have enough resources to meet its obligations. An LLC with no money, no insurance, and significant liabilities looks like a sham. Courts are more likely to pierce the veil of an undercapitalized entity. This doesn't mean the LLC needs millions of dollars, but it does need enough to operate legitimately.

Respect Formalities

While LLCs are less formal than corporations, they still require basic maintenance. Keep records. File annual reports. Pay franchise taxes. Update operating agreements when circumstances change. These actions demonstrate that the entity is real, not just a paper fiction.

Single-Property LLCs vs. Portfolio LLCs

Once investors move beyond one property, structure matters even more. The question becomes: should each property have its own LLC, or should multiple properties share one entity?

Single-Property LLCs: Maximum Isolation

Under this approach, each property is owned by a separate entity. Property A is owned by ABC Properties LLC. Property B is owned by XYZ Holdings LLC. Property C is owned by Maple Street Rentals LLC. Each is distinct.

How It Works

Liability from one property cannot reach another because they are legally separate. If a major judgment is entered against ABC Properties LLC, the creditor can seize Property A, but cannot touch Property B or Property C. Those are owned by different entities. The judgment is isolated.

Risk is fully compartmentalized. A catastrophic loss on one property does not jeopardize the rest of the portfolio. This is the highest level of real estate asset protection available without exotic offshore structures.

The Cost of Isolation

This structure is highly effective for asset protection, but more expensive to maintain. Each LLC requires its own formation documents, its own annual filings, its own franchise taxes, and often its own bank account. The administrative burden multiplies with each property.

For a portfolio of ten properties, this means ten LLCs, ten tax returns (if taxed separately), ten sets of records, and ten annual compliance obligations. The cost in time and money is real.

When Single-Property LLCs Make Sense

For higher-risk properties or larger portfolios, this is often the gold standard. If you own properties with significant liability exposure (multi-family buildings, properties in litigious jurisdictions, older buildings with code violations), isolating each one is worth the cost.

It also makes sense when the value of the portfolio justifies the expense. If your real estate holdings are worth several million dollars, spending a few thousand dollars per year on entity maintenance is a reasonable insurance premium.

Portfolio LLCs: Efficiency with Tradeoffs

A portfolio LLC owns multiple properties under one entity. ABC Properties LLC might own Property A, Property B, and Property C simultaneously.

The Benefits

Lower administrative cost is the primary advantage. One entity means one formation, one set of annual filings, one bank account (usually), and one tax return (if the LLC is disregarded for tax purposes or files as a partnership). This simplifies management significantly.

Fewer filings and less complexity make portfolio LLCs attractive to smaller investors or those with lower-risk properties. If you own three single-family rentals in stable neighborhoods with good tenants and strong insurance, the portfolio approach may be appropriate.

The Risk Concentration Problem

The tradeoff is risk concentration. If one property generates a major claim, all properties in the entity are exposed. The creditor can reach the entire portfolio because it's all owned by the same legal entity.

Imagine a serious injury occurs at Property A. A jury awards a $2 million judgment. Your insurance covers $1 million. The remaining $1 million judgment attaches to the LLC. The creditor can now force the sale of Property B and Property C to satisfy that judgment, even though those properties had nothing to do with the injury. Equity across the portfolio is at risk.

This is the fundamental weakness of the portfolio structure. It sacrifices isolation for convenience.

When Portfolio LLCs Make Sense

Portfolio structures may be appropriate for lower-risk properties. Single-family homes in good repair, well-maintained duplexes, and properties with stable, long-term tenants carry less risk than high-turnover apartment buildings or properties with deferred maintenance.

Similar property types also work better in a portfolio structure. Grouping similar properties together (all single-family rentals, or all small commercial buildings) creates a more coherent risk profile than mixing property types.

Smaller investors balancing cost and protection may find the portfolio approach acceptable early in their investing career. As the portfolio grows and the value increases, migrating to single-property LLCs becomes more justifiable.

There is no universal answer, only informed tradeoffs. The decision depends on property values, risk profiles, cash flow, administrative capacity, and personal risk tolerance.

Homestead Exemptions and State Differences

Primary residences receive unique treatment under U.S. law. These protections are called homestead exemptions, and they vary dramatically by state.

What Is a Homestead Exemption?

A homestead exemption protects some or all of the equity in your primary residence from certain creditors. If a creditor obtains a judgment against you, the homestead law may prevent them from forcing the sale of your home to satisfy that debt.

The amount of protection depends entirely on where you live. Protection levels vary widely.

States with Unlimited or Very High Homestead Protection

Some states offer unlimited homestead protection. In Florida and Texas, for example, the equity in your primary residence is fully protected regardless of value (subject to acreage limits). If your home is worth $5 million and you own it free and clear, that equity is generally unreachable by most judgment creditors.

Other states offer very high caps. California provides up to $600,000 in homestead protection depending on age, marital status, and other factors. Massachusetts offers up to $500,000. These states provide substantial shelter for home equity.

States with Low or Moderate Homestead Protection

Other states cap protection at relatively low amounts. New Jersey, for example, provides no statutory homestead exemption at all. Pennsylvania offers no meaningful homestead protection. Delaware caps the exemption at $50,000 for people over 65, and provides nothing for younger homeowners.

In these states, significant home equity is exposed. A judgment creditor can force the sale of your home, pay off any mortgages, give you the exempt amount (if any), and take the rest.

States Requiring Formal Declarations

Some states require you to file a formal homestead declaration to claim the exemption. This is a document recorded with the county that establishes your intent to use the property as your primary residence. If you don't file it, you may lose the protection.

Other states grant the homestead exemption automatically without requiring a filing. The protection applies simply because the property is your primary residence.

Understanding your state's rules is essential. Assumptions are dangerous.

What Homestead Protection Does Not Cover

Homestead exemptions generally do not protect against certain types of claims:

Mortgages and Voluntary Liens

If you have a mortgage on your home, the homestead exemption does not prevent foreclosure. The lender can still take the property if you default. Voluntary liens (those you agreed to) survive the homestead protection.

Property Taxes

If you fail to pay property taxes, the government can sell your home to satisfy the tax debt. Homestead laws do not shield you from tax liens.

Certain Federal Claims

Federal tax liens, federal student loan judgments, and other federal claims may override state homestead protections. Federal law can preempt state exemptions in specific circumstances.

Liabilities Directly Related to the Property

If a contractor performs work on your home and you don't pay, the contractor can file a mechanic's lien and potentially force a sale. Homestead exemptions typically do not protect against claims directly arising from the property itself.

They are powerful, but not absolute. Homestead protection is one layer of defense, not a complete shield.

Strategic Considerations

Because homestead protection is state-specific, moving states can change protection dramatically. If you relocate from Florida (unlimited exemption) to New Jersey (no exemption), your asset protection posture shifts overnight.

Planning must account for future relocation. If you might move for work, retirement, or family reasons, consider the homestead laws in your likely destination. Don't assume the protection you have today will follow you.

Excess equity may still be exposed. Even in states with high exemptions, if your home equity significantly exceeds the cap, the excess is vulnerable. A $1 million home with no mortgage in a state with a $500,000 exemption leaves $500,000 exposed.

Relying blindly on homestead laws without understanding their limits is a common mistake. These laws provide valuable protection, but they are not a substitute for comprehensive planning.

Landlord-Specific Risks

Landlords face a unique and persistent risk profile. The nature of the landlord-tenant relationship creates exposures that other property owners don't encounter.

Common Landlord Liabilities

Landlords are responsible for maintaining safe, habitable properties. When they fail, claims follow. These include:

Slip-and-Fall Injuries

Icy sidewalks, broken stairs, uneven flooring, and poor lighting all create slip-and-fall risk. These are among the most common premises liability claims. They often involve serious injuries (broken hips, traumatic brain injuries, spinal damage) and generate significant verdicts.

Unsafe Conditions

Broken railings, exposed wiring, malfunctioning heating systems, and structural defects can injure tenants or guests. Landlords have a duty to maintain the property in a reasonably safe condition. Breaching that duty creates liability.

Habitability Claims

Most states impose an implied warranty of habitability on residential landlords. This means the property must be fit for human habitation. Lack of heat, non-functioning plumbing, pest infestations, and water damage can all breach this warranty. Tenants can sue for damages, withhold rent, or terminate the lease.

Mold and Environmental Allegations

Mold claims have become increasingly common. Tenants allege that mold exposure caused respiratory problems, neurological damage, or other health issues. These claims are difficult to defend, expensive to litigate, and often result in settlements even when causation is questionable.

Other environmental hazards include lead paint, asbestos, radon, and carbon monoxide. Landlords can face liability for failing to disclose known hazards or for negligently maintaining systems that produce these risks.

Fair Housing Violations

Federal and state fair housing laws prohibit discrimination based on race, color, religion, sex, national origin, familial status, and disability. Some states add additional protected classes. Violating these laws can result in substantial damages, penalties, and attorney's fees. Even unintentional discrimination can create liability.

Contractor and Vendor Disputes

Landlords hire contractors, property managers, landscapers, and other vendors. Disputes over unpaid bills, defective work, or injuries caused by these third parties can generate claims. Sometimes the landlord is held vicariously liable for a contractor's negligence.

Why Landlord Claims Are Dangerous

Many landlord claims involve serious injuries. A tenant who falls down a flight of stairs due to a broken railing may suffer permanent disability. A child exposed to lead paint may experience developmental delays. These are not minor claims.

Many landlord claims involve sympathetic plaintiffs. Juries are naturally sympathetic to injured tenants, especially when the landlord is perceived as wealthy or negligent. The tenant-landlord relationship carries inherent power imbalance, and juries often side with the tenant.

Many landlord claims involve aggressive litigation. Plaintiff's attorneys in premises liability and habitability cases often work on contingency. They have an incentive to maximize the settlement or verdict. They are skilled at presenting emotional, compelling cases.

These factors increase both settlement pressure and verdict risk. Even weak claims can be expensive to defend. Strong claims can produce catastrophic judgments.

Insurance Is Necessary, but Not Sufficient

Landlord insurance and umbrella coverage are essential. Every landlord should carry comprehensive general liability insurance and consider an umbrella policy for additional coverage.

But claims frequently exceed policy limits. A serious injury with long-term disability can generate a verdict in the millions. If your policy limit is $1 million and the verdict is $3 million, you are personally liable for the difference (unless you have entity protection).

Claims frequently trigger exclusions. Insurance policies contain numerous exclusions. Intentional acts, pollution, mold, and certain types of discrimination may not be covered. If a claim falls within an exclusion, you are uninsured.

Claims can involve uninsured periods. If you fail to renew your policy, switch carriers and leave a gap, or cancel coverage, you may be uninsured when a claim arises. Claims can also relate to incidents that occurred before you purchased coverage.

Asset protection planning assumes that insurance may fail at the worst possible time. Insurance is the first line of defense, but it cannot be the only line.

Personal Guarantees and Financing Risks

Real estate is typically financed with debt. Lenders provide mortgages, and landlords use leverage to acquire properties. But financing introduces its own asset protection risks.

Personal Guarantees

Lenders often require personal guarantees on loans to LLCs, especially for smaller investors. A personal guarantee means you personally promise to repay the loan if the entity cannot. This guarantee is enforceable even if the property is held in an LLC.

If the LLC defaults and you've signed a personal guarantee, the lender can pursue your personal assets. The entity structure provides no protection against this liability because you voluntarily agreed to personal responsibility.

Personal guarantees can undo entity protection. If a significant portion of your financing involves personal guarantees, the asset protection benefit of entity ownership is reduced. You remain personally exposed to the debt, even if operational liabilities are isolated.

Cross-Collateralization

Some loans include cross-collateralization clauses. This means multiple properties serve as collateral for a single loan, or one loan is secured by multiple properties. If you default on the loan, the lender can foreclose on all the collateralized properties, not just the one that generated the loss.

Cross-collateralization creates the same risk concentration problem as a portfolio LLC. A problem with one property can jeopardize multiple properties.

Blanket Liens

A blanket lien is similar. The lender takes a lien against all of your properties (or all properties owned by the entity) to secure a loan. If you default, every property under the lien is at risk.

These practices can reconnect properties to personal assets. Even if you've carefully structured each property in a separate LLC, financing terms can undermine that separation. A blanket lien across multiple LLCs effectively pools the risk.

Understanding financing terms is as important as choosing the right entity. Before signing any loan documents, read carefully. Ask questions. Understand what you're personally guaranteeing and what collateral you're pledging. Negotiate where possible to limit personal exposure.

The Real Estate Asset Protection Mindset

Effective real estate asset protection is not about avoiding responsibility. It is about containing risk so that one mistake, one injury, one lawsuit does not destroy everything you've built.

Core Principles

Isolate Properties

Where feasible, separate high-risk properties from each other and from personal assets. Use entity structures to create legal boundaries. The goal is to ensure that a loss on one property does not cascade across the entire portfolio.

Maintain Strong Insurance

Carry adequate liability coverage on every property. Consider umbrella policies for additional protection. Review policies annually. Understand exclusions. Ensure coverage is continuous.

Respect Entity Boundaries

If you use LLCs, treat them as real. Keep separate bank accounts. Sign documents in the entity's name. Don't commingle funds. Pay entity expenses from entity accounts. These formalities preserve the legal protection.

Document Everything

Keep thorough records of maintenance, repairs, tenant communications, and lease agreements. Documentation is your defense in litigation. If you can prove you maintained the property, addressed complaints promptly, and complied with the law, you're far less likely to lose.

Plan for Worst-Case Scenarios Without Panic

Asset protection is planning for things going wrong. This doesn't mean you expect disaster. It means you acknowledge that accidents happen, tenants sue, and insurance sometimes fails. Preparing for these possibilities is prudent, not paranoid.

What Poor Planning Looks Like

Poorly structured investors rely on hope. They hope nothing bad will happen. They hope their insurance will cover everything. They hope the tenant won't sue. They hope the jury will be reasonable.

Hope is not a strategy. Hope is the absence of planning.

Poorly structured investors also make these mistakes:

- Holding all properties personally because "it's simpler"
- Using one LLC for all properties to "save money"
- Commingling personal and business funds because "it's just easier"
- Letting insurance lapse because "nothing ever happens"
- Ignoring maintenance complaints because "tenants always complain"
- Failing to document anything because "I'll remember"

These choices are not malicious. They are human. But they are also costly.

Looking Ahead

In the next chapter, we will examine retirement accounts and statutory protections: assets that receive special treatment under the law and often form the backbone of long-term protection strategies.

Real estate builds wealth slowly. Lawsuits destroy it quickly. Structure determines which outcome prevails.

The difference between a protected portfolio and an exposed one is not luck. It is intention, discipline, and informed decision-making. The tools exist. The question is whether you will use them.

6

Retirement Accounts and Statutory Protections

Not all assets are treated equally under the law. Some assets, particularly retirement accounts, receive special statutory protection that makes them among the safest holdings in any asset protection plan. These protections exist by design, reflecting public policy choices to encourage long-term savings and prevent individuals from becoming dependent on public support later in life.

Understanding how these protections work, and where they end, is essential. Retirement accounts can be powerful anchors in an asset protection strategy, but only when their limits and conditions are respected.

Why Retirement Accounts Are Uniquely Protected

Retirement accounts are protected not primarily by contracts or entities, but by statute. Statutes are laws that override many creditor claims automatically. Think of them as a legal shield built directly into the code that governs these accounts.

These protections are strong because they are embedded in federal law, courts apply them routinely without requiring you to prove anything special, and creditors face limited remedies even when they win a lawsuit against you. The protection isn't something you have to argue for or defend in court. It simply exists.

In many cases, retirement accounts are the last assets creditors can reach, even after successful lawsuits. A creditor might win a judgment against you, obtain liens on your property, garnish your wages, and seize your bank accounts, but your 401(k) or IRA may remain completely untouchable.

This makes retirement accounts especially valuable for professionals with liability exposure (doctors, lawyers, consultants, engineers, architects), business owners who face the risk of lawsuits or business failure, individuals approaching or in retirement who need to protect their life savings, and anyone concerned about long-term financial security in an increasingly litigious world.

Unlike other asset protection tools, statutory protections do not require ongoing maintenance or complex structures. You don't need to file annual reports, pay franchise taxes, or maintain corporate formalities. Once your money is in a protected retirement account, the protection is automatic. It travels with the account wherever it goes, as long as the account maintains its qualified status.

This simplicity is a tremendous advantage. Many asset protection strategies fail because people don't maintain them properly. Retirement account protection, by contrast, is virtually maintenance-free.

Federal vs. State Protections: Understanding the Two-Tier System

Retirement account protection is governed by a combination of federal and state law. Understanding the difference is important because it affects how secure your accounts really are. The interplay between these two systems can be confusing, but it's worth taking the time to understand.

Federal Protections: The Gold Standard

Certain retirement plans are protected under federal law regardless of which state you live in. This uniformity is one of their greatest strengths. Whether you live in California or Florida, New York or Texas, the federal protections remain the same.

The most important federal protections apply to most employer-sponsored plans (like 401(k)s, 403(b)s, and traditional pension plans) and plans governed by ERISA (the Employee Retirement Income Security Act of 1974). ERISA is the comprehensive federal law that sets minimum standards for most voluntarily established retirement and health plans in private industry.

These protections are among the strongest available and offer several key advantages. They are unlimited in amount, meaning there is no dollar cap on protection. Whether you have $50,000 or $5 million in your 401(k), the entire balance is protected. They are automatic, meaning you don't have to do anything special to claim them. The protection exists simply by virtue of the account being an ERISA-qualified plan. And they are resistant to state-level exceptions, meaning individual states cannot pass laws that weaken these federal protections.

Federal protection typically applies in bankruptcy proceedings and often outside of bankruptcy as well. This dual protection is significant. If you file for bankruptcy, your ERISA-qualified retirement accounts are excluded from your bankruptcy estate entirely. Creditors cannot touch them. But even if you never file for bankruptcy, if a creditor sues you and wins a judgment, they generally still cannot reach your ERISA-protected retirement accounts.

This means creditors usually cannot touch these funds even if they sue you successfully. They might be able to garnish your paycheck, put a lien on your house, or seize your savings account. But your 401(k) remains protected.

The Supreme Court has consistently reinforced these protections. In cases involving creditor claims against ERISA plans, the Court has made clear that Congress intended these accounts to have strong protection, and courts should not create exceptions unless Congress has explicitly provided for them.

State Protections: A Patchwork of Rules

State law governs individual retirement accounts (IRAs), both traditional and Roth, non-ERISA plans (such as certain governmental and church plans), and certain exemptions that apply outside of bankruptcy proceedings.

State protections vary widely from one state to another, creating a patchwork of rules that can be difficult to navigate. Some states, like Florida and Texas, fully exempt IRAs from creditor claims with no dollar limit. Others cap protection at specific dollar amounts. For example, California currently caps IRA protection at approximately $1.5 million (adjusted for inflation), while other states may have caps of $500,000, $1 million, or other amounts.

Some states require that funds be "reasonably necessary" for retirement, which introduces a subjective standard that can lead to uncertainty. A court might look at your age, your other assets, your income, and your lifestyle to determine how much of your IRA is truly necessary for your retirement. Amounts deemed excessive might lose their protection.

Because state law varies so dramatically, retirement planning must consider where you live and where you may move in the future. Moving from a state with strong IRA protections to one with weak protections could suddenly expose your retirement savings to creditor claims. Conversely, moving to a state with stronger protections might enhance your asset protection, though you typically need to establish residency before the new state's exemptions apply.

This variability creates planning opportunities but also pitfalls. If you're considering a move, especially later in life or when facing potential liability, the strength of retirement account protection in your destination state should be part of your decision-making process. This may sound extreme, but when you have decades of savings at stake, the legal environment matters.

Some states also distinguish between contributory IRAs (funded by your own contributions and employer contributions rolled over from qualified plans) and rollover IRAs (funded only by rollovers from employer plans). In states that make this distinction, rollover IRAs sometimes receive stronger protection because they represent funds that would have been fully protected if they had remained in the ERISA plan.

IRAs vs. Employer Plans: Not All Retirement Accounts Are Equal

From an asset protection perspective, not all retirement accounts are equal. The type of account you have matters significantly, and understanding these differences can inform important financial decisions.

Employer-Sponsored Plans: Maximum Protection

Employer-sponsored plans, including 401(k) plans, 403(b) plans, profit-sharing plans, and traditional pension plans, typically offer strong federal protection under ERISA, protection from most creditors both inside and outside bankruptcy, and limited exposure even in litigation.

They are often the gold standard for creditor protection. If you have the choice between leaving money in an employer plan or rolling it into an IRA, the employer plan usually provides stronger protection. This is especially true if you live in a state with weak IRA protections or if you have a large account balance that exceeds your state's IRA exemption cap.

Many people automatically roll over their 401(k) when they leave a job, often at the encouragement of financial advisors who want to manage the assets. But from a pure asset protection standpoint, this can be a mistake. If your former employer's plan allows you to keep your money there, and if the plan offers reasonable investment options and fees, leaving the money in the ERISA-protected 401(k) may provide superior creditor protection.

This doesn't mean you should never roll over a 401(k). Investment options, fees, convenience, and estate planning considerations all matter. But asset protection should be part of the analysis, especially if you face meaningful liability risks.

Individual Retirement Accounts: Strong but Variable

IRAs receive significant protection in most states, but the protection comes with important caveats. Protection may be capped at a certain dollar amount depending on your state. While most states provide generous protection, the existence of caps means that very large IRA balances may be partially exposed in some jurisdictions.

State law plays a larger role in determining protection levels, which introduces variability and uncertainty. What works in one state may not work in another.

Inherited IRAs may be treated differently, often with weaker protection. We'll explore this in more detail below, but it's worth noting here that an IRA you inherit from someone else generally does not receive the same level of protection as an IRA you funded yourself.

While IRAs are still highly valuable and offer substantial protection in most states, they require closer attention to jurisdiction and structure. You can't simply assume your IRA is protected. You need to know the specific rules in your state.

For individuals with high liability risk or very large account balances, this difference matters. A surgeon with $3 million in retirement savings might have all of it protected if it's in a 401(k), but only $1.5 million protected if it's in an IRA in a state with that cap.

Roth Accounts: Same Protection, Different Tax Treatment

Both Roth 401(k)s and Roth IRAs generally receive the same creditor protection as their traditional counterparts. A Roth 401(k) receives the same ERISA protection as a traditional 401(k). A Roth IRA receives the same state-law protection as a traditional IRA.

The choice between traditional and Roth accounts should be driven primarily by tax considerations, not asset protection. Both offer strong protection. The question is whether you'd rather pay taxes now (Roth) or later (traditional).

Rollovers and Transitions: Proceed with Caution

Moving funds from an employer plan to an IRA is one of the most common financial transactions in America. Millions of people do it every year when they change jobs or retire. But from an asset protection perspective, this seemingly routine transaction has important implications.

A rollover can improve flexibility and investment options, giving you access to a much broader range of investments than most employer plans offer. It can also simplify your financial life by consolidating multiple retirement accounts in one place. And it can facilitate estate planning by giving you more control over beneficiary designations and distribution options.

But a rollover can also reduce certain protections. By moving money from an ERISA-protected 401(k) to a state-law-protected IRA, you may be moving from unlimited federal protection to limited state protection.

Improper rollovers can unintentionally weaken asset protection. The way you document the rollover and the timing of the transfer both matter. A direct rollover, where funds move directly from the employer plan to the IRA without you ever touching the money, is generally treated more favorably than an indirect rollover, where you receive a check and then have 60 days to deposit it into an IRA.

If you are concerned about creditor protection, consult with an advisor before rolling over a large employer plan balance into an IRA. This is especially important if you have significant liability exposure, if you live in a state with IRA protection caps, or if you have an unusually large account balance.

For some people, the right answer may be to leave funds in the employer plan indefinitely, even decades after leaving the job. For others, rolling over makes sense. But it should be a deliberate decision, not an automatic one.

In some cases, a partial rollover might make sense. You could roll over enough to get the investment flexibility you want while leaving a substantial amount in the ERISA-protected plan as a creditor-proof safety net.

Inheritance Considerations: Planning Beyond Your Lifetime

Asset protection does not end at death. What happens to your retirement accounts after you pass away is a critical part of planning. In fact, for many people, protecting their beneficiaries from creditors, divorce, and poor decisions is just as important as protecting themselves.

Inherited Retirement Accounts: A Weaker Shield

In many jurisdictions, inherited retirement accounts receive weaker creditor protection than accounts you own yourself. This is a critical and often overlooked point.

When you own an IRA, it's protected because it represents your retirement security. Courts recognize that you need this money to avoid becoming a public burden in your old age. But when your child or grandchild inherits your IRA, it's no longer necessary for their retirement in the same way. They may be decades away from retirement. They likely have their own retirement accounts. As a result, courts in many states have ruled that inherited IRAs deserve less protection.

Beneficiaries may lose statutory exemptions that protected the original owner. In some states, an inherited IRA receives no protection at all. In others, it receives some protection but less than the beneficiary's own retirement accounts would receive.

The Supreme Court addressed this issue in a 2014 case called Clark v. Rameker 573 U.S. 122 (2014), ruling that inherited IRAs are not "retirement funds" within the meaning of the federal bankruptcy exemption. This means that in bankruptcy, inherited IRAs may receive no federal protection at all. They may still be protected by state law, but that varies widely.

Divorce and bankruptcy risks increase for beneficiaries when they inherit retirement accounts outright. If your son inherits your $500,000 IRA and then gets divorced two years later, that IRA may be considered a marital asset subject to division. If your daughter inherits your IRA and then files for bankruptcy, it may be seized by creditors.

This reality has significant implications for estate planning decisions, beneficiary designations on your accounts, and trust-based planning strategies.

Leaving retirement assets outright to beneficiaries may expose those assets to risks the original owner never faced. For example, if your child inherits your IRA and then gets divorced or sued, the inherited IRA may be vulnerable even though it was protected when you owned it. Your lifetime of careful savings could be lost not because of anything you did wrong, but because of events in your beneficiary's life that you couldn't predict.

Using Trusts for Inherited Accounts: A Powerful Solution

Properly designed trusts can preserve the tax advantages of inherited retirement accounts (though the rules changed significantly with the SECURE Act of 2019, which generally requires inherited accounts to be distributed within 10 years rather than stretched over the beneficiary's lifetime). They can also provide creditor protection for beneficiaries, control distributions over time to prevent beneficiaries from squandering the inheritance, and protect against divorce and mismanagement.

A trust named as the beneficiary of your retirement account can shield the inherited retirement assets from your beneficiary's creditors, divorcing spouse, and poor financial decisions. The trust can specify how and when distributions are made, ensuring the money is used wisely.

For example, instead of leaving your $1 million IRA directly to your daughter, you could leave it to a trust for her benefit. The trust could provide that distributions are made to her for health, education, maintenance, and support, but creditors cannot reach the trust assets. If she gets divorced, the IRA remains protected. If she gets sued, creditors cannot touch it. And if she struggles with financial management, the trustee can control the pace of distributions.

Trust planning is not about distrust. It is about foresight and protecting the people you care about from circumstances they cannot predict or control. It's not assuming your children will make bad decisions. It's recognizing that bad things can happen to good people, and that a well-structured trust can provide protection against those events.

The tax rules for retirement accounts and trusts are complex, and they changed significantly in recent years. Working with an attorney who understands both estate planning and retirement account taxation is essential. A poorly drafted trust can create tax disasters. A well-drafted trust can provide both protection and tax efficiency.

Divorce and Retirement Assets: When Protection Isn't Enough

Divorce represents one of the most significant threats to retirement assets, even with strong statutory protections in place. In fact, asset protection laws that shield retirement accounts from creditors often provide no protection at all in divorce.

The reason is simple: retirement accounts accumulated during marriage are generally considered marital property subject to division between spouses. Courts have the authority to divide marital property equitably (or equally, depending on the state), and they routinely order retirement accounts to be split.

Key considerations include the fact that retirement accounts are often considered marital property subject to division, division may be mandatory regardless of asset protection strategies, Qualified Domestic Relations Orders (QDROs) govern how employer plans are divided in divorce, and courts can order retirement accounts to be split between spouses regardless of whose name is on the account.

Asset protection planning cannot override family law. If a court determines that your retirement account is marital property, it can be divided in a divorce regardless of creditor protections. A 401(k) that is completely protected from business creditors can still be split 50/50 with a spouse in a divorce.

However, understanding this exposure can inform prenuptial planning and agreements. A well-drafted prenuptial agreement can specify that retirement accounts remain separate property, preventing them from being divided in divorce. This is particularly important in second marriages or when one spouse enters the marriage with substantial retirement savings.

Understanding divorce exposure can also inform account structuring decisions and contribution strategies during marriage. In community property states, contributions to retirement accounts during marriage are generally community property regardless of whose name is on the account.

In equitable distribution states, the rules are more complex but generally lead to similar results.

If you're concerned about protecting retirement assets in the event of divorce, consider how pre-marital retirement assets are documented and segregated, whether a prenuptial or postnuptial agreement makes sense for your situation, how contributions are made during marriage, and what your overall asset allocation looks like between spouses.

It's also worth noting that not all states treat all retirement accounts the same way in divorce. Some states treat defined benefit pensions differently than 401(k)s. Some give special consideration to unvested benefits. Understanding your state's specific rules can inform planning decisions.

Statutory Protection Is Powerful but Not Absolute

Retirement accounts enjoy exceptional protection, but they are not invincible. There are important exceptions you need to understand. Believing your retirement accounts are completely untouchable can lead to complacency and poor planning.

Common exceptions include certain tax claims. The IRS can reach retirement accounts for unpaid taxes. If you owe back taxes to the federal government, the IRS has the authority to levy your IRA or 401(k) to satisfy the debt. State tax authorities may have similar powers.

Domestic support obligations, including child support and alimony, can also reach retirement accounts. Courts can order retirement funds to be used to satisfy support obligations. This makes sense from a policy perspective: we don't want deadbeat parents hiding assets in retirement accounts while their children go without support.

Improper withdrawals can also eliminate protection. Taking money out of a retirement account removes its protected status. Once funds are withdrawn, they become regular assets subject to creditor claims. If you take a distribution from your 401(k) and deposit it in your checking account, those funds are no longer protected. Creditors can reach them.

Loss of protected status through misuse is another concern. If you use a retirement account for non-retirement purposes, you may forfeit its protection. For example, borrowing against your 401(k) to fund a business venture could jeopardize its protected status in some circumstances.

Using retirement accounts as day-to-day liquidity or as a regular source of cash can erode both tax benefits and asset protection benefits. Every early withdrawal triggers taxes and penalties. And every withdrawal removes protected assets from the shelter of the retirement account.

These accounts are designed for retirement, and using them for other purposes can have serious consequences. The tax penalties alone (generally 10% for withdrawals before age 59½, plus regular income tax) make early withdrawals expensive. Add in the loss of asset protection, and the cost becomes even higher.

There are also certain types of creditors that may have special access to retirement funds. In addition to tax authorities and domestic support obligations, some courts have held that creditors with claims based on fraud or intentional misconduct may be able to reach otherwise protected retirement accounts. The theory is that people shouldn't be able to defraud others and then hide behind asset protection laws.

Contribution Strategies: Maximizing Protection

If retirement accounts offer strong protection, it makes sense to maximize contributions to them, especially if you face liability risks. Every dollar in a protected retirement account is a dollar that creditors generally cannot reach.

For business owners and high-income professionals, this suggests several strategies:

Max out contributions to employer-sponsored plans first, especially if you have a 401(k), 403(b), or other ERISA-protected plan. For 2024, you can contribute up to $23,000 to a 401(k) if you're under 50, or $30,500 if you're 50 or older. If you own your own business, you may be able to contribute even more through profit-sharing contributions.

Consider defined benefit plans for maximum contributions. If you're self-employed or own a small business, a defined benefit pension plan can allow for much larger contributions than a 401(k). In some cases, you can contribute $200,000 or more per year to a defined benefit plan. These plans are complex and require actuarial calculations, but for the right situation, they can provide tremendous asset protection value.

Use SEP IRAs and SIMPLE IRAs if you're self-employed without employees. These are easier to administer than defined benefit plans but still allow for meaningful contributions.

Don't overlook spousal IRAs. Even if one spouse doesn't work, you can contribute to an IRA for that spouse as long as the working spouse has enough earned income. This effectively doubles your IRA contribution capacity.

Time contributions strategically. If you're facing a lawsuit or anticipate liability, making large retirement account contributions immediately before the claim arises can sometimes be challenged as a fraudulent transfer. Courts may allow creditors to reach those contributions if they were made to defraud creditors. But regular, ongoing contributions made as part of normal financial planning are generally protected.

Bankruptcy Considerations: Federal Exemptions

If you file for bankruptcy, both federal and state exemptions may apply to your retirement accounts. The rules are complex, but understanding the basics can help you plan.

ERISA-qualified plans (401(k)s, pensions, etc.) are excluded from your bankruptcy estate entirely. This means they don't even count as an asset in your bankruptcy. You keep them, period.

IRAs receive protection up to a certain limit in bankruptcy under federal law, currently about $1.5 million (adjusted for inflation every three years). This is a federal floor, meaning it applies even if your state provides less protection. But if your state provides more protection, you may be able to claim the state exemption instead.

Rollover IRAs from qualified plans may receive unlimited protection in bankruptcy. Some courts have held that funds rolled over from ERISA plans retain their unlimited protection even after being rolled into an IRA. Other courts disagree. This is an unsettled area of law.

The interplay between federal bankruptcy exemptions and state exemptions can be confusing. When you file for bankruptcy, you generally have the option to choose either the federal exemption scheme or your state's exemption scheme. You can't mix and match. Some states, however, have "opted out" of the federal exemptions, meaning you must use the state exemptions.

For retirement planning purposes, the key takeaway is that substantial retirement account balances are generally protected in bankruptcy, but if you have extremely large account balances, consulting with a bankruptcy attorney before filing can help you understand exactly how much protection you'll receive.

Real-World Example: The Power of Retirement Account Protection

Consider a physician who built a successful practice over 30 years. He diligently contributed to his 401(k) and eventually accumulated $2.5 million in retirement savings. He also accumulated other assets: a home worth $800,000, investment accounts worth $600,000, and $200,000 in cash savings.

At age 58, he faced a malpractice lawsuit. Despite having malpractice insurance, the claim exceeded his coverage by $1.2 million. A jury awarded the plaintiff $1.5 million beyond his insurance coverage.

Without retirement account protection, the doctor would have faced financial devastation. The creditor could have forced the sale of his home, seized his investment accounts and cash, and potentially garnished his wages. He would have been starting over financially just as he approached retirement.

But with retirement account protection, the outcome was very different. His 401(k) was completely protected under federal ERISA law. The $2.5 million remained untouchable. The creditor could reach his other assets, but his retirement remained intact.

Yes, he lost his investment accounts and most of his cash savings. He had to downsize his home. But he didn't lose everything. His retirement security remained intact. At age 65, he could retire with his 401(k) providing for his needs.

This example illustrates why retirement accounts are such powerful asset protection tools. They provide a floor beneath which you cannot fall, a guaranteed level of security that creditors cannot penetrate.

Integrating Retirement Accounts Into a Broader Plan

The strongest asset protection strategies treat retirement accounts as anchors, not catch-alls. They should be one part of a comprehensive approach, not your only strategy.

Retirement accounts work best when combined with adequate insurance coverage (malpractice, liability, umbrella policies), supported by entity planning (like LLCs for business assets or rental properties), and integrated with estate planning and trust structures to protect beneficiaries.

Over-reliance on any single protection, no matter how strong, is risky. A balanced approach that uses multiple layers of protection is almost always more effective. Think of it like layered security: insurance to prevent claims from becoming judgments, entities to separate risky assets from safe ones, and retirement accounts as a protected reserve that creditors cannot reach.

For business owners, this might mean operating the business through an LLC or corporation to limit personal liability, maintaining substantial liability insurance, maximizing contributions to ERISA-protected retirement plans, and using trusts for estate planning to protect beneficiaries.

For professionals, it might mean maintaining adequate professional liability insurance, maximizing retirement contributions, potentially using a professional LLC or PC where allowed, and keeping investment assets separate from business assets.

For retirees, it might mean keeping substantial assets in protected retirement accounts rather than taking large lump-sum distributions, using trusts to protect beneficiaries from creditors and divorce, maintaining umbrella liability insurance, and structuring home ownership to maximize applicable exemptions.

The key is to view retirement accounts not as a complete solution, but as one powerful tool in a comprehensive strategy.

Common Mistakes to Avoid

As you think about using retirement accounts for asset protection, be aware of common mistakes that can undermine your planning:

Taking early withdrawals. Every withdrawal removes protected assets from shelter. Unless you absolutely need the money, leave it in the protected account.

Automatically rolling over employer plans. The default assumption that you should always roll over a 401(k) when you leave a job ignores the asset protection implications. Sometimes leaving money in the employer plan is smarter.

Ignoring state-specific rules. If you live in a state with weak IRA protections, you need to know that. Don't assume your IRAs are fully protected without checking your state's laws.

Failing to plan for beneficiaries. Leaving retirement accounts outright to beneficiaries without considering the loss of creditor protection is a missed opportunity. Trust-based planning can preserve protection for the next generation.

Making fraudulent transfers. Moving large amounts of money into retirement accounts right before filing for bankruptcy or right after learning about a lawsuit can be challenged as a fraudulent transfer. Regular contributions are protected; last-minute sheltering of assets may not be.

Not coordinating with other planning. Retirement account planning should be integrated with your overall financial plan, estate plan, and asset protection strategy. Working with advisors who understand all these pieces is essential.

The Bottom Line

Retirement accounts represent one of the most powerful asset protection tools available to ordinary Americans. They are simpler than trusts, stronger than LLCs in many cases, and more accessible than offshore structures.

Their protection is automatic, requires no ongoing maintenance, and applies to millions of Americans who may not even realize they have asset protection in place. But like any tool, they must be used correctly. Understanding the differences between ERISA plans and IRAs, federal and state protections, and the treatment of inherited accounts is essential.

When used as part of a comprehensive strategy, retirement accounts provide a foundation of security that can withstand most creditor challenges. They allow you to build wealth knowing that at least a portion of what you accumulate will be there when you need it, protected from the uncertainties of lawsuits, business failures, and other financial setbacks.

Looking Ahead

In the next chapter, we will explore Domestic Asset Protection Trusts (DAPTs), one of the most debated and misunderstood tools in modern asset protection planning. While retirement accounts offer straightforward, statutory protection, DAPTs represent a more complex and controversial approach that involves creating trusts in special jurisdictions designed to shield assets from creditors.

Retirement accounts protect wealth quietly and consistently. Understanding their strengths and limitations allows you to build around them with confidence and create a more secure financial future. They are the foundation. Now let's examine the more sophisticated structures that can be built on top of that foundation.

7

Domestic Asset Protection Trusts

Domestic Asset Protection Trusts (commonly called DAPTs) occupy a unique and often controversial place in asset protection planning. To some people, they are an elegant solution that allows individuals to protect assets while retaining beneficial access. To others, they are overpromised, misunderstood, and occasionally misused. Both views contain elements of truth.

This chapter explains what DAPTs are, how they work, where they are strong, where they are vulnerable, and most importantly, who they are actually appropriate for. We'll break down complex legal concepts into practical terms and help you understand whether a DAPT might make sense for your situation.

What a DAPT Is and How It Works

A Domestic Asset Protection Trust is a self-settled trust created under the laws of certain U.S. states that allow the person who creates the trust (the grantor) to also be a beneficiary.

To understand why this matters, you need to know a bit of trust law history. Traditionally, U.S. trust law followed a simple rule: if you create a trust for your own benefit, your creditors can reach it. The reasoning was straightforward. If you could benefit from assets, those assets should be available to people you owe money to. Otherwise, you could simply move all your assets into a trust, claim you don't own them anymore, and avoid your obligations.

DAPTs are an exception to that rule, but only in specific states and only under specific conditions. Beginning in the 1990s, several states passed laws allowing people to create trusts for their own benefit that creditors could not easily access. These states were competing for trust business and the fees that come with it.

Basic Structure

A typical DAPT involves several key components:

The grantor is the person who creates the trust and transfers assets into it. This is you, if you're setting one up.

An independent trustee must be located in a DAPT-friendly state. This cannot be you, and it cannot be someone completely under your control. Most people use a professional trustee like a trust company or bank. This trustee has legal discretion over distributions.

The grantor as a discretionary beneficiary means you can potentially receive distributions from the trust, but you have no guaranteed right to them. The trustee decides whether and when to make distributions.

Spendthrift provisions are clauses in the trust document that specifically restrict creditor access and prevent beneficiaries from transferring their interests.

If properly established and maintained, creditors may be unable to reach trust assets, even though the grantor may still benefit from them. The key word here is "may." Protection is never absolute.

States That Allow Self-Settled Trusts

Not all states recognize DAPTs. Only a limited number of states have enacted statutes allowing self-settled asset protection trusts. As of now, approximately 19 states have some form of DAPT legislation, including Alaska, Delaware, Nevada, South Dakota, Wyoming, Tennessee, and others.

These statutes vary significantly in strength, scope, and creditor exceptions. Some states have more protective laws than others, and the differences matter tremendously in practice.

Key differences include:

Statutes of limitation for creditor claims determine how long a creditor has to challenge a transfer to a DAPT. Some states allow only two years, while others allow four or more. A shorter statute of limitations offers better protection.

Types of creditors excluded from protection vary by state. All DAPT states exclude certain creditors like ex-spouses owed alimony or child support, but some states have broader exceptions than others.

Requirements for trustees and administration differ significantly. Some states require only that the trustee be located in the state. Others require that some trust administration activities occur there or that some trust assets be physically held there.

Burdens of proof placed on creditors can be higher or lower depending on the state. Some states require creditors to prove fraudulent transfer by "clear and convincing evidence" rather than the lower "preponderance of the evidence" standard.

Because of these differences, where a DAPT is established matters just as much as how it is drafted. This is why people often call these statutes a "race to the bottom" or, more charitably, a "race to the top," depending on your perspective.

Strengths of Domestic Asset Protection Trusts

DAPTs offer several meaningful advantages when used correctly. Understanding these benefits helps you evaluate whether they're worth the cost and complexity.

Retention of Benefit

Unlike traditional irrevocable trusts, a DAPT allows:

Continued discretionary access to assets. You don't have to completely walk away from your wealth. If you need money for medical expenses, retirement, or other purposes, the trustee can potentially distribute funds to you.

Potential income and principal distributions. The trust can pay you income it generates, or even give you back some of the principal you contributed, all at the trustee's discretion.

Psychological comfort for grantors. Many people struggle with the idea of giving away assets irrevocably, even if it's for asset protection. DAPTs offer a middle ground. You're not completely cut off from the assets, which makes the decision emotionally easier.

This makes DAPTs attractive to individuals reluctant to give up control entirely. For many people, especially those who have worked their whole lives to accumulate wealth, the thought of transferring assets to a trust they can never benefit from is simply too much to bear. DAPTs solve that problem.

Onshore Simplicity

Compared to offshore structures, DAPTs:

Operate within the U.S. legal system. Everything happens under American law, in American courts, with American trustees. There's no need to navigate foreign legal systems or worry about political instability in other countries.

Are easier to administer. You can communicate with your trustee easily, in the same time zone, speaking the same language. Meetings can happen in person if needed. Documents don't need to be shipped internationally.

Avoid foreign reporting regimes. Offshore trusts trigger extensive IRS reporting requirements that are burdensome and create audit risk. DAPTs require much simpler reporting.

Feel more familiar to clients and advisors. Both you and your attorney or financial advisor likely understand U.S. trust law reasonably well. Offshore planning often involves unfamiliar legal concepts and requires specialized expertise.

For moderate-risk profiles, this simplicity can be appealing. If you're a doctor worried about malpractice claims or a business owner concerned about lawsuits but not facing extreme or immediate risk, the added complexity of going offshore may not be justified.

Statutory Creditor Protection

When effective, DAPTs:

Limit creditor remedies. Even if a creditor can prove a claim, the DAPT statute may limit what they can do. In some cases, they might only be able to reach distributions actually made to you, not the trust principal itself.

Impose high burdens of proof. As mentioned, some states require creditors to prove fraudulent transfer by clear and convincing evidence, a significantly higher standard than the normal civil litigation standard.

Discourage speculative litigation. If a potential plaintiff knows you have a DAPT and understands the legal hurdles involved in attacking it, they may be less likely to sue in the first place. Even if they do sue, they may be more willing to settle for less.

They can meaningfully improve settlement leverage in certain scenarios. When you're negotiating with someone who has sued you or threatened to sue you, the existence of a properly structured DAPT can change the dynamics. The other side knows that even if they win a judgment, collecting may be difficult or impossible.

Limitations and Risks of DAPTs

Despite their appeal, DAPTs have real limitations that must be understood clearly. Being honest about these weaknesses is essential. Too many people set up DAPTs with unrealistic expectations and end up disappointed or worse.

Interstate Enforcement Risk

The most significant weakness of DAPTs is interstate uncertainty. This deserves your careful attention because it's the issue that keeps asset protection attorneys up at night.

While a DAPT may be valid under the law of the state where it is created, courts in other states are not always required to honor that protection, especially if:

The grantor resides elsewhere. If you live in California but create a Nevada DAPT, a California court may decide that California law governs the dispute, not Nevada law. Since California doesn't recognize DAPTs, the protection might disappear.

The creditor claim arises elsewhere. If the lawsuit that leads to a judgment against you happens in a non-DAPT state, that state's courts may simply ignore the DAPT statute.

Public policy conflicts exist. Some states have strong public policy against allowing people to shield their own assets from creditors. Courts in these states may refuse to enforce DAPT protections on public policy grounds.

The legal issue here involves complex questions about conflict of laws, the Full Faith and Credit Clause of the Constitution, and the tension between state sovereignty and interstate commerce. Courts have discretion in deciding which state's law applies, and reasonable judges can disagree.

A court may decide to apply its own state's law rather than the DAPT statute. This has happened in several reported cases, though outcomes vary significantly based on the specific facts.

This uncertainty does not mean DAPTs never work, but it does mean they are not bulletproof. You cannot and should not rely on a DAPT as your only line of defense. Think of it as one layer in a comprehensive strategy, not as an impenetrable shield.

Creditor Exceptions

Most DAPT statutes exclude certain claims, such as:

Child support and alimony. No state will allow you to shield assets from obligations to your children or former spouse. These obligations are considered so important as a matter of public policy that asset protection planning cannot defeat them.

Certain tort claims. Some states exclude tort claims that arose before the trust was funded or that arose from actions taken before the trust existed. If you injure someone and then create a DAPT, that person's claim will not be blocked.

Government or tax claims. The IRS and other government agencies can typically reach DAPT assets for tax debts, regulatory fines, and similar obligations. States want to attract trust business, but they're not willing to let people hide assets from the government.

These exceptions can significantly reduce effectiveness for individuals with predictable exposure in those areas. If you're going through a contentious divorce, have unpaid child support, or owe substantial taxes, a DAPT will provide little to no benefit.

Timing Sensitivity

DAPTs are extremely sensitive to timing. This cannot be emphasized enough. When you create and fund a DAPT matters just as much as how you do it.

Transfers made after a claim arises are almost always vulnerable. If someone has already sued you, or already has a judgment against you, transferring assets to a DAPT will likely be set aside as a fraudulent transfer.

Transfers made when a claim is foreseeable are also problematic. If you reasonably should have known that someone was going to sue you, even if they haven't yet, the transfer can be attacked. For example, if you're a surgeon and you know you made a serious mistake during surgery, you can't quickly set up a DAPT before the patient realizes what happened.

Transfers that result in insolvency will be challenged. If funding the DAPT leaves you unable to pay your existing debts, creditors can argue that the transfer was fraudulent and should be reversed.

A DAPT created too late may offer no protection at all. In fact, it might make things worse by angering the judge and making you look like you're trying to hide assets. Courts do not look kindly on last-minute asset protection planning.

The key takeaway is that DAPTs must be created and funded well in advance of any problems, ideally when your financial situation is stable and you have no claims or lawsuits pending or foreseeable.

Cost and Maintenance

DAPTs require:

Independent trustees. Professional trustees charge annual fees based on the value of trust assets. These fees can range from 0.5% to 1.5% or more of trust assets annually, depending on the complexity and size of the trust.

Ongoing administration. The trust needs to file tax returns, maintain records, and ensure compliance with the DAPT statute's requirements. This means accounting fees and administrative work every year.

Professional drafting. A properly structured DAPT requires an experienced attorney who understands both trust law and asset protection planning. This is not a do-it-yourself project. Initial legal fees can easily run from $5,000 to $25,000 or more.

Annual maintenance. Beyond trustee fees, you'll have ongoing legal and accounting costs for reviews, amendments, and compliance.

They are not "set it and forget it" solutions and may be inappropriate for smaller estates. If you have $200,000 in assets, spending $10,000 to set up a DAPT and $3,000 per year to maintain it probably doesn't make economic sense. Generally, DAPTs are most appropriate for individuals with at least $500,000 to $1 million in assets that need protection.

Interstate Risk and Court Enforcement

DAPTs exist in a legal tension between state sovereignty, constitutional principles, and public policy. Understanding this tension helps explain why outcomes can be unpredictable.

The U.S. Constitution's Full Faith and Credit Clause generally requires states to honor the judgments and laws of other states. However, there are exceptions, particularly when honoring another state's law would violate the forum state's strong public policy.

Many states have laws or case precedents holding that self-settled trusts are against public policy. When a creditor with a judgment from one of these states tries to collect from a DAPT established in a DAPT-friendly state, a conflict arises.

Courts have discretion, and outcomes can depend heavily on:

The facts of the case. Did the grantor move to the DAPT state, or do they still live elsewhere? Are the trust assets physically located in the DAPT state? Does the trustee actually perform meaningful functions there? The stronger the connection to the DAPT state, the more likely the protection will hold.

The judge. Some judges are sympathetic to asset protection planning and view it as legitimate. Others see it as an abuse of the legal system designed to help wealthy people avoid their obligations. The judge's philosophy matters.

The connection between the trust and the DAPT state. If the only connection to the DAPT state is that the trust document says it's governed by that state's law, courts may not be impressed. If the trustee is there, assets are there, and administration actually happens there, the protection is stronger.

This unpredictability is why DAPTs are best viewed as risk-reduction tools, not guarantees. They are not force fields that make creditors bounce off harmlessly.

They may deter lawsuits, improve negotiating leverage, and survive many claims, but they should not be relied upon as a single line of defense. Think of them as one tool in your toolbox, valuable but not sufficient on their own.

Who Should Use a DAPT

DAPTs may be appropriate for individuals who:

Have moderate to elevated liability exposure. This includes professionals like doctors, dentists, and lawyers who face malpractice risk. It includes business owners who might be sued by customers, employees, or vendors. It includes real estate investors who worry about premises liability.

Want onshore asset protection. If you're uncomfortable with offshore planning (and many people are), a DAPT offers a U.S.-based alternative. You avoid the complexity, reporting requirements, and psychological discomfort of going offshore.

Are planning well in advance. You cannot see a lawsuit on the horizon. Your financial situation is stable. You're thinking five, ten, or twenty years ahead. This advance planning is critical to effectiveness.

Have sufficient assets to justify the cost. Generally, this means at least $500,000 to $1 million in assets, though the exact threshold depends on your risk profile and other factors.

Understand and accept legal uncertainty. You need to go into this with eyes open, knowing that a DAPT might not work if challenged in court. You're comfortable with that uncertainty because you recognize that partial protection is better than no protection.

They work best when combined with:

Strong insurance. Malpractice insurance, general liability insurance, umbrella policies, and other coverage should be your first line of defense. Insurance pays claims so your assets never come into play.

Entity planning. Operating businesses through limited liability companies (LLCs) or corporations, holding real estate in separate entities, and using proper business structures all provide additional protection.

Conservative behavior. Asset protection planning is not a license to act recklessly. The best protection is not getting sued in the first place. That means treating people fairly, honoring your commitments, and not taking unnecessary risks.

Who Should Not Use a DAPT

DAPTs are generally a poor fit for:

Individuals facing active or imminent claims. If you've already been sued, already have a judgment against you, or know that someone is about to sue you, it's too late for a DAPT. Not only will it likely fail to protect you, but it may also make you look bad in court.

Those seeking "guaranteed" protection. If you need certainty, DAPTs cannot provide it. The interstate enforcement risk is real and cannot be eliminated. If your risk is severe enough that you need guaranteed protection, you may need to consider offshore planning or simply maintaining comprehensive insurance.

People unwilling to relinquish legal ownership. To create a DAPT, you must actually transfer assets to the trust. You no longer own them. The trustee does. If you want to maintain complete control and ownership, a DAPT won't work for you.

Low net worth individuals. If you don't have substantial assets to protect, the cost of establishing and maintaining a DAPT exceeds the benefit. There are simpler, less expensive asset protection strategies for people with modest wealth.

Anyone looking for secrecy or shortcuts. DAPTs are not offshore bank accounts. They must be properly disclosed on your tax returns. They require professional administration. They don't hide assets; they protect them through legal mechanisms. If you're looking for a way to hide money from creditors, the government, or an ex-spouse, a DAPT is not the answer and will likely get you into serious trouble.

Using a DAPT for the wrong reasons often produces the worst outcomes. People who set up DAPTs too late, with unrealistic expectations, or without proper professional guidance often end up wasting money and potentially making their situation worse.

DAPTs in Context: A Balanced Perspective

Domestic Asset Protection Trusts are neither magic nor meaningless. They are context-dependent tools with legitimate uses and real limitations.

Their effectiveness depends on:

Timing. Create and fund the trust well before any problems arise. Years in advance is ideal.

Jurisdiction. Choose a state with strong DAPT statutes and favorable case law. Work with trustees and attorneys who have deep experience in that jurisdiction.

Asset type. Some assets are easier to protect than others. Liquid financial assets like stocks, bonds, and cash are generally good candidates. Closely held businesses, real estate, and other less liquid assets can be more complicated.

Behavior. How you act after creating the DAPT matters. Don't treat trust assets as your personal piggy bank. Don't make excessive distributions to yourself. Follow the formalities and let the trustee exercise real discretion.

Integration with other protections. A DAPT should be part of a comprehensive plan that includes insurance, entity structuring, and smart business practices. It should never be your only strategy.

Used thoughtfully, they can enhance an asset protection plan. They add a meaningful layer of protection that can deter lawsuits, improve settlement outcomes, and provide peace of mind.

Used carelessly, they can create false confidence and unnecessary expense. Worse, they can make you look like you're trying to hide assets, which can anger judges and juries.

Practical Considerations for Implementation

If you're seriously considering a DAPT, here are some practical steps and considerations:

Work with experienced professionals. Find an attorney who regularly creates DAPTs and understands the nuances of different state statutes. Your general estate planning attorney may not have this expertise.

Choose the right state. Research which states have the strongest protections for your particular situation. Popular choices include Nevada, South Dakota, Delaware, and Alaska, but others may be appropriate depending on your circumstances.

Fund the trust properly. Don't just transfer everything at once without thinking. Consider which assets are most at risk and most appropriate for trust ownership. Be mindful of tax consequences.

Maintain proper formalities. Keep good records. Don't treat trust assets as your own. Let the trustee make real decisions about distributions. The more seriously you take the trust structure, the more likely it is to hold up if challenged.

Review and update regularly. Laws change. Your circumstances change. Review your DAPT at least every few years to ensure it still makes sense and complies with current law.

Be patient. Remember that many DAPT statutes have statutes of limitations that run for several years. The protection gets stronger over time as potential fraudulent transfer claims expire.

Looking Ahead

In the next chapter, we will step outside the United States to examine offshore asset protection: why it exists, how it differs from domestic planning, and when it may offer advantages that no U.S.-based structure can replicate.

Offshore planning is more complex, more expensive, and comes with significant additional reporting requirements. But for some people facing serious risks, it offers a level of protection that DAPTs simply cannot match.

Understanding DAPTs prepares you to evaluate those differences clearly and without ideology. You'll be able to compare domestic and offshore options rationally and make the choice that best fits your situation, your risk profile, and your comfort level.

Asset protection is not about finding the perfect, bulletproof solution. It's about understanding the available tools, their strengths and limitations, and building a strategy that makes sense for you.

PART III: Offshore Asset Protection

8

Why Offshore Protection Exists

Offshore asset protection is one of the most misunderstood topics in personal finance and law.

For some, the very word "offshore" evokes secrecy, wrongdoing, or an attempt to escape responsibility. For others, it suggests a flawless solution that places assets permanently beyond reach. Both reactions are emotional, and both are inaccurate.

Offshore asset protection exists for a much simpler reason: legal systems have limits, and not all legal systems operate the same way.

This chapter explains why offshore protection developed, what problems it is designed to address, and how to evaluate it rationally without fear, hype, or ideology.

The Limits of U.S. Courts

U.S. courts are powerful, but their power is not absolute.

American courts exercise authority over people and entities subject to U.S. jurisdiction, assets located within the United States, and entities formed under U.S. law. That authority weakens considerably when assets are held outside the country, under foreign law, or by foreign trustees or institutions.

This is not a loophole. It is a basic principle of international law: courts generally cannot enforce their judgments beyond their borders without cooperation from foreign governments and legal systems.

While U.S. courts can issue judgments, order disclosures, and penalize noncompliance, they cannot directly seize assets held in jurisdictions that do not recognize U.S. judgments. A judge in New York cannot simply reach into a bank in the Cook Islands and withdraw funds. The judgment must first be recognized and enforced by the courts in that foreign jurisdiction, a process that may be difficult, expensive, or impossible depending on local law.

This practical limitation is the foundation of offshore asset protection. It does not make assets disappear. It creates distance and additional legal hurdles that creditors must overcome.

Jurisdiction Shopping, Explained Legally

The term "jurisdiction shopping" is often used pejoratively, as if selecting favorable laws is inherently dishonest. But in legal practice, it is routine and entirely accepted.

Jurisdiction shopping simply means choosing the laws that will govern your affairs from among the lawful options available to you.

This happens constantly in everyday business and personal planning. Corporations choose states of incorporation based on favorable corporate laws (Delaware being the most famous example). Contracts specify which state's or country's laws will govern disputes. Financial institutions select regulatory regimes that align with their business models. Trusts are governed by the laws of chosen jurisdictions, which may differ dramatically in their protections and flexibility.

Offshore asset protection is an extension of this principle across international borders.

Different countries have different creditor remedies, burdens of proof, statutes of limitation, and rules for recognizing foreign judgments. Some jurisdictions make it extremely difficult for creditors to attack trusts or collect on foreign judgments. Others impose higher standards of proof or shorter time windows for bringing claims.

Selecting a jurisdiction with debtor-friendly laws is no more unethical than choosing a state with favorable tax or business statutes. Businesses do this all the time when they incorporate in Delaware or Nevada. What matters is that the choice is legal, transparent, and made in advance of any legal trouble.

When Domestic Strategies Are Not Enough

For many people, U.S.-based planning is sufficient. Insurance, business entities, retirement accounts, and domestic trusts solve most asset protection problems effectively and at reasonable cost.

Offshore strategies exist for the exceptions.

Domestic planning may be insufficient when liability exposure is unusually high, when assets significantly exceed insurance limits, when risks are unpredictable or catastrophic in nature, when public visibility increases the likelihood of litigation, or when jurisdictional neutrality is desired for international families or businesses.

Certain professionals (doctors, lawyers, architects), business owners, real estate investors, and wealthy families face risks that are not easily capped or insured. A surgeon may carry $5 million in malpractice insurance, but a catastrophic outcome could result in a judgment far exceeding that amount. A business owner may face liability from products, partnerships, or ventures that insurance does not fully cover. In these cases, domestic tools may reduce exposure but not meaningfully deter determined claimants with large potential recoveries at stake.

Offshore protection introduces distance, complexity, and cost into the litigation equation. It does not hide assets, but it changes the economics of pursuing them.

How Offshore Protection Changes the Equation

Offshore structures do not make lawsuits impossible. They make them harder and more expensive to pursue successfully.

They may prevent automatic enforcement of U.S. judgments, requiring creditors to relitigate claims abroad under different legal standards. They may impose higher burdens of proof, requiring creditors to prove their case again from scratch in a foreign court. They may shorten limitation periods, giving creditors less time to act. They may increase legal costs dramatically, as creditors must hire foreign attorneys and navigate unfamiliar legal systems. And they introduce uncertainty about the outcome, since foreign courts may not view claims the same way U.S. courts do.

This shift in the litigation landscape often discourages contingency-fee litigation and speculative claims. If a plaintiff's attorney knows that winning a judgment in the U.S. is only the first step, and that collecting will require expensive foreign litigation with uncertain prospects, the case becomes far less attractive. The economics no longer favor pursuit.

Importantly, offshore protection does not eliminate legal responsibility. It changes leverage in settlement negotiations. A creditor with a valid claim may still prevail, but the increased difficulty and cost of collection often leads to negotiated settlements on more favorable terms for the debtor.

Separating Emotion From Facts

Few topics in asset protection generate stronger emotional reactions than offshore planning. These reactions tend to fall into two categories: fear-based objections and fantasy-based expectations. Neither is helpful.

Fear-Based Objections

Common fears include beliefs that offshore planning must be illegal, that the IRS will automatically target you, that only criminals engage in such planning, or that moving assets offshore is somehow unpatriotic.

These concerns are rooted more in perception and media coverage than in law. Offshore planning is widely used by multinational corporations, pension funds, endowments, and wealthy families, often with full regulatory oversight and reporting. Major companies structure operations across dozens of countries. Universities hold endowment assets in foreign jurisdictions. None of this is illegal or improper.

Legality depends on compliance, not geography. Offshore planning becomes illegal only when it involves hiding assets from the IRS, lying on required disclosure forms, or transferring assets to defraud existing creditors. Done properly, with full reporting and proper timing, it is entirely lawful.

The IRS requires extensive reporting of foreign assets and accounts, but owning foreign assets is not itself suspicious or prohibited. Millions of Americans hold foreign investments, work abroad, or maintain international business interests. What matters is that you report accurately and pay taxes owed.

Fantasy-Based Expectations

On the other extreme are unrealistic beliefs that offshore means completely untouchable, that no one can ever find offshore assets, that courts are powerless to do anything about them, or that moving assets offshore frees you from U.S. legal obligations.

These beliefs are equally dangerous and will lead to severe legal consequences.

Offshore assets are discoverable through legal process. Courts can compel you to disclose them under penalty of contempt. They are reportable to the IRS through forms like the FBAR and Form 8938. They remain subject to court orders directed at you personally, even if the court cannot reach the assets directly. And they are vulnerable if you engage in poor behavior (like contempt of court) or bad timing (like transferring assets after a claim arises).

Offshore protection is not invisibility. It is resistance. It makes collection harder, not impossible. It increases leverage in negotiations. But it does not place you above the law or shield you from consequences if you violate court orders or lie to authorities.

Offshore Protection Is Only a Tool

Using offshore planning does not say anything about your ethics, politics, or intentions. It reflects a decision about risk management and the level of protection you believe is appropriate for your circumstances.

Good offshore planning is conservative, boring, thoroughly documented, and fully compliant with all reporting requirements. It does not rely on secrecy or deception. It relies on the simple jurisdictional reality that courts in one country cannot easily seize assets held under the laws of another country.

The goal is not to evade legitimate obligations. The goal is to create a strong enough defense that frivolous or excessive claims become uneconomical to pursue, and legitimate claimants are motivated to settle reasonably rather than engage in expensive international litigation.

The Cost of Misinformation

The greatest risk in offshore planning is not legal. It is conceptual.

People either avoid offshore tools entirely due to irrational fear, or they use them improperly due to hype and unrealistic expectations about what offshore protection can accomplish. Both approaches lead to poor outcomes.

Those who avoid offshore planning out of fear may leave themselves exposed to risks that could have been managed. Those who embrace it with unrealistic expectations may face contempt charges, tax penalties, or criminal prosecution for failing to comply with reporting requirements or court orders.

Understanding offshore protection requires a clear-eyed assessment of your actual risk level, an honest evaluation of whether domestic alternatives are sufficient, and a willingness to accept the trade-offs involved (including cost, complexity, and reporting obligations).

There is no universal solution, only solutions appropriate to specific circumstances.

Looking Ahead

In the next chapter, we will examine offshore asset protection trusts in detail: how they work mechanically, why certain jurisdictions are favored by planners, and what makes these trusts fundamentally different from domestic trusts in terms of legal protections and creditor remedies.

Offshore protection exists because the world is not governed by a single legal system. Each country has its own laws, courts, and enforcement mechanisms. Understanding that fact, and planning within that reality, allows you to make intelligent decisions about asset protection rather than emotional ones driven by fear or fantasy.

9

Offshore Asset Protection Trusts

Offshore Asset Protection Trusts (OAPTs) represent the strongest form of personal asset protection available today when set up properly. However, they are also among the most widely misunderstood financial planning tools. This comprehensive guide will walk you through everything you need to know about how these trusts work, why they differ from domestic options, and what you should realistically expect if you are considering one.

What Offshore Asset Protection Trusts Are Not

Before we dive into how these trusts work, it's crucial to clear up common misconceptions. Offshore asset protection trusts are not about hiding money from the government. They are not designed to help you avoid paying taxes you legitimately owe. They are not tools for escaping legal responsibility for your actions.

These trusts work because certain foreign countries have deliberately designed their legal systems to resist outside claims. When combined with careful planning and full legal compliance, these systems can provide protections that no U.S.-based structure can reliably match. The protection comes from legitimate legal frameworks, not from secrecy or deception.

Understanding the Fundamental Differences

How U.S. Trust Law Works

To understand why offshore trusts are different, you first need to understand how trusts work in the United States.

U.S. trust law is ultimately governed by several foundational principles. First, it operates within the framework of U.S. constitutional principles and federal law. Second, it gives broad authority to judges to interpret trust documents and reach outcomes they consider equitable or fair. Third, it includes strong protections for creditors who are seeking payment from debtors.

In practical terms, this means that U.S. courts have substantial power to look inside trust structures, reinterpret their terms, and order assets to be made available to creditors if the judge believes that is the fair outcome. Courts can pierce through formalities if they believe a trust is being used primarily to avoid legitimate obligations.

How Offshore Trust Jurisdictions Operate Differently

Offshore trust jurisdictions have taken a fundamentally different approach. Popular jurisdictions for asset protection trusts include the Cook Islands, Nevis, Belize, and several others. These countries have made deliberate choices about how their legal systems treat trusts and creditor claims.

First, many of these jurisdictions do not recognize judgments from foreign courts, including U.S. courts. This means that even if you lose a lawsuit in California or New York and a judge orders you to pay damages, that judgment has no automatic legal effect in the Cook Islands. The creditor cannot simply take that U.S. judgment and use it to seize assets held in a Cook Islands trust.

Second, these jurisdictions require creditors to start their lawsuits over from the beginning in the local courts. The creditor must hire local attorneys, follow local procedures, and prove their case all over again under the laws of that jurisdiction. This is not a simple or inexpensive process.

Third, these jurisdictions impose strict procedural requirements that are deliberately difficult to meet. These requirements might include very short statutes of limitation (the time window in which a lawsuit must be filed), high standards of proof (sometimes requiring proof beyond a reasonable doubt, similar to criminal cases), and requirements to post substantial bonds or deposits before pursuing a claim.

These differences are not loopholes or accidents. They are intentional policy choices made by these countries to attract trust business and provide strong protections to people who properly establish trusts under their laws.

The Public Policy Orientation

Many offshore trust jurisdictions have made an explicit economic decision to favor asset owners over creditors. This policy orientation shows up in multiple ways.

These jurisdictions tend to design their trust laws to discourage lawsuits filed without strong evidence. They impose procedural hurdles that filter out weak or speculative claims. They limit what creditors can do to collect debts, even when those debts are legitimate.

These policies are completely legal and transparent. The laws are publicly available. The countries promote their trust-friendly legal systems openly as a way to attract international business and professional fees.

In contrast, U.S. courts frequently prioritize different values. American judges often focus on giving creditors access to assets and reaching outcomes they consider fair, even if that means looking past the formal structure of a trust or other legal entity. U.S. courts tend to be skeptical of structures that appear designed primarily to keep assets away from creditors, particularly when those creditors have legitimate claims.

This difference in judicial philosophy creates the foundation for why offshore trusts can provide stronger protection than domestic alternatives.

The Critical Role of Foreign Trustees

One of the key features that makes an offshore asset protection trust effective is that it must have a foreign trustee. This is not optional or merely technical. It is fundamental to how the structure works.

Why the Trustee Must Be Foreign

If a U.S. person directly controls a trust, a U.S. court can order that person to hand over assets or make distributions to creditors. The court has jurisdiction over anyone physically present in the United States. A judge can hold that person in contempt, impose fines, or even order jail time for refusing to comply with court orders.

This means that if you are the trustee of your own trust, or if your lawyer or accountant in the United States serves as trustee, the entire structure can be unwound with a single court order. The trust provides no meaningful protection.

A properly structured offshore trust places legal control with a licensed, independent trustee located in a foreign country. This trustee is subject to foreign law and foreign court jurisdiction, not U.S. jurisdiction. A U.S. court cannot directly order a trustee in the Cook Islands to do anything. The court has no enforcement power over someone who is not in the United States and not subject to U.S. law.

This separation of control is what creates the protection. When your assets are legally controlled by someone outside the reach of U.S. courts, those courts cannot force distributions or asset transfers through direct orders.

Keeping Influence Without Ownership

Many people worry about "losing control" of their assets when they transfer them to a foreign trustee. This concern is understandable. After all, you are placing substantial wealth in the hands of someone in another country who you may have never met in person.

Offshore trusts address this concern through several legal mechanisms that allow you to maintain influence while keeping legal control separate.

Trust Protectors: A trust protector is an independent party (often another professional or trusted-advisor) who has the power to oversee the trustee. The protector might have the authority to remove and replace the trustee if the trustee is not performing properly or not following the trust's terms. The protector serves as a check on the trustee's power and provides accountability.

Reserved Powers: Under the laws of many offshore jurisdictions, you can reserve certain powers for yourself without destroying the asset protection features of the trust. For example, you might reserve the power to replace investment managers, direct how funds are invested (within certain parameters), or specify which beneficiaries receive distributions and when. The key is that these reserved powers must be carefully defined and must not give you the ability to simply demand that the trustee hand assets back to you.

Letters of Wishes: A letter of wishes is a non-binding document that provides guidance to the trustee about your intentions and preferences. You might express preferences about how you would like assets invested, when you would like distributions made to beneficiaries, or how you would like the trust administered. While the trustee is not legally required to follow these wishes, professional trustees generally give them substantial weight when making decisions. The letter of wishes allows you to communicate your intentions without exercising direct legal control.

Duress Clauses: One of the most important protective mechanisms in an offshore trust is the duress clause, sometimes called a flee clause or forced repatriation clause. This provision states that if you are ever ordered by a court to do something that would harm the trust or force assets back to the United States, the trustee is required to ignore your instructions. The clause recognizes that you are under duress (being coerced by a court) and instructs the trustee to act independently to protect the trust assets. This clause is what allows the trust to remain protected even if a U.S. court orders you to bring the assets home or make them available to creditors.

The Critical Balance

The critical point to understand is that your influence must be indirect and properly structured. You can have input into how the trust is managed. You can communicate with the trustee. You can make recommendations and express preferences. But you cannot have direct, unilateral control over the assets.

Informal arrangements or direct control defeat the entire purpose of the structure. If you maintain the practical ability to control the trust assets as if they were still in your personal name, a court will likely disregard the trust structure entirely. The entire arrangement can fail, and you will have spent substantial money and effort for nothing.

Worse, if you set up an offshore trust but continue to control it directly in violation of its terms, you may face accusations of fraud or contempt of court. The consequences can be severe.

How Claim Hurdles Actually Work

Offshore asset protection trusts do not work by eliminating claims against you. They work by making those claims extraordinarily difficult, expensive, and uncertain to pursue. Let's break down exactly how this works in practice.

The Recognition Problem

Imagine you are sued in a U.S. court and you lose. The plaintiff obtains a judgment against you for $5 million. In the United States, that judgment is a powerful tool. The plaintiff can use it to garnish your wages, place liens on your property, seize your bank accounts, and force sales of assets you own.

Now imagine that your primary assets are held in a properly structured Cook Islands trust. The plaintiff takes that U.S. judgment to the Cook Islands and attempts to use it to claim the trust assets.

Here is what happens: nothing. The Cook Islands do not automatically recognize U.S. civil court judgments. The judgment has no legal effect there. It is, from the perspective of Cook Islands law, just a piece of paper from a foreign country.

If the creditor wants to pursue the trust assets, they must file a completely new lawsuit in the Cook Islands courts. They must hire Cook Islands attorneys who are licensed to practice in that jurisdiction. They must follow Cook Islands court procedures and rules of evidence. They must prove their case all over again under Cook Islands law.

This requirement alone dramatically increases the cost, time, and uncertainty for anyone trying to reach your assets. Many creditors will decide it is not worth the expense or risk.

Statutes of Limitation

Even if a creditor is willing to file a new lawsuit in the offshore jurisdiction, they face strict time limits.

Many offshore jurisdictions have very short statutes of limitation for fraudulent transfer claims. A fraudulent transfer is a legal concept that allows creditors to undo transfers of assets that were made to avoid paying debts. In the United States, statutes of limitation for fraudulent transfer claims are typically four to six years, and in some cases longer.

In the Cook Islands, for example, the statute of limitation for fraudulent transfer claims is one to two years from the date of the transfer, depending on the circumstances. If a creditor does not file their lawsuit within that narrow window, the claim is barred forever. The assets are permanently protected.

This creates a powerful incentive to establish offshore trusts well before any claims arise. If you transfer assets to an offshore trust and the statute of limitation expires before anyone files a claim, those assets become effectively unreachable.

Higher Standards of Proof

In the United States, most civil lawsuits are decided using a "preponderance of the evidence" standard. This means the plaintiff only needs to prove their case is more likely true than not, essentially a 51% threshold.

Many offshore jurisdictions impose a much higher standard for fraudulent transfer claims. Some require proof "beyond a reasonable doubt," which is the same standard used in criminal cases. This is an extraordinarily high bar. The creditor must prove not just that you probably transferred assets to avoid a claim, but that this is virtually certain.

Additionally, offshore jurisdictions often require creditors to prove actual fraudulent intent, not just constructive fraud. Constructive fraud is a legal concept that treats certain transfers as fraudulent based on circumstances (such as transferring assets while insolvent) even without proof of intent. Many offshore jurisdictions do not recognize constructive fraud at all. The creditor must prove you specifically intended to defraud them, which is far more difficult.

Bond Requirements

Some offshore jurisdictions require creditors to post a substantial bond (deposit money with the court) before they are allowed to pursue a claim. This bond is meant to cover the defendant's legal costs if the creditor loses.

If a creditor must post a bond of $100,000 or more just to file a lawsuit, and they face the risk of losing that money entirely if they do not win, many will reconsider whether the pursuit is worthwhile. This requirement filters out creditors who are not absolutely confident in their case.

No Contingency Fee Advantage

In the United States, many lawsuits are pursued on a contingency fee basis. This means the plaintiff's attorney only gets paid if they win the case, typically taking a percentage of the recovery. This arrangement makes it economically feasible to pursue lawsuits even if the plaintiff has no money to pay lawyers upfront.

In many offshore jurisdictions, contingency fee arrangements are prohibited or highly impractical. Plaintiffs must pay all legal costs upfront. They must pay their attorneys by the hour, pay court filing fees, pay for expert witnesses, and cover all other litigation expenses out of pocket.

For a plaintiff with limited resources, this makes pursuing an offshore claim economically impossible, even if their underlying case has merit. The upfront cost and financial risk are simply too high.

This reality discourages lawsuits that are driven more by leverage and the threat of costs than by actual legal merit. It levels the playing field and ensures that only creditors with strong cases and substantial resources will pursue claims in the offshore jurisdiction.

Costs, Timelines, and Realistic Expectations

Offshore trusts are not simple or inexpensive planning tools. They require serious commitment, both financial and operational. Let's look at what is actually involved.

Initial Setup Costs

Setting up an offshore asset protection trust involves multiple professionals and significant legal work. Typical expenses include:

Legal Fees for Drafting and Setup: You will need experienced attorneys who specialize in offshore trust planning. These attorneys must be familiar with both U.S. tax and asset protection law and the laws of the offshore jurisdiction you choose. Legal fees for establishing an offshore trust typically range from $15,000 to $50,000 or more, depending on the complexity of your situation and the jurisdiction selected.

Trustee Acceptance and Establishment Fees: Professional offshore trustees charge fees to review your situation, perform due diligence, and accept the role of trustee. These establishment fees typically range from $5,000 to $15,000. The trustee will want to verify that you are not transferring assets to avoid existing known claims, that the assets are coming from legitimate sources, and that you are not engaged in illegal activity.

Asset Transfer Costs: Transferring assets into the trust may involve additional legal, accounting, and administrative expenses. If you are transferring real estate, you will need deeds prepared and recorded. If you are transferring business interests, you may need corporate resolutions and amendments to operating agreements. If you are transferring investment accounts, you will need to work with financial institutions to retitle accounts.

Ongoing Annual Costs

Offshore trusts are not a one-time expense. They require ongoing maintenance and administration.

Annual Trustee Fees: Professional offshore trustees charge annual administration fees to manage the trust, maintain records, prepare reports, and ensure compliance with local law. Annual trustee fees typically range from $5,000 to $15,000 or more per year, depending on the size of the trust and the complexity of its investments and activities.

Tax Preparation and Compliance Costs: Offshore trusts create significant tax reporting obligations. You will need to file annual returns reporting your interest in the foreign trust, reporting foreign bank accounts, and potentially reporting foreign assets. These reporting requirements are complex and the penalties for failing to file are severe. You will need experienced accountants who specialize in international tax compliance. Annual tax preparation costs for an offshore trust typically range from $3,000 to $10,000 or more.

Legal and Advisory Fees: You will need ongoing legal and advisory support to ensure the trust continues to operate properly, to make updates as laws change, and to address any issues that arise. Budget for several thousand dollars per year in ongoing legal and professional fees.

Who Should Consider Offshore Trusts

Given these costs, offshore trusts are best suited for individuals with:

Substantial Net Worth: As a practical matter, offshore trusts typically only make economic sense for individuals with a net worth of several million dollars or more. If you have a net worth of $500,000, spending $30,000 to set up a trust and $15,000 per year to maintain it is probably not a good use of resources. If you have a net worth of $10 million, these costs are more reasonable relative to the protection provided.

High Liability Exposure: Offshore trusts are most appropriate for people who face significant and ongoing liability risks. This might include business owners who could face lawsuits related to their company's operations, doctors or other professionals who face malpractice exposure, real estate investors with multiple properties and tenant relationships, or individuals with complex financial situations that create ongoing legal risk.

Long-Term Planning Horizons: Offshore trusts are not short-term solutions. They require a commitment to maintaining the structure for many years. If you might need to unwind the trust in a year or two, the setup costs are probably not justified. Offshore trusts work best when viewed as a permanent or long-term structure.

Timeline Considerations

Timing is absolutely critical when it comes to offshore asset protection trusts. These trusts must be established well before any claim or lawsuit arises against you.

The Advance Planning Requirement: If you set up an offshore trust after you are already aware of a potential claim, the transfer of assets to the trust is likely to be considered a fraudulent transfer. This means a court can undo the transfer and make the assets available to creditors. Even worse, transferring assets to an offshore trust with the intent to avoid a known claim can result in criminal charges for fraud.

The protection an offshore trust provides improves as time passes. Every month and year that goes by without a claim being filed strengthens your position. Statutes of limitation begin to expire. The transfer looks more like routine estate planning and less like a reactive move to avoid a specific creditor.

Seasoning Period: Many advisors recommend allowing assets to "season" in the trust for at least a year or more before you can be confident in the protection. The longer assets have been in the trust, the harder it is for a creditor to argue the transfer was made specifically to avoid their claim.

Last-Minute Planning Fails: Offshore planning set up after a claim arises is rarely effective and often creates serious problems. If you are already being sued, or if you are aware of facts that could give rise to a lawsuit, transferring assets offshore is likely to be viewed as fraudulent. You may face contempt of court charges, sanctions, increased damages, and potentially even criminal liability.

The bottom line is that offshore asset protection planning must be proactive, not reactive.

What to Realistically Expect

It is important to have realistic expectations about what an offshore trust can and cannot do.

What Offshore Trusts Do Not Do:

Offshore trusts do not guarantee complete immunity from legal action. You can still be sued. Creditors can still obtain judgments against you personally. The trust protects the assets, not you as an individual.

Offshore trusts do not eliminate your tax or disclosure reporting obligations. You must continue to report all income generated by trust assets on your tax returns. You must file annual reports disclosing your interest in the foreign trust and any foreign bank accounts. You must comply with all U.S. tax laws. The trust does not provide tax benefits or allow you to hide income from the IRS.

Offshore trusts do not prevent lawsuits from being filed against you. Anyone can file a lawsuit claiming you owe them money. The trust does not make you immune from being sued or from having to defend yourself in court.

What Offshore Trusts Actually Do:

What offshore trusts actually accomplish is changing the leverage dynamics in your favor. When a creditor knows your primary assets are in a properly structured offshore trust, they know pursuing those assets will be expensive, time-consuming, and uncertain. This knowledge changes the negotiation dynamic. You are in a much stronger position to settle claims on reasonable terms rather than being forced to accept unfavorable settlements because you have no protection.

Offshore trusts significantly increase the strength of your legal defense in worst-case scenarios. If you face a catastrophic lawsuit, such as a multi-million dollar judgment, the offshore trust can protect your wealth even when other strategies fail. It serves as a last line of defense.

Offshore trusts discourage claims that lack strong merit. Plaintiffs and their attorneys are less likely to pursue speculative lawsuits if they know the defendant's assets are protected. The trust filters out weak claims that are based more on the hope of a quick settlement than on actual legal merit.

Think of offshore trusts as catastrophe insurance rather than everyday planning tools. You hope you never need the protection, but if you do face a true catastrophe, the trust can preserve your wealth and financial security.

When Offshore Trusts Work Best

Offshore trusts are most effective when used as part of a comprehensive asset protection strategy, not as standalone solutions.

Layered Defense Strategy

The strongest asset protection plans combine multiple layers of defense. This might include:

Domestic Asset Protection Tools: Limited liability companies (LLCs) for business activities and real estate holdings, liability insurance policies, domestic asset protection trusts in friendly U.S. states, retirement accounts and other exempt assets, and prenuptial or postnuptial agreements for marital asset protection.

Offshore Trust as the Final Layer: The offshore trust serves as the ultimate backstop. It protects wealth that cannot be adequately protected through domestic tools. It provides security if all other layers of protection fail.

This layered approach ensures that most claims are resolved through earlier layers of defense (insurance, settlement, domestic legal structures) without ever reaching the offshore trust. The offshore trust remains in reserve for the worst-case scenario.

Full Legal Compliance

Offshore trusts only work when they are supported by fully compliant behavior with all laws.

You must file all required tax returns and pay all taxes owed. You must comply with all disclosure and reporting requirements, including annual reports on foreign trusts, foreign bank accounts, and foreign assets. You must not use the trust to hide income or evade taxes.

You must ensure the trust is established before any claims arise, not as a reactive measure to avoid a known creditor. You must work with professional, licensed trustees who follow proper procedures and maintain appropriate records.

Any hint of non-compliance or illegal activity will destroy the trust's effectiveness and can expose you to criminal liability. Courts will not protect structures that are being used for illegal purposes.

Conservative, Not Aggressive Use

Offshore trusts work best when used conservatively and maintained over time. Aggressive tactics, such as moving assets in and out of the trust frequently, trying to exercise direct control, or attempting to use the trust for active business operations rather than passive asset holding, increase the risk that the structure will fail when challenged.

The most effective offshore trusts are established, funded, and then largely left alone. Assets remain in the trust long-term. The structure is simple and straightforward. There is a clear separation between the grantor (you) and the trustee.

Professional Management

Working with experienced professionals is essential. This includes:

Specialized Attorneys: You need attorneys who focus specifically on offshore asset protection planning and who are familiar with both U.S. law and the laws of the jurisdiction where the trust will be established.

Reputable Offshore Trustees: The trustee should be a licensed, professional trustee company with a long track record and strong reputation. Avoid cut-rate or unlicensed trustees. The trustee is the cornerstone of the entire structure.

Experienced Tax Advisors: International tax compliance is complex. You need accountants who specialize in foreign trust reporting and who can ensure you meet all filing requirements.

Trying to save money by using inexperienced professionals or attempting to set up an offshore trust without expert guidance is virtually certain to fail.

The Serious Consequences of Getting It Wrong

Improperly structured offshore trusts fail quickly and can create severe consequences. Understanding the risks is as important as understanding the benefits.

Common Errors That Cause Failure

Retaining Direct Control: If you maintain the practical ability to control trust assets as if they were still yours, a court will disregard the trust structure. This includes maintaining signature authority on trust bank accounts, directing investment decisions unilaterally, or treating trust assets as if they are available for your personal use. The trust must have real, independent control by the foreign trustee.

Using Unlicensed or Unprofessional Trustees: Some people try to save money by using a friend, relative, or unlicensed service provider as the offshore trustee. This is a recipe for disaster. Courts are highly skeptical of trustee arrangements that are not conducted at arm's length with licensed professionals. An unlicensed or nominal trustee provides no real protection.

Ignoring Tax Compliance and Reporting Obligations: Failing to file required tax returns, failing to report the foreign trust, or failing to report foreign bank accounts and assets can result in severe civil and criminal penalties. Beyond the penalties, non-compliance destroys the credibility of the entire structure. A court is not going to protect assets in a trust that was used to hide income from the IRS.

Setting Up the Trust Reactively: Establishing an offshore trust after a problem has already started, after you become aware of a potential claim, or in response to a lawsuit virtually guarantees the transfer will be considered fraudulent. Courts see through reactive planning and will unwind it.

Failing to Follow Formalities: Offshore trusts require proper documentation, regular trustee meetings and minutes, proper accounting and record-keeping, and compliance with the formalities required by the jurisdiction's law. Treating the trust casually or failing to maintain proper records undermines its effectiveness.

Consequences of Failure

When offshore planning fails, the consequences can be severe.

Complete Loss of Asset Protection: The most obvious consequence is that the trust provides no protection at all. The assets can be reached by creditors just as if they were in your own name. You will have spent tens of thousands of dollars and years of effort for nothing.

Contempt of Court Charges: If a court orders you to repatriate assets from an offshore trust and you claim you cannot comply (because of the duress clause or trustee independence), but the court finds you actually retain control, you can be held in contempt. Contempt can result in substantial fines and even jail time until you comply with the court's order.

Criminal Liability for Fraud: If you transfer assets to an offshore trust with the intent to defraud creditors, or if you make false statements to a court about your control over the trust or the location of assets, you can face criminal prosecution for fraud. Criminal penalties can include substantial fines and imprisonment.

Tax Evasion Charges: If you fail to report foreign trusts, foreign accounts, or income generated by trust assets, you can face criminal prosecution for tax evasion. The IRS takes offshore tax compliance extremely seriously, and the penalties for willful violations are severe.

Increased Damages and Penalties: Courts often impose enhanced damages, penalties, or sanctions against defendants who attempt to use offshore structures improperly or who are not fully transparent about their assets. Your efforts to protect assets can backfire and result in you owing even more than you would have without the offshore structure.

The stakes are high. This is why it is absolutely critical to work with experienced professionals, to establish the trust properly, to maintain full compliance with all laws, and to use the structure conservatively and appropriately.

Key Takeaways

Offshore asset protection trusts are powerful tools, but they must be understood clearly and used carefully.

These trusts work because of legitimate legal structures in foreign jurisdictions. They are not about hiding assets or breaking rules. They are about using legal systems that have deliberately chosen to provide strong protections to trust assets and to make it difficult and expensive for creditors to pursue claims.

Protection comes from separation of control and legal hurdles. The foreign trustee, the requirement for creditors to restart lawsuits in the offshore jurisdiction, the high standards of proof, and the procedural obstacles all combine to create powerful protection. But this protection only works if the structure is properly established and maintained.

Timing and compliance are critical. Offshore trusts must be established well before any claims arise. They must be supported by full compliance with all tax and reporting obligations. They must be managed professionally and conservatively.

Offshore trusts are not for everyone. They require substantial resources to establish and maintain. They are best suited for individuals with significant wealth and high liability exposure who are committed to long-term planning.

Offshore trusts are one layer in a comprehensive strategy. They work best when combined with domestic asset protection tools, insurance, and conservative business and personal practices. They serve as catastrophe insurance, not everyday planning.

The consequences of getting it wrong are severe. Improperly structured offshore trusts fail and can result in contempt charges, criminal liability, and increased damages. Working with experienced professionals and following the rules is not optional.

When used appropriately, by the right people, in the right circumstances, with proper professional guidance, offshore asset protection trusts can provide a level of protection that no domestic structure can match. They offer peace of mind and security in worst-case scenarios. But they are serious undertakings that must be approached with care, realism, and a commitment to doing things the right way.

Looking Ahead

In the next chapter, we will examine offshore companies and banking structures. We will look at how these entities work together with offshore trusts, what specific roles they play in asset protection planning, and why compliance and transparency matter just as much as the legal structure itself. We will also address common misconceptions about offshore banking and explain the realities of how these financial relationships actually function in practice.

10

Offshore Companies and Banking

When most people hear the term "offshore," they think of secrecy, tax evasion, or hidden money. Movies and news stories have created a mythology around offshore accounts that has little to do with reality.

The truth is far less dramatic and far more practical.

Offshore companies and bank accounts are often discussed as if they were synonymous with offshore asset protection. In reality, they are supporting tools, not standalone solutions.

Used properly, offshore companies and banking add flexibility, diversification, and structural separation. Used improperly, they create compliance risk without meaningful protection.

This chapter explains what offshore entities and bank accounts actually do, how they fit into an asset protection strategy, and why compliance (not secrecy) is the deciding factor in whether offshore planning succeeds or fails.

What Does "Offshore" Actually Mean?

Let's start with a simple definition: "offshore" simply means outside your home country.

If you're a U.S. citizen or resident, an offshore company is one formed under the laws of another country. An offshore bank account is an account held at a financial institution located outside the United States.

That's it. There's nothing inherently illegal, suspicious, or even unusual about it.

Many successful businesses operate internationally. Many families have legitimate reasons to hold assets in multiple countries. Major corporations maintain subsidiaries around the world. Wealthy families often have banking relationships in multiple financial centers. International professionals frequently maintain accounts in countries where they work or invest.

The difference between legitimate offshore planning and problematic offshore planning comes down to three things: purpose, structure, and compliance.

Purpose means you have a genuine reason for the offshore structure beyond simply trying to hide assets or evade obligations. Legitimate purposes include international business operations, investment diversification, managing assets in multiple countries, or protecting wealth from unstable political or economic conditions.

Structure means the offshore components are properly designed, legally formed, and integrated into a comprehensive plan. Random offshore entities created without professional guidance rarely provide meaningful protection.

Compliance means you follow all applicable laws, file all required reports, and maintain complete transparency with tax and regulatory authorities. This is where many people get into serious trouble. The consequences of non-compliance can far exceed any benefits the offshore planning was supposed to provide.

Offshore LLCs and IBCs Explained

Offshore companies generally fall into two broad categories:

- **Offshore LLC-style entities:** These are limited liability companies formed under foreign law. They function similarly to U.S. LLCs but are governed by the laws of another country. Popular jurisdictions include Nevis, Cook Islands, Belize, and several others.

- **International Business Companies (IBCs):** These are corporations designed specifically for international business and asset holding. They're common in jurisdictions like the British Virgin Islands, Panama, and the Bahamas.

While names vary by jurisdiction (some call them "exempted companies," others use "private companies" or similar terms), their functions are similar.

What Offshore Companies Are Designed to Do

Offshore companies are legal entities created under foreign law. They can:

- **Hold assets** such as real estate, investments, or intellectual property. The company becomes the legal owner of these assets, not you personally.
- **Own bank and brokerage accounts** in their own name. The accounts belong to the company, adding a layer of separation between you and the underlying funds.
- **Serve as subsidiaries** in larger corporate or trust structures. They can be components of a multi-layered protection plan.
- **Separate ownership from individuals**, creating a legal buffer. When properly structured (usually within a trust), this separation can make it much harder for creditors to reach the underlying assets.
- **Enter contracts and conduct business activities.** They are legal persons under foreign law, capable of signing contracts, buying and selling property, and engaging in commercial transactions.

They are legal persons under foreign law, capable of owning property, entering contracts, and conducting business just like a domestic company would.

What Offshore Companies Are Not

This is where many misunderstandings begin. Offshore companies are not:

Anonymous shields against liability. Modern international regulations require transparency about ownership. The days of truly anonymous offshore companies are over. International agreements like the Common Reporting Standard (CRS) and regulations under FATCA (Foreign Account Tax

Compliance Act) require banks and governments to share information about account holders and company owners.

Substitutes for trusts. Companies and trusts serve different functions and have different legal characteristics. A company is an entity that owns things. A trust is a legal relationship where one party holds assets for the benefit of another. They work together, but one cannot replace the other in a proper asset protection plan.

Automatically protected from creditors. Without additional structure, a company you own can be attacked just like any other asset. If you own 100% of an offshore company's shares, a court can order you to turn over those shares to satisfy a judgment. The foreign location doesn't prevent this.

Exempt from U.S. reporting. U.S. persons must report their interests in foreign entities regardless of where those entities are formed. The reporting requirements are extensive, and the penalties for non-compliance are severe.

Tax havens that eliminate your tax obligations. U.S. citizens and residents are taxed on worldwide income regardless of where it's earned or held. Forming an offshore company doesn't change this fundamental reality.

By themselves, offshore companies offer limited asset protection. Their value comes from how they are integrated into a broader plan, typically involving trusts, proper capitalization, and careful compliance.

The Critical Distinction: Asset-Holding vs. Operating Entities

One of the most important concepts in offshore planning is the difference between companies that hold assets and companies that operate businesses. Confusing these two purposes is a common and expensive mistake.

Asset-Holding Entities

Asset-holding companies are designed to be passive containers. Their job is to:

Own investments like stocks, bonds, or fund positions. The company holds a diversified portfolio managed by investment advisors, but it doesn't trade frequently or engage in active business.

Hold cash reserves for future use or emergency access. These might be funds set aside for family needs, future opportunities, or unexpected situations.

Own intellectual property such as patents, trademarks, or copyrights. The company licenses these to operating businesses but doesn't actively operate a business itself.

Serve as passive containers with minimal day-to-day activity. The company exists primarily to hold assets, not to generate active income.

These entities should:

- Have **minimal business activity**. They might receive investment income, license fees, or rental payments, but they're not out signing contracts with customers or hiring employees.
- **Avoid entering contracts with third parties** when possible. The fewer business relationships the company has, the less exposure it has to potential liability.
- **Generate little to no liability.** Because they're not operating a business, they're not creating the kind of risks that operating businesses face.
- **Exist primarily as ownership vehicles.** Their purpose is to hold assets, not to do things.

Why this matters for asset protection: When paired with an offshore trust, asset-holding entities are especially effective because creditors must penetrate multiple layers to reach underlying assets. The trust owns the company, the company owns the assets, and each layer adds friction and legal complexity to any attack.

Example: An offshore LLC owned by a Cook Islands trust holds a diversified investment portfolio worth $2 million. The LLC doesn't operate a business or sign contracts. It simply holds investments managed by a professional investment advisor. The LLC has a bank account and a brokerage account, both in the LLC's name.

If someone sues you personally, they cannot directly access the LLC because you don't own it. The trust owns it. And they cannot easily force the trust to distribute assets because of the trust's protective provisions. The Cook Islands trust includes language that allows the trustee to refuse distributions when doing so would expose assets to creditors.

Even if the creditor obtains a judgment against you personally, they must navigate Cook Islands law to attack the trust, then attack the LLC, then access the underlying accounts. Each step requires foreign legal proceedings, foreign attorneys, and significant expense. Many creditors will give up rather than pursue this expensive and uncertain process.

Operating Entities

Operating entities are fundamentally different. They:

- **Provide goods or services** to customers or clients. They have active revenue-generating operations.
- **Enter contracts regularly** with vendors, customers, and partners. Every contract is a potential source of liability.
- **Employ workers or contractors.** Employment relationships create significant legal exposure.
- **Generate revenue through active business operations.** They're making money by doing things, not just holding things.
- **Create liability through normal business activities.** Customers can sue over defective products. Employees can make claims. Contracts can be breached. Accidents can happen on business premises.

Operating businesses are inherently exposed to risk. Even well-run businesses face lawsuits. This is why you buy liability insurance. But insurance has limits, and some claims exceed those limits.

For Asset Protection Purposes

Operating risk should be isolated. Keep the dangerous business separate from valuable assets. Don't let your operating company own your investment portfolio.

Valuable assets should be held elsewhere. Your operating business should own only what it needs to operate. Everything else should be in protected structures.

Personal guarantees should be minimized. Every personal guarantee you sign exposes your personal assets to business risk. Sometimes personal guarantees are unavoidable (many commercial leases require them), but minimize them whenever possible.

Why this matters: Using offshore entities as operating businesses without proper planning often increases risk rather than reducing it. You add compliance complexity, reporting obligations, and international legal exposure without gaining meaningful protection.

Example: Someone forms a Nevis LLC to run their consulting business, thinking it will protect their assets. They live in California, their clients are in the U.S., and they provide services personally from their home office.

The Nevis LLC adds significant reporting requirements. They must file Form 5471 with their tax return, reporting detailed information about the foreign corporation. They must comply with Nevis regulations. They may need to file annual reports with Nevis authorities.

But the Nevis LLC provides essentially no protection. Why? Because the business activity occurs in the U.S. A client who sues for professional malpractice will file in California court. The court has jurisdiction over the consultant personally. The fact that the business is technically owned by a Nevis LLC is irrelevant. The court can still reach the consultant's personal assets.

All the consultant accomplished was adding complexity and cost without gaining protection.

The Correct Approach: Separation

The proper structure separates these functions:

Operating businesses are held in domestic entities (or offshore entities in countries where you actually operate). If you run a consulting business in Texas serving Texas clients, use a Texas LLC. If you operate a hotel in Costa Rica, a Costa Rican entity might make sense.

Valuable assets are held in protected structures like trusts and asset-holding entities. Your investment portfolio, cash reserves, and intellectual property should not be in the operating company.

Operating entities lease or license what they need from asset-holding entities. If the operating business needs to use a patent, it licenses it from the asset-holding company for a fair market rate. If it needs to use equipment, it leases it.

If the operating business gets sued, the assets are elsewhere and protected. The creditor can take the operating business, but the valuable assets are in separate structures.

This separation is the foundation of intelligent business planning, whether domestic or international.

Example of proper separation: You own a successful landscaping business in Florida. Your business structure looks like this:

A Florida LLC operates the landscaping business. It owns the trucks, equipment, and supplies needed for operations. It has a modest bank account for payroll and operating expenses. It carries substantial liability insurance.

The business is profitable, generating $300,000 per year in net income. But you don't accumulate wealth in the operating LLC. Instead, you pay yourself a reasonable salary and take distributions.

Those distributions go into a separate structure: a Cook Islands trust that owns an offshore LLC. That offshore LLC holds your investment portfolio (now worth $1.5 million) and cash reserves.

If a customer sues your landscaping business and wins a judgment that exceeds your insurance, they can take the Florida LLC. But your $1.5 million investment portfolio is elsewhere, in a structure that's very difficult to attack.

This is separation. This is how sophisticated planning works.

Offshore Bank Accounts: Benefits and Limits

Offshore bank accounts are one of the most visible (and misunderstood) components of offshore planning. Let's separate fact from fiction.

The Real Benefits of Offshore Banking

Offshore banking can legitimately provide:

1. Jurisdictional diversification

Just as you diversify investments across asset classes (stocks, bonds, real estate), you can diversify banking relationships across jurisdictions. If there's a banking crisis, currency controls, or political instability in one country, your assets in another jurisdiction remain accessible.

Think about what happened in Cyprus in 2013. The government imposed capital controls and actually confiscated a portion of bank deposits to fund a bailout. Account holders couldn't access their money. Large deposits were reduced by significant percentages.

Or consider Argentina's history of currency controls, where citizens couldn't freely convert pesos to dollars or move money out of the country. During various crises, people with accounts solely in Argentina found themselves trapped.

If you have banking relationships in multiple stable jurisdictions, you're not dependent on the stability of any single country's banking system or government.

2. Reduced political or banking-system risk

Some countries have more stable banking systems, stronger property rights, or more predictable legal environments than others. This isn't about tax evasion. It's about stability.

Switzerland has a centuries-old tradition of banking stability and strong property rights. Singapore has a well-regulated, sophisticated banking system. These jurisdictions didn't become major financial centers by accident. They earned that status through consistent adherence to the rule of law.

Diversifying where you bank can reduce your exposure to problems in any single system. If you're worried about the U.S. banking system's stability, holding some assets in a Swiss or Singaporean bank provides a hedge against that risk.

3. Separation from domestic disputes

In asset protection contexts, offshore banking adds friction to enforcement. A creditor with a U.S. judgment must navigate foreign legal systems, comply with foreign procedures, and often prove their case again under foreign law.

This doesn't make collection impossible, but it makes it more expensive and time-consuming. And that changes the economics of collection. If pursuing offshore assets will cost $100,000 in legal fees with no guarantee of success, many creditors will decide it's not worth it, even if the account has $200,000 in it.

The calculation changes from "Can I collect?" to "Is collection economically rational?" Often, the answer becomes "no."

4. Access to international markets

Some investments, currencies, or financial products are easier to access through offshore accounts. Want to invest in European bonds? Asian stocks? Emerging market funds? An offshore account may provide better access to these opportunities than a domestic U.S. brokerage.

This can be particularly valuable for internationally-minded investors who want true global diversification, not just U.S.-based funds that invest internationally.

The Critical Limits of Offshore Banking

Now for what offshore bank accounts do not do:

1. They do not hide money from courts

Modern banking regulations require extensive reporting and cooperation between countries. The U.S. has tax information exchange agreements with dozens of countries. Banks in those countries report U.S. account holders to the IRS.

If a U.S. court orders you to disclose your offshore accounts, you must comply. The disclosure obligation applies to you personally, not to the bank. If you refuse, you can be held in contempt of court. That means jail time until you comply.

2. They do not eliminate reporting obligations

U.S. persons must report foreign bank accounts exceeding certain thresholds on the Report of Foreign Bank and Financial Accounts (FBAR). If your foreign accounts exceeded $10,000 in aggregate value at any point during the year, you must file the FBAR.

These reports go to the Treasury Department's Financial Crimes Enforcement Network (FinCEN). They're not optional. They're not suggestions. They're mandatory legal requirements.

You may also need to file Form 8938 (Statement of Specified Foreign Financial Assets) with your tax return if you exceed certain higher thresholds.

3. They do not prevent disclosure under court order

Courts can compel you to provide information, sign authorizations, or take actions regarding your offshore accounts. If you're in litigation, you may be required to:

- Disclose the existence and location of all offshore accounts during discovery.
- Provide account statements and transaction histories.
- Sign authorizations allowing the bank to release information directly to the court or to opposing counsel.
- Transfer funds back to the U.S. if ordered to do so.

Refusing these court orders can land you in jail for contempt. The judge doesn't care that your money is in Switzerland. The judge has jurisdiction over you personally, and can compel you to take actions within your power.

4. They do not stop litigation by themselves

Opening an offshore bank account doesn't prevent someone from suing you. It doesn't make you judgment-proof. It simply means that if someone wins a judgment, enforcing it against offshore assets requires additional steps.

The lawsuit proceeds normally. If you lose, you have a judgment against you. The offshore account doesn't change that. It only affects the enforcement process after the judgment is entered.

The Reality: Friction, Not Invisibility

The protection offshore banking provides is friction, not invisibility.

Think of it like this: a simple combination lock on a storage unit provides almost no security against a determined thief with bolt cutters. But it does deter casual thieves who are looking for easy targets. They'll move on to unlocked units.

Similarly, a creditor who would give up after discovering your bank account is offshore wasn't a serious creditor to begin with. But a creditor who must:

- Navigate foreign legal procedures in an unfamiliar legal system.
- Hire foreign counsel (expensive and difficult to coordinate).
- Overcome foreign asset protection laws that may be more protective

than U.S. laws.

- Potentially re-litigate their claim under foreign law if the foreign court doesn't automatically recognize the U.S. judgment.
- Spend significant additional time and money (often $50,000 to $200,000 or more).
- Wait months or years for foreign court proceedings to conclude.

...may decide that continuing isn't worth the cost, even if they believe they would eventually succeed.

This is especially true if the potential recovery is uncertain. If you have $150,000 in an offshore account and pursuing it will cost $100,000 with no guarantee of success, the creditor faces a difficult decision. Many will negotiate a settlement instead.

This friction is the real benefit of offshore banking, not invisibility.

Banking Compliance Is Conservative by Nature

It's important to understand how offshore banks actually operate in the modern world.

Banks are highly regulated and deeply conservative institutions. They:

- **Cooperate with lawful requests from authorities.** If the U.S. government properly requests information under a tax treaty or mutual assistance agreement, foreign banks comply. They have no choice. Non-compliance would jeopardize their ability to do business internationally.
- **Close accounts that appear risky or noncompliant.** Banks don't want problem customers. If you appear to be evading taxes, hiding assets improperly, or engaged in anything questionable, the bank will simply close your account. They don't need a reason. They don't want the regulatory risk.
- **Perform extensive due diligence on customers.** Opening an offshore account today requires providing extensive documentation: passport, proof of address, source of funds documentation, tax identification numbers, and often detailed questionnaires about the purpose of the account.

- **Monitor transactions for suspicious activity.** Banks watch for patterns that might indicate money laundering, tax evasion, or other illegal activity. Large cash deposits, frequent transfers to high-risk countries, or transactions that don't make sense given your stated business will trigger reviews.

- **Report to their own regulators.** Banks must comply with regulations in their own jurisdictions. Those regulations increasingly require reporting on foreign account holders and cooperation with international authorities.

The idea that offshore banks will help you hide assets or evadc obligations is a dangerous myth. Modern banks operate under international agreements that require cooperation and transparency. The era of true bank secrecy ended years ago.

Offshore banking is a tool for stability and diversification, not secrecy.

Compliance Requirements: A Plain-English Overview

If there's one point to take away from this chapter, it's this: **compliance is the price of legitimacy.**

U.S. persons with offshore structures must comply with multiple reporting regimes. These requirements are serious but manageable with proper guidance. Let's break them down in plain English.

Common Reporting Obligations

Depending on your structure and activity, your obligations may include:

1. Reporting foreign bank accounts (FBAR)

If you have foreign financial accounts exceeding $10,000 in aggregate at any point during the year, you must file a Report of Foreign Bank and Financial Accounts (FBAR) with the Treasury Department by April 15 (with automatic extension to October 15 if you file an extension for your tax return).

This includes bank accounts, brokerage accounts, and certain other financial accounts. It doesn't matter if you earned any income on these accounts. The reporting requirement is based solely on the account balances.

The $10,000 threshold is aggregate, meaning you add up all your foreign accounts. If you have a checking account in Canada with $4,000, a savings account in the UK with $3,000, and a brokerage account in Switzerland with $5,000, you've exceeded the threshold ($12,000 total) and must file.

The FBAR is filed electronically through FinCEN's BSA E-Filing System. It's separate from your tax return.

2. Reporting ownership in foreign companies (Form 5471, Form 8865)

If you own or control a foreign corporation or partnership, you may need to file information returns with your tax return. These forms report the company's activities, ownership structure, and financial information.

Form 5471 (Information Return of U.S. Persons With Respect to Certain Foreign Corporations) is required if you:

- Own 10% or more of a foreign corporation (by vote or value).
- Are an officer or director of a foreign corporation in which a U.S. person owns 10% or more.
- Acquire or dispose of stock that results in ownership of 10% or more.
- Have other specified relationships with a foreign corporation.

The form requires detailed financial information about the foreign corporation, including balance sheets, income statements, and various schedules reporting transactions between you and the corporation.

Form 8865 (Return of U.S. Persons With Respect to Certain Foreign Partnerships) serves a similar function for foreign partnerships and LLCs treated as partnerships for tax purposes.

These forms are complex and time-consuming. They're also strictly required. Failure to file can result in penalties of $10,000 per form, per year, and the IRS can prevent you from claiming deductions or credits related to the foreign entity.

3. Reporting trust relationships (Form 3520, Form 3520-A)

If you create, fund, or benefit from a foreign trust, or if you receive distributions or gifts from one, you must report these relationships.

Form 3520 (Annual Return To Report Transactions With Foreign Trusts and Receipt of Certain Foreign Gifts) is filed by:

- U.S. persons who create or transfer assets to a foreign trust.

- U.S. beneficiaries who receive distributions from a foreign trust.
- U.S. persons who receive large gifts or bequests from foreign persons.

Form 3520-A (Annual Information Return of Foreign Trust With a U.S. Owner) is the trust's own information return. It reports the trust's income, assets, and distributions. The foreign trustee is responsible for filing this form, but if they don't, you (as the U.S. owner/beneficiary) may be required to file it.

The penalty for failing to file Form 3520 is the greater of $10,000 or 35% of the gross value of any property transferred to the trust. For failing to file Form 3520-A, the penalty is 5% of the trust's gross assets.

These are not trivial penalties.

4. Declaring foreign income (Form 8938, FATCA)

Under the Foreign Account Tax Compliance Act (FATCA), you must report specified foreign financial assets exceeding certain thresholds on Form 8938 (Statement of Specified Foreign Financial Assets).

The thresholds vary based on your filing status and whether you live in the U.S.:

For single taxpayers living in the U.S.: $50,000 on the last day of the year or $75,000 at any point during the year.

For married taxpayers filing jointly and living in the U.S.: $100,000 on the last day of the year or $150,000 at any point during the year.

Higher thresholds apply if you live abroad.

Form 8938 requires reporting foreign bank accounts, foreign brokerage accounts, foreign stock or securities, interests in foreign entities, and various other foreign financial assets.

This is in addition to (not instead of) FBAR reporting. Yes, you may need to report the same accounts on both forms. The forms serve different purposes and go to different agencies (FBAR goes to FinCEN, Form 8938 goes to the IRS with your tax return).

5. Other potential filings

Depending on your specific situation, other forms may be required:

- Form 8621 for investments in certain foreign mutual funds (PFICs).
- Form 926 for transfers to foreign corporations.
- Form 8858 for foreign disregarded entities.

Various other specialized forms for specific situations.

This is why professional guidance is essential. The maze of reporting requirements is complex, and missing even one form can trigger penalties.

The Consequences of Non-Compliance

Failure to comply with these requirements can result in:

- **Civil penalties starting at $10,000 per violation.** For willful violations of FBAR requirements, the penalty can be up to 50% of the account balance, or $100,000, whichever is greater. That's per year, per account.
- **Criminal penalties including fines and imprisonment.** Willful failure to file FBAR can result in criminal prosecution, with fines up to $250,000 and imprisonment up to five years.
- **Penalties far exceeding the value of the planning itself.** I've seen cases where people owed more in penalties than they had in their offshore accounts. The penalty structure can quickly spiral out of control.
- **IRS audits and increased scrutiny.** Once you're on the IRS's radar for offshore non-compliance, expect heightened scrutiny of all your tax matters for years to come.
- **Loss of the protection you were trying to create.** If your offshore structure is deemed non-compliant or created for illegal purposes, courts may disregard it entirely, eliminating any protection you thought you had.

The government takes offshore reporting seriously. The penalties are not theoretical. Every year, people face devastating financial consequences for failing to comply with offshore reporting requirements.

The IRS has special programs (like the Offshore Voluntary Disclosure Program and Streamlined Filing Compliance Procedures) for people who want to come into compliance after years of non-reporting. These programs exist because the problem is so common. Don't become another case study in what happens when offshore compliance is ignored.

What Compliance Means in Practice

Compliance requires:

1. Accurate recordkeeping

You need to maintain clear records of:

- Account balances throughout the year (especially the maximum balance).
- All transactions involving foreign accounts or entities.
- Ownership percentages and changes in ownership.
- Distributions received from foreign trusts or entities.
- Foreign income earned, even if not distributed.
- Source of funds documentation showing where money came from.

Keep everything organized and accessible. If you're ever audited, you'll need to produce documentation quickly and completely. Digital copies are fine, but have backups. Store important documents in multiple secure locations.

2. Timely filings

These forms have deadlines. Missing them creates problems even if you eventually file.

FBAR: April 15 (automatic extension to October 15 if you file a tax return extension).

Forms 5471, 8865, 8938, 3520, 3520-A: Filed with your tax return (typically April 15 for calendar year taxpayers, or October 15 if you file an extension).

Set up systems to ensure nothing is missed. Many people use calendar reminders, tax software prompts, or rely on their CPA to track all required filings. Whatever system you use, it needs to be reliable.

3. Coordination between advisors

Your attorney, CPA, and offshore service providers need to communicate. Make sure everyone knows what everyone else is doing.

Your attorney creates the offshore trust structure. Your CPA needs to know about it to file the required forms. Your offshore trustee needs to provide information to your CPA for the required filings. If any link in this chain breaks, compliance fails.

Have an annual meeting (even if virtual) where all your advisors discuss your structure, confirm what forms need to be filed, and ensure everyone has the information they need.

4. Conservative assumptions

When in doubt about whether something needs to be reported, report it. The cost of over-reporting is minimal (maybe an extra hour of your CPA's time). The cost of under-reporting can be catastrophic (penalties of tens or hundreds of thousands of dollars).

If you're not sure whether an account exceeds the $10,000 threshold, file the FBAR. If you're not sure whether a foreign entity requires Form 5471, ask your CPA and err on the side of filing. If you're uncertain about anything, get professional advice and document that you sought guidance.

Privacy vs. Secrecy

Here's an important distinction: compliance does not require public disclosure of your assets or loss of privacy. It requires lawful reporting to tax and regulatory authorities.

Your offshore accounts and structures remain private from:

- **Neighbors.** Your FBAR filing doesn't get posted on your neighborhood Facebook group.
- **Business competitors.** Your Form 5471 doesn't appear in public databases.
- **Potential litigants** (until they have a judgment and discovery rights). Someone thinking about suing you cannot simply request your offshore account information. They need a judgment first, then discovery rights, then court orders.
- **The general public.** Tax returns and related forms are confidential. The IRS doesn't publish your financial information.

But they are not secret from:

- **The IRS.** They get complete information about your offshore accounts and entities.
- **Other relevant government agencies.** Treasury Department, FinCEN, and potentially others depending on your situation.
- **Courts with jurisdiction over you.** If you're in litigation, courts can compel disclosure of offshore accounts through the discovery process.

This is exactly how it should be. Privacy is legitimate. Secrecy from lawful authorities is not.

You can (and should) structure your affairs to maintain privacy from casual observers and potential adversaries. But you cannot (and should not try to) maintain secrecy from the government.

Understanding this distinction is critical to successful offshore planning.

Why Offshore Companies Fail Without Trusts

One of the most common offshore planning mistakes is relying on companies alone. This deserves its own section because it's such a frequent and expensive error.

The Problem with Companies Alone

If you own an offshore company directly (meaning you personally own the shares), here's what happens:

You remain the ultimate owner. The company is your asset, subject to claims against you. If someone obtains a judgment against you personally, they can seize your shares in the company, just like they could seize shares you own in Apple or Google.

Courts can compel action. A judge can order you to transfer assets, sign documents, or distribute funds from the company. You might think, "But the company is in Nevis! The judge can't touch it!" Wrong. The judge has jurisdiction over you personally. If you refuse the order, you go to jail for contempt.

Asset protection is weak. You're essentially playing a jurisdiction game without changing the fundamental ownership structure. You still own the company. You still control it. You can still be forced to transfer it or liquidate it.

Compliance is complex. You have all the reporting obligations (Form 5471, FBAR, Form 8938) without the benefits of proper structure.

Example: You form a Cook Islands LLC and transfer $500,000 to it. You own the LLC directly. You think your assets are protected because they're "offshore."

Then you get sued. You lose. The judgment is $400,000.

The court orders you to bring the money back from the Cook Islands and pay your creditor. If you refuse, the court holds you in contempt. Contempt means jail. You sit in a jail cell until you comply with the court's order.

"But the LLC is in Cook Islands!" you protest. "You can't make me bring it back!"

The judge explains: "I'm not ordering the Cook Islands to do anything. I'm ordering you, personally, to take actions that are within your power. You own the LLC. You control it. You can transfer the funds. Do so, or remain in jail."

This is called a "turnover order," and it's perfectly legal. The foreign location of the company doesn't prevent the court from exercising jurisdiction over you personally.

You have three choices:

- Comply with the order and lose your $400,000.
- Refuse and go to jail indefinitely (some people have spent years in jail for contempt in asset protection cases).
- Try to prove you genuinely cannot comply (but if you formed the company and you control it, this argument fails).
- The offshore company provided no meaningful protection.

How Trusts Change the Equation

When an offshore company is owned by a properly structured offshore trust, the dynamic changes completely:

You no longer own the company. The trust owns it. You are a beneficiary, not an owner. This isn't a technicality. It's a fundamental change in ownership structure.

Courts cannot compel actions you cannot take. You cannot transfer what you don't own. You cannot order distributions from a trust you don't control. The trustee (not you) makes decisions about trust assets.

The trust's protective provisions apply. Well-drafted offshore trusts include provisions that prevent distributions in response to creditor pressure. These provisions instruct the trustee to deny distribution requests that would result in assets going to creditors.

Multiple layers protect assets. The creditor must attack the trust (governed by foreign law), then the company (also foreign), then the underlying assets (in foreign accounts). Each layer adds friction, expense, and legal complexity.

Example: Same $500,000, but this time it's in a Cook Islands LLC owned by a Cook Islands trust. You're a beneficiary of the trust, but you don't own it and you don't control it.

You get sued. You lose. Same $400,000 judgment.

The court orders you to bring the money back. But this time, you genuinely cannot comply. You don't own the LLC. The trust owns it. You can't order the trust to distribute money to you. The trustee makes that decision, not you.

"Ask the trustee to make a distribution," the court says.

"I did," you respond. "The trustee declined. The trust agreement includes an anti-duress provision that prohibits distributions when I'm under compulsion from creditors. The trustee is following the terms of the trust."

The court is frustrated, but stuck. You genuinely cannot comply with a turnover order because you don't control the assets. The court can't hold you in contempt for failing to do something genuinely beyond your power.

Can the creditor still pursue the assets? Potentially, but now they must:

- Hire attorneys in Cook Islands.
- File a claim in Cook Islands courts.
- Overcome Cook Islands asset protection laws (which are specifically designed to resist foreign judgments).

- Prove the transfer to the trust was fraudulent under Cook Islands law (a very high burden).
- Wait for Cook Islands court proceedings to conclude (often years).

This is expensive ($100,000 or more in legal fees) and uncertain (Cook Islands law strongly favors trust settlors over creditors). Many creditors will negotiate a settlement rather than pursue this path.

This is why offshore companies work best as components within trust structures, not as standalone solutions.

The Correct Structure

A proper offshore asset protection structure typically looks like this:

You (as grantor/settlor) create and fund the trust. You transfer assets to the trust during a period when you have no creditor threats. This is critical: the transfer must happen before any claims arise, or it may be deemed a fraudulent transfer.

The trust (an independent legal entity) owns the offshore company. The trust is the shareholder of the LLC or IBC. Not you. You have no ownership interest in the company.

The offshore company holds the actual assets (accounts, investments, etc.). The company has bank accounts in its own name, brokerage accounts, and holds the cash and securities.

You are a beneficiary of the trust (not an owner). You can potentially receive distributions from the trust, but you cannot demand them, control them, or force the trustee to make them.

This layered approach provides real protection because:

- **Control is separated from beneficial interest.** You benefit from the trust, but you don't control it.
- **Foreign law governs the trust.** U.S. courts must respect the foreign law governing the trust structure.
- **The trustee has legal authority to refuse improper demands.** When creditors come calling, the trustee says no, and it's not your decision.
- **Creditors must navigate multiple legal systems and**

structures. Each layer is a hurdle. Most creditors won't jump all of them.

Offshore Planning Without Illusions

Let's be very clear about what successful offshore planning actually looks like in the real world.

Successful offshore planning is:

- **Transparent** (to authorities, properly disclosed). Everything is reported to the IRS and other relevant agencies. Nothing is hidden from the government.
- **Boring** (no exotic schemes or aggressive strategies). Properly structured offshore planning is methodical and conservative. It follows established legal principles.
- **Heavily documented** (every decision and transaction recorded). You maintain meticulous records of all transfers, decisions, and communications with trustees.
- **Professionally managed** (experienced trustees and advisors). You work with reputable trustees in well-regarded jurisdictions, and you pay for quality professional advice.
- **Compliant** (all reporting requirements met). Every required form is filed on time, every year, without exception.
- **Long-term focused** (not a quick fix for current problems). You establish these structures years before you need them, as part of comprehensive wealth planning.

Successful offshore planning is not:

- **Exciting.** It's paperwork, compliance, and conservative legal structures.
- **Mysterious.** Everything is documented and explainable.
- **Secret.** Authorities know exactly what you have and where it is.
- **A magic wand.** It doesn't solve all problems or eliminate all risks.
- **A way to hide assets.** Modern regulations make truly hiding assets essentially impossible.

- **A way to avoid taxes.** U.S. persons pay tax on worldwide income, period.
- **A solution to current litigation.** If you're already being sued, it's too late for offshore planning (transferring assets after a claim arises is fraudulent transfer).

Red Flags to Watch For

If a promoter, advisor, or service provider promises any of the following, walk away immediately:

- **Anonymity** (modern regulations require transparency). Anyone promising you can remain anonymous hasn't been paying attention to international regulations for the past 15 years.
- **Invisibility** (you cannot hide reportable assets). Claims that "the IRS will never know" are false and dangerous.
- **Guaranteed protection** (no structure is impenetrable). Anyone guaranteeing you'll never lose assets to creditors is lying. Asset protection is about making collection difficult and expensive, not impossible.
- **Tax elimination** (U.S. persons pay tax on worldwide income). Schemes claiming you can eliminate taxes through offshore structures are tax fraud waiting to be discovered.
- **No reporting obligations** (false and dangerous). If someone tells you that you don't need to report offshore accounts or entities, they're setting you up for massive penalties.
- **Quick solutions to pending litigation** (likely fraudulent transfer). If you're already being sued and someone promises offshore planning will solve your problem, they're describing fraud.

These promises indicate either incompetence or dishonesty. Either way, involvement with such advisors will end badly.

The Professional Standard

Legitimate offshore planning professionals will:

- **Ask detailed questions about your situation.** They need to understand your assets, risks, family situation, and goals before recommending any structure.

- **Discuss compliance requirements upfront.** They'll explain all the reporting obligations and costs before you commit to anything.
- **Warn you about limitations and risks.** They'll be clear about what offshore planning can and cannot do.
- **Provide written documentation of everything.** Every recommendation, every step of implementation, and every ongoing obligation will be documented in writing.
- **Coordinate with your existing advisors.** They'll insist on involving your CPA and domestic attorney to ensure everyone is on the same page.
- **Focus on long-term legal protection, not short-term evasion.** The conversation will be about building sustainable, compliant structures, not quick fixes or clever schemes.

If someone promises easy solutions or downplays compliance with the law, that's a massive red flag. Walk away and find different counsel.

Integrating Offshore Companies Into a Layered Strategy

When used correctly, offshore companies:

- **Add structural separation** between you and your assets. Multiple legal entities create distance that makes it harder for creditors to reach underlying assets.
- **Improve asset mobility** if you need to relocate or reorganize. If you need to move to another country, having assets already held internationally makes that transition easier.
- **Support trust planning** as holding vehicles within trust structures. The trust owns the company, the company holds the accounts. This layering is the foundation of strong protection.
- **Enhance resilience** through geographic and legal diversification. You're not dependent on the stability or fairness of any single legal system.

They do not replace domestic planning. They complement it.

A Complete Picture

A sophisticated asset protection plan might include all of the following components:

- **Domestic LLC holding operating business.** Your active business operates through a U.S. entity in the state where you do business. This keeps operations simple and compliant.
- **Domestic irrevocable trust holding personal residence.** Your home is protected through a domestic asset protection trust or a qualified personal residence trust. This provides estate planning benefits along with some creditor protection.
- **Offshore trust in a strong jurisdiction** (Cook Islands, Nevis). This is the centerpiece of your offshore planning, providing strong protection for liquid assets.
- **Offshore LLC owned by the offshore trust, holding liquid investments.** The LLC is the actual account holder for brokerage and bank accounts. It's owned by the trust, not by you.
- **Domestic trust for estate planning purposes.** Separate from asset protection, you may have domestic trusts for estate tax planning, providing for minor children, or managing assets for family members.
- **Proper insurance covering predictable risks.** Liability insurance, malpractice insurance, umbrella policies. Insurance handles the first layer of protection against common risks.

Each component serves a specific purpose. Each has advantages and limitations. Together, they create overlapping layers of protection that are much stronger than any single tool alone.

The Role of Offshore Components

In this complete picture, the offshore components:

- **Hold liquid, mobile assets** that could be targeted in litigation. Cash and securities are easily seized by creditors. Keeping them offshore adds protection.
- **Provide a final layer of protection** if domestic structures are compromised. If someone penetrates your domestic planning, the

offshore structures provide a fallback position.

- **Create additional obstacles for creditors.** Even sophisticated creditors face significant challenges pursuing assets through foreign jurisdictions and multiple legal structures.
- **Preserve options if relocation becomes necessary.** If you ever need to leave the U.S. (or if you're from another country and might return home), having assets already structured internationally makes that transition much easier.

But they don't do everything. You still need domestic planning, proper business structure, and appropriate insurance.

Common Mistakes to Avoid

Let's review the most common offshore planning mistakes so you can avoid them:

1. Forming entities without a clear purpose

Don't create offshore companies just because it seems sophisticated or because you heard other wealthy people do it. Every entity should serve a specific function in your plan. If you can't clearly explain why a particular entity exists, it probably shouldn't exist.

2. Ignoring compliance

This is the fastest way to turn an asset protection plan into a liability. The penalties for non-compliance with offshore reporting requirements can far exceed the value of the assets you're trying to protect. Compliance is non-negotiable.

3. Waiting until litigation begins

Offshore structures must be in place well before problems arise. Transferring assets after a claim appears (or even when a claim is reasonably foreseeable) is a fraudulent transfer. Courts will unwind the transfer and you'll face both the original creditor and potential fraud liability.

The right time to implement offshore planning is when everything is going well, when you have no creditor threats, and when you can make decisions calmly and deliberately.

4. Using offshore entities for active business

Keep operating businesses domestic (or in countries where you actually operate). Use offshore structures for asset holding only. Running an active business through offshore entities adds complexity without adding protection, and often creates more problems than it solves.

5. Believing in secrecy

Modern offshore planning is about structure and diversification, not hiding assets. The secrecy model is dead. It was killed by international regulations over the past two decades. Accept this reality upfront and plan accordingly.

6. Doing it yourself

This is specialized work requiring expertise in international law, tax law, and asset protection principles. Mistakes are expensive. Do-it-yourself offshore planning almost always ends badly. The cost of proper professional guidance is far less than the cost of fixing mistakes or paying penalties.

7. Using low-quality providers

The cheapest option is rarely the best in offshore planning. Discount offshore incorporation services often provide entities without proper structure, without appropriate guidance, and without addressing compliance requirements. You save a few thousand dollars upfront and create tens of thousands of dollars in problems later.

This is not an area to cut corners. Work with experienced, reputable professionals who have track records of successful implementations.

The Bottom Line: Infrastructure, Not Magic

Offshore companies and banking are not shortcuts to asset protection. They are infrastructure.

Like roads, bridges, and electrical systems, good infrastructure is:

- **Built properly from the start.** Cutting corners during construction creates problems that are expensive or impossible to fix later.
- **Maintained consistently.** Annual filings, ongoing compliance, regular reviews with advisors. Infrastructure requires maintenance.
- **Invisible when working correctly.** If your offshore structures are properly established and maintained, they operate quietly in the background. You don't think about them until you need them.

- **Expensive when it fails.** Failed infrastructure causes catastrophic problems. A bridge collapse, a power grid failure, a compromised asset protection structure, all create damage far exceeding the cost of proper maintenance.

When offshore structures are built correctly, they quietly support long-term protection. They don't promise miracles. They provide steady, reliable diversification and structural separation.

That's not exciting. But it works.

It works because it's based on sound legal principles, not clever tricks. It works because it's fully compliant with laws and regulations. It works because it creates genuine legal obstacles that creditors must overcome, not paper barriers that courts ignore.

Looking Ahead

In the next chapter, we will examine international diversification beyond formal structures: foreign real estate, international brokerage accounts, and geographic exposure. We'll explore how these elements contribute to resilience without the complexity of offshore entities.

The goal is to understand your options completely, so you can make informed decisions about which tools serve your specific situation best.

Offshore planning is one option among many. It's not right for everyone. But for those who need it, understanding how it actually works (rather than how it's portrayed in movies) is the first step toward making it work properly.

If you have significant liquid assets ($500,000 or more), face elevated liability risks in your profession or business, or have legitimate international connections or concerns about domestic stability, offshore planning may be appropriate. But it's a significant commitment requiring ongoing compliance, professional guidance, and realistic expectations.

Done right, it's boring, compliant, and effective. Done wrong, it's expensive, risky, and potentially criminal.

Choose boring and compliant. Every time.

11

International Diversification as Risk Management

Not all asset protection involves complex legal structures. Sometimes, protection comes from not having everything in one place.

International diversification is one of the oldest and simplest forms of risk management. Long before modern trusts and entities existed, families spread assets across borders to reduce exposure to any single legal, political, or economic system.

This chapter explains how international diversification works as an asset protection strategy, how it differs from secrecy-based thinking, and how to approach foreign assets rationally rather than emotionally.

Legal Diversification vs. Secrecy

The most important distinction in international diversification is intent. Many people confuse legitimate international diversification with illegal concealment. The difference is not subtle, and understanding it can save you from serious legal trouble.

What Legal Diversification Means

Legal diversification is about:

- **Reducing concentration risk.** Just as you would not put all your investments in a single stock, you should not keep all your assets subject to a single legal system. If that system becomes unstable, your entire financial position becomes vulnerable.
- **Accessing multiple legal systems.** Different countries offer different legal frameworks, protections, and investment opportunities. Having assets in multiple jurisdictions gives you options and flexibility.
- **Increasing resilience.** When your wealth is spread across borders, you are less vulnerable to localized economic downturns, political changes, or legal developments in any one place.
- **What Secrecy Is (And Why It Fails)**

Secrecy, by contrast, is about:

- **Hiding assets.** Concealing what you own from creditors, courts, or tax authorities.
- **Evading disclosure.** Failing to report assets when legally required to do so.
- **Avoiding responsibility.** Trying to escape legitimate obligations through concealment.

The former approach is lawful and widely practiced by wealthy families, corporations, and sophisticated investors. The latter is illegal and almost always fails. Modern financial transparency laws, international information-sharing agreements, and sophisticated discovery tools make hiding assets nearly impossible.

How Legal Diversification Works

International diversification works in plain sight. Assets are owned, reported, and managed transparently. Their protection comes not from concealment, but from geography and jurisdiction.

When you own property in France, maintain a brokerage account in Singapore, or hold investments in Canada, you are not hiding anything. You report these assets on your tax returns. You disclose them in legal proceedings when required. But their location creates practical and legal barriers that make them more difficult for creditors to reach quickly or easily.

Think of it like having backup systems. If one fails, others continue functioning. The key is transparency about what you own, where it is, and why it is there.

Foreign Real Estate

Foreign real estate is one of the most tangible and straightforward forms of international diversification. It is also one of the oldest. For centuries, families have purchased property abroad to preserve wealth across generations and political changes.

Asset Protection Characteristics

Foreign real estate offers several natural protections:

Governed by local property law. Real estate is always subject to the laws of the country where it sits. A U.S. court cannot simply order property in Italy to be sold. Any legal action must proceed through the Italian legal system, using Italian procedures, in the Italian language.

Outside direct reach of U.S. courts. While a U.S. court can order you personally to take actions regarding foreign property, it cannot directly seize or sell that property. Enforcement requires cooperation from foreign courts, which may or may not be granted.

Requires local legal action to seize. A creditor must file a separate lawsuit in the foreign country, hire local attorneys, navigate that country's legal procedures, and obtain a judgment there. This process is expensive, time-consuming, and uncertain.

These factors create natural enforcement barriers. They do not make the property untouchable, but they make it significantly harder and more expensive to reach than assets sitting in a U.S. bank account.

How Protection Depends on Structure

The level of protection depends heavily on:

Ownership structure. Who legally owns the property? If you own it in your personal name, a U.S. court can order you to transfer it or cooperate in its sale. If it is owned by a foreign entity or trust, the analysis becomes more complex.

Local creditor laws. Some countries offer strong protections for property owners. Others make seizure relatively easy. Understanding the local legal landscape is essential.

Political stability. Property in a country with weak rule of law, frequent political upheaval, or a history of asset seizures may create more risk than it solves.

Direct personal ownership may offer limited protection. Entity or trust ownership may improve outcomes, but only if done correctly and for legitimate reasons.

Practical Risks and Tradeoffs

Foreign real estate introduces several practical challenges:

Local legal complexity. Every country has different property laws, tax rules, inheritance regulations, and ownership restrictions. What works in one place may be illegal or impractical in another.

Currency risk. If you purchase property in euros, pounds, or pesos, you are exposed to exchange rate fluctuations. A property that maintains its local value may lose value in dollar terms if the currency weakens.

Management challenges. Managing property from thousands of miles away, in a different time zone, language, and legal system, is inherently difficult. You need local help, which introduces cost and trust issues.

Potential illiquidity. Foreign real estate can be harder to sell quickly than U.S. property, especially if you need to repatriate funds or deal with capital controls.

Asset protection should never ignore operational reality. A protected asset that cannot be managed or sold effectively may create new problems. The goal is to improve your overall position, not to create an untouchable asset that becomes a burden.

When Foreign Real Estate Makes Sense

Foreign real estate works best when:

- You have personal or business reasons to own property in that location.
- You understand the local market and legal system, or have trusted

advisors who do.

- The property serves multiple purposes: personal use, investment, diversification.
- You can afford to hold it long-term and are not dependent on quick liquidity.

It rarely makes sense to buy foreign property solely for asset protection, especially in a jurisdiction you know nothing about.

Foreign Brokerage Accounts

Foreign brokerage accounts allow investors to hold financial assets outside the U.S. banking and brokerage system. They have become more accessible in recent years, though still require more effort to establish than domestic accounts.

What They Offer

Foreign brokerage accounts allow you to:

Hold international securities directly. You can invest in foreign stocks, bonds, and funds without going through U.S. intermediaries.

Reduce reliance on a single financial system. If U.S. markets or financial institutions face disruption, you have assets held elsewhere.

Access non-U.S. markets. Some investments are only available through foreign brokers, particularly in emerging markets or specialized sectors.

From an asset protection perspective, they provide diversification, not immunity. They make enforcement more complicated, but they do not make assets disappear or become unreachable.

Protection Considerations

Foreign brokerage accounts:

Are subject to foreign law. The account is governed by the laws and regulations of the country where the brokerage is located. This can provide advantages, but also introduces unfamiliar rules and procedures.

May complicate enforcement. A U.S. creditor must navigate international legal processes to reach assets held abroad. This is more difficult than reaching a domestic account, but far from impossible.

Remain reportable and discoverable. You must report foreign financial accounts to the IRS (typically using the FBAR form). If you are involved in litigation, you must disclose these accounts during discovery. Hiding them is illegal and will likely be discovered.

They should be viewed as part of a broader financial strategy, not a defensive wall that will stop all creditors.

Custodian Risk Matters

The safety of any brokerage account depends as much on the institution holding it as on the legal protections of the jurisdiction.

Key factors include:

The custodian. Is the brokerage firm well-established, properly regulated, and financially sound? Large, reputable institutions in stable countries are far safer than unknown firms in obscure jurisdictions.

Local investor protections. Does the country have insurance schemes (like SIPC in the U.S.) that protect investors if a brokerage fails? What happens to foreign customers if something goes wrong?

Regulatory oversight. Strong financial regulation reduces the risk of fraud, mismanagement, or sudden account freezes.

Choosing reputable jurisdictions and institutions is essential. The goal is to diversify risk, not to trade one set of risks for worse ones.

Tax and Reporting Obligations

Foreign accounts come with additional paperwork:

FBAR reporting. If your foreign financial accounts exceed $10,000 in aggregate at any point during the year, you must file FinCEN Form 114.

FATCA reporting. Depending on the value of your foreign assets, you may need to file Form 8938 with your tax return.

Tax treatment. Foreign investments may generate foreign tax liabilities, and you may need to claim foreign tax credits to avoid double taxation.

These obligations are not optional. Failing to report foreign accounts can result in severe penalties, including criminal prosecution in extreme cases.

Political and Legal Risk Considerations

International diversification reduces some risks but introduces others. Moving assets abroad is not a one-way improvement. It is a tradeoff that must be evaluated carefully.

Political Risk

When considering any foreign jurisdiction, you need to assess:

- **Rule of law.** Does the country have a stable legal system that respects property rights and enforces contracts? Or is the system arbitrary, corrupt, or subject to political interference?

- **Property rights history.** Has the government ever seized private property, imposed capital controls, or nationalized assets? Even if this happened decades ago, it reveals something about the country's attitude toward private ownership.

- **Capital controls.** Some countries restrict the movement of money across borders. You might be able to get funds into the country easily but struggle to get them out when needed.

- **Government stability.** Countries experiencing political turmoil, economic crisis, or leadership transitions carry additional risk. Today's friendly regime may become tomorrow's hostile one.

Diversifying into unstable jurisdictions may increase risk rather than reduce it. The point is not to move assets somewhere exotic, but somewhere stable and reliable.

Legal Risk

Legal systems vary widely around the world. Key differences include:

- **Contract enforcement.** How reliably do courts enforce agreements? In some countries, even clear contracts may not be honored if one party has political connections.

- **Property rights.** Are ownership rights clearly defined and protected? Or are they ambiguous, contested, or subject to change?

- **Judicial independence.** Are courts independent of political influence, or are they tools of the government? An independent judiciary is critical for protecting property rights.

Understanding these differences matters more than chasing favorable headlines or tax rates. A zero-tax jurisdiction with weak rule of law may offer less real protection than a higher-tax country with strong institutions.

Concentration Still Matters

Diversification only works if it is actually diverse. Common mistakes include:

- **Putting too much in one foreign country.** If you move 80% of your wealth to Panama, you have not diversified. You have simply replaced U.S. concentration risk with Panama concentration risk.
- **Choosing similar jurisdictions.** Three different Caribbean island nations may seem like diversification, but they often have similar legal systems, economic vulnerabilities, and political risks.
- **Following trends blindly.** Popular jurisdictions become popular for a reason, but that does not mean they are right for your situation.

Diversification works best when:

- Assets are spread thoughtfully across truly different systems.
- Jurisdictions are chosen deliberately based on your needs, not generic advice.
- No single foreign country becomes a new point of failure.

Replacing one concentrated risk with another is not progress.

International Diversification Is Not a Substitute for Planning

Foreign assets do not replace the fundamental tools of asset protection. They complement them.

International diversification improves resilience. It adds another layer of complexity for creditors and reduces your exposure to any single system. But it does not determine outcomes in disputes.

Insurance still protects you from liability.

Entity planning still shields business assets from personal claims.

Trust structures still provide creditor protection and estate planning benefits.

Foreign assets enhance these strategies, but they cannot replace them. A proper asset protection plan uses multiple tools in coordination.

Think of international diversification as adding geographic spread to an already solid foundation, not as a substitute for building that foundation in the first place.

When International Diversification Makes Sense

International diversification is not for everyone. It adds complexity, cost, and reporting obligations. It makes sense in certain situations and is unnecessary or counterproductive in others.

Good Candidates for International Diversification

You may benefit from international diversification if you:

- **Have substantial assets.** If your net worth is in the millions, the benefits of diversification may outweigh the costs and complexity. For smaller estates, the juice may not be worth the squeeze.

- **Face systemic or political risk concerns.** If you believe the U.S. legal, economic, or political system faces serious long-term risks, spreading assets internationally provides a hedge.

- **Want geographic balance.** If you already have international business interests, family abroad, or spend significant time in other countries, holding assets there makes practical sense.

- **Are comfortable managing complexity.** International diversification requires ongoing attention, professional advice, and tolerance for unfamiliar systems. If this sounds overwhelming, it may not be right for you.

When It Does Not Make Sense

International diversification is rarely appropriate:

- **As a reaction to immediate threats.** If you are already being sued or facing a creditor claim, moving assets abroad looks like fraudulent transfer and will make things worse.

- **When you cannot afford proper advice.** Setting up foreign structures incorrectly can create tax problems, reporting failures, and legal exposure worse than having no diversification at all.
- **If you are trying to hide assets.** This will fail, and the consequences will be severe.
- **When simpler domestic options exist.** If your primary concern is liability protection, domestic trusts, entities, and insurance may provide equivalent or better protection with far less complexity.

Keeping Perspective

The goal of international diversification is not to outrun the law. It is to avoid overreliance on any single system.

When approached calmly and legally, diversification:

- **Reduces tail risk.** Extreme outcomes in any one jurisdiction become less likely to destroy your entire financial position.
- **Improves stability.** Multiple systems provide redundancy and options when one system faces problems.
- **Enhances flexibility.** Assets in different places give you choices about where to live, invest, or conduct business.

When approached emotionally, particularly out of fear or panic, it leads to poor decisions. People choose unsuitable jurisdictions, set up structures incorrectly, fail to report assets properly, or trust the wrong advisors.

International diversification is a long-term strategy that works best when implemented thoughtfully, with proper advice, and in coordination with your overall financial plan.

Looking Ahead

In the next chapter, we will turn to compliance, ethics, and reality checks: why transparency matters, how asset protection fails in practice, and how to avoid the most costly mistakes.

International diversification is a strategy of balance, not escape. Understanding that difference keeps it effective.

PART IV: Compliance, Ethics, and Reality Checks

12

Taxes, Reporting, and Transparency

Asset protection and taxes are often discussed in the same breath, and just as often confused. Many people assume that if a strategy protects assets, it must also reduce taxes. Others believe that moving assets into certain structures or jurisdictions makes them invisible to tax authorities. Both assumptions are wrong, and believing them can lead to serious consequences.

Asset protection is about legal risk. Taxation is about income, ownership, and reporting. While the two can intersect, they operate under different rules and must be addressed separately.

This chapter explains why asset protection does not automatically lower taxes, what U.S. persons are required to disclose, and why transparency is not a weakness but a foundation for durable protection.

Why Asset Protection Does Not Reduce Taxes by Default

Asset protection structures are designed to change who can reach your assets, not who is taxed on them.

Think of it this way: moving money from your personal bank account to an LLC bank account changes who can sue to get that money. It does not change who owes taxes on the income that money generates. The IRS still expects you to report it, pay taxes on it, and comply with all the same rules you followed before.

In most cases:

- Income remains taxable to the same person
- Gains are reported as usual
- Deductions and credits follow existing rules

Simply placing assets in an LLC, a trust, or an offshore company does not eliminate your tax obligations. The IRS does not care where your assets are held. It cares about who controls them, who benefits from them, and where the income comes from.

What Determines Tax Treatment

Tax results depend on several factors:

- Tax classification of the entity (corporation, partnership, disregarded entity, grantor trust, etc.)
- Residency of the owner or beneficiary
- Source of income (U.S. or foreign)
- Applicable tax treaties between countries

For example, if you create a foreign LLC and you are the sole owner, the IRS will typically treat it as a disregarded entity. That means all income flows directly to you and is taxed on your personal return, just as if the LLC did not exist. The structure may provide asset protection, but it provides no tax benefit.

Similarly, if you establish a domestic irrevocable trust but retain too much control or benefit, the IRS may treat you as the owner for tax purposes. You lose access to the assets for creditor protection, but you still pay taxes on the trust's income.

This creates a common trap. People set up structures thinking they will get both asset protection and tax savings. They end up with asset protection but unexpected tax bills, additional filing requirements, or both. The structure works for what it was designed to do, but the tax surprise can be financially painful.

The Tax Code Does Not Reward Asset Protection

Here is an important truth: the tax code does not give you a break just because you put assets out of reach of creditors.

If you transfer $500,000 into an irrevocable trust to protect it from lawsuits, the IRS does not say, "Good job protecting yourself, here is a tax deduction." Instead, the IRS asks, "Who controls this trust? Who benefits from it? What income does it generate?" Then it taxes accordingly.

If you retain control or benefit from the trust, you pay taxes on the income even though you cannot freely access the principal. If you give up control and benefit entirely, the trust may pay its own taxes at trust tax rates, which are often higher than individual rates. Either way, there is no tax benefit from the protection itself.

Asset protection planning that ignores tax consequences often creates expensive surprises. You may end up with a structure that protects you from lawsuits but generates unexpected tax bills, additional filing requirements, or both.

Separation of Goals Matters

Good planning distinguishes between:

- Asset protection goals (limiting liability, shielding assets from creditors)
- Tax planning goals (managing tax exposure, deferring income, maximizing deductions)

These goals are not opposed to each other, but they are not the same. When they are conflated, structures are misused and compliance failures follow.

For instance, some people set up offshore companies thinking they will both protect assets and avoid U.S. taxes. In reality, U.S. citizens and residents are taxed on worldwide income regardless of where it is earned or held. The offshore company may offer asset protection benefits, but it does not change the tax obligation. Worse, it adds complex reporting requirements that, if missed, can trigger severe penalties.

The lesson is simple: design your asset protection plan for protection. Design your tax plan for taxes. Make sure the two work together, not against each other.

When Tax and Asset Protection Conflict

Sometimes the best structure for asset protection creates a worse tax outcome, and vice versa.

For example, a single-member LLC provides good liability protection and is tax-neutral. All income flows to you, and you report it on your personal return just as you would without the LLC. Simple and clean.

But if you want stronger protection, you might add a second member or convert to a partnership structure. Now you have a separate tax return to file, potential self-employment tax issues, and more complexity. The protection improved, but the tax compliance burden increased.

Or consider an irrevocable trust. If you give up too much control, the trust becomes a separate taxpayer. Trust tax brackets are compressed, meaning the trust hits the highest tax rate much faster than an individual would. You gain asset protection but pay higher taxes on the same income.

These are not failures. They are trade-offs. The key is understanding them before you commit to a structure, not discovering them afterward when it is too late to adjust.

The Myth of the Tax-Free Offshore Account

One of the most persistent and dangerous myths is that moving money offshore eliminates U.S. taxes.

It does not.

U.S. citizens and residents are taxed on their worldwide income. It does not matter if the money is in a bank in Switzerland, the Cayman Islands, or Singapore. If you earned it, if you control it, or if you benefit from it, the IRS expects you to report it and pay taxes on it.

Opening a foreign bank account does not create a tax deduction. It does not shelter income. It does not reduce your tax bill. What it does create is additional reporting requirements, and failing to meet those requirements can result in penalties that dwarf any tax you might have owed.

The offshore account may provide asset protection benefits. It may make it harder for a creditor to freeze your funds quickly. But it provides zero tax benefit to a U.S. person unless structured in very specific ways that require extensive professional guidance and full compliance with U.S. tax law.

Required Disclosures for U.S. Persons

U.S. tax law is based on citizenship and residency, not geography. This makes the United States almost unique in the world.

If you are a U.S. citizen, green card holder, or tax resident, you must report:

• Worldwide income (from any country) • Foreign financial accounts (bank accounts, brokerage accounts, etc.) • Ownership in foreign entities (corporations, partnerships, trusts) • Interests in foreign trusts (whether as grantor, beneficiary, or otherwise)

This applies regardless of:

- Where the assets are physically located
- Whether income is distributed to you
- Whether the account is "active" or dormant
- Whether the foreign entity conducts business

Disclosure is mandatory, not optional. The IRS has spent decades building enforcement mechanisms to ensure compliance, and those mechanisms have teeth.

What "Worldwide Income" Actually Means

Worldwide income means exactly what it sounds like. Every dollar you earn, no matter where it comes from, must be reported to the IRS.

This includes:

- Salary from a foreign employer
- Rental income from foreign property
- Interest from foreign bank accounts
- Dividends from foreign stocks
- Business income from foreign operations
- Capital gains from selling foreign assets

- Royalties, fees, or payments from foreign sources

It also includes income you never actually receive. If a foreign company you own earns a profit, you may owe U.S. taxes on that profit even if the money stays in the company and you never bring it to the United States.

The only exceptions are narrow and specific. You may qualify for the Foreign Earned Income Exclusion if you live and work abroad, which allows you to exclude a certain amount of foreign wages from U.S. taxes. You may get a credit for foreign taxes paid to avoid double taxation. But these are exceptions, not loopholes, and they require proper reporting to claim.

The default rule is simple: if you earned it anywhere in the world, the IRS wants to know about it.

How the IRS Finds Unreported Foreign Assets

Many people wonder how the IRS would ever know about a foreign account or entity. The answer is: they have multiple ways to find out.

Foreign Account Tax Compliance Act (FATCA): This law requires foreign financial institutions to report accounts held by U.S. persons directly to the IRS. Banks around the world comply because the penalties for not complying are severe. If you open an account abroad, there is a good chance the IRS already knows about it.

When FATCA was first introduced, many foreign banks simply closed the accounts of U.S. customers rather than deal with the reporting requirements. Others complied fully. Either way, the days of secret foreign bank accounts are over. The banks report your name, your account number, the balance, and the income earned. The IRS receives this information automatically.

Information exchange agreements: The U.S. has agreements with dozens of countries to share tax information. Even countries traditionally seen as private banking havens now share data with the IRS.

Switzerland, once famous for banking secrecy, now exchanges information with the IRS. So do Luxembourg, Liechtenstein, Panama, and the Cayman Islands. The network of information exchange is global and growing.

Whistleblowers and leaks: Former bank employees, disgruntled business partners, and data breaches have all exposed unreported foreign accounts. The IRS pays whistleblowers a percentage of what they recover.

In the past decade, major leaks like the Panama Papers and the Paradise Papers exposed thousands of offshore accounts. The IRS used this information to pursue non-compliant taxpayers. Whistleblowers who come forward with evidence of tax evasion can receive 15% to 30% of what the IRS collects as a result.

Indirect evidence: Audits, divorce proceedings, bankruptcy filings, and customs declarations can all reveal foreign holdings.

If you go through a divorce and your spouse's lawyer discovers a foreign account, that information may end up with the IRS. If you declare expensive items at customs, the IRS may wonder where you got the money to buy them. If you file for bankruptcy and fail to list foreign assets, that is fraud, and the trustee will report it.

The assumption that foreign assets are invisible is outdated and dangerous.

Why "The IRS Will Never Know" Is a Lie

Some promoters of offshore structures still tell clients, "The IRS will never find out." This is not just wrong. It is reckless.

The IRS has powerful tools, aggressive enforcement priorities, and a long memory. Non-compliance may not catch up with you immediately, but it often catches up eventually. And when it does, the penalties are severe.

Even if the IRS does not find out on their own, life events create exposure. Divorce, death, business disputes, and legal battles all bring financial information into the open. Once that happens, there is no putting it back.

The safer assumption is that the IRS will find out. Plan accordingly.

Common Reporting Obligations

While specifics depend on individual circumstances, common obligations include:

Report of Foreign Bank and Financial Accounts (FBAR)

If you have financial interest in or signature authority over foreign financial accounts with an aggregate value exceeding $10,000 at any time during the year, you must file an FBAR with the Financial Crimes Enforcement Network (FinCEN). This is separate from your tax return.

Foreign financial accounts include:

- Bank accounts
- Brokerage accounts
- Mutual funds
- Life insurance policies with cash value
- Accounts held by entities you control

The $10,000 threshold is aggregate. If you have three foreign accounts worth $4,000 each, you exceed the threshold and must file.

When the threshold is measured: The $10,000 threshold is not based on the average balance or the year-end balance. It is based on the highest aggregate balance at any point during the year. If your accounts totaled $11,000 for a single day in July and then dropped to $8,000 for the rest of the year, you still must file.

What "signature authority" means: You do not have to own an account to have a reporting obligation. If you have authority to sign checks, move money, or otherwise control an account, you must report it. This can apply to employees who manage company accounts, trustees who oversee trust accounts, or anyone else with account access.

How to file: FBAR is filed electronically through FinCEN's BSA E-Filing System. It is not part of your tax return. The deadline is April 15, with an automatic extension to October 15. You do not need to request the extension. It applies automatically.

Form 8938: Statement of Specified Foreign Financial Assets

This form is filed with your tax return and requires disclosure of foreign financial assets if they exceed certain thresholds (which vary based on filing status and whether you live in the U.S.). The thresholds are higher than FBAR, but the reporting is more detailed.

Thresholds for U.S. residents:

- Single or married filing separately: $50,000 on the last day of the year or $75,000 at any time during the year
- Married filing jointly: $100,000 on the last day of the year or $150,000 at any time during the year

Thresholds for U.S. residents living abroad are higher:

• Single or married filing separately: $200,000 on the last day of the year or $300,000 at any time during the year • Married filing jointly: $400,000 on the last day of the year or $600,000 at any time during the year

What must be reported: Form 8938 covers more than just bank accounts. It includes foreign stocks, foreign bonds, foreign partnership interests, foreign mutual funds, and interests in foreign entities. It also requires you to report the maximum value during the year, not just the year-end value.

Overlap with FBAR: Many foreign accounts must be reported on both FBAR and Form 8938. The forms are not duplicates. They have different thresholds, different filing locations, and different penalty structures. You cannot skip one just because you filed the other.

Form 5471: Information Return of U.S. Persons With Respect To Certain Foreign Corporations

If you own stock in a foreign corporation, you may need to file Form 5471. The requirements depend on the level of ownership and the category of filer. Even minority shareholders can have filing obligations in certain situations.

Categories of filers:

- Category 1: U.S. shareholders of certain foreign corporations that were Section 965 specified foreign corporations at any time during the tax year
- Category 2: U.S. officers or directors of a foreign corporation in which a U.S. person acquired stock
- Category 3: U.S. persons who acquire, dispose of, or own 10% or more of a foreign corporation
- Category 4: U.S. persons who control a foreign corporation
- Category 5: U.S. shareholders of a controlled foreign corporation (CFC)

The rules are complex, but the basic idea is simple: if you have significant involvement with a foreign corporation, the IRS wants detailed information about it.

What the form requires: Form 5471 is not a short form. Depending on your category, you may need to provide financial statements for the foreign corporation, details about transactions between the corporation and U.S. persons, and information about the corporation's income and assets. The form can run dozens of pages for a single foreign corporation.

Why it matters: Failure to file Form 5471 can result in a $10,000 penalty per form, plus additional penalties for continued failure. If the foreign corporation is a controlled foreign corporation (CFC), there are additional reporting and tax consequences, including the potential for deemed income inclusion under Subpart F rules.

Form 3520: Annual Return To Report Transactions With Foreign Trusts and Receipt of Certain Foreign Gifts

If you create a foreign trust, transfer money to a foreign trust, or receive distributions from a foreign trust, you must file Form 3520. This form is also required if you receive gifts or bequests from foreign persons exceeding certain thresholds.

When the form is required:

- You create a foreign trust
- You transfer money or property to a foreign trust
- You receive a distribution from a foreign trust
- You receive a gift or bequest from a foreign person exceeding $100,000 (or $16,388 from a foreign corporation or partnership in 2023, adjusted annually for inflation)

What the form covers: Form 3520 requires detailed information about the trust, the transfer, or the gift. For foreign trusts, you must identify the trustee, describe the trust's assets, and report all transactions with the trust. For foreign gifts, you must identify the donor and describe the gift.

Why foreign gifts are reportable: The IRS wants to distinguish between gifts and unreported income. If you receive $200,000 from a foreign person, the IRS needs to know whether it is a legitimate gift or disguised income. Form 3520 provides that disclosure.

Form 3520-A: Annual Information Return of Foreign Trust With a U.S. Owner

If you are treated as the owner of a foreign trust (a "grantor" under U.S. tax rules), the trust itself must file Form 3520-A, and you must attach a copy to your personal return.

Who files: The foreign trust files Form 3520-A. As the U.S. owner, you are responsible for ensuring the trust files it. You must also attach the Foreign Grantor Trust Owner Statement (part of Form 3520-A) to your personal tax return.

What it covers: Form 3520-A requires the trust to provide a full accounting of its income, deductions, and transactions. It essentially treats the foreign trust as a transparent entity for U.S. tax purposes, ensuring that you report all the trust's income on your personal return.

Why this matters for grantor trusts: If you are the grantor of a foreign trust, you are taxed on all the trust's income whether or not you receive distributions. The trust does not pay U.S. taxes, but you do. Form 3520-A ensures the IRS has a record of that income.

Other Reporting Forms

Depending on your situation, you may also need to file:

- **Form 8865:** For ownership interests in foreign partnerships
- **Form 926:** For transfers of property to a foreign corporation
- **Form 8621:** For ownership of passive foreign investment companies (PFICs), such as foreign mutual funds
- **Form 5472:** For certain transactions between a foreign-owned U.S. corporation and related parties

Each of these forms has its own thresholds, requirements, and penalties. The reporting burden can be significant, especially if you have multiple foreign entities or accounts.

Why So Many Forms?

The IRS uses multiple forms to capture different types of information. FBAR focuses on accounts and balances. Form 8938 focuses on assets and their value. Form 5471 focuses on ownership and control of foreign corporations. Form 3520 focuses on transactions with foreign trusts.

Each form serves a specific purpose, and together they create a comprehensive picture of your foreign financial activity. The overlap is intentional. It allows the IRS to cross-check information and identify inconsistencies.

The Cost of Non-Compliance

Failure to comply with reporting requirements is one of the fastest ways to turn asset protection planning into a liability.

Financial Penalties

Penalties for non-compliance can be severe:

FBAR violations: Up to $10,000 per violation for non-willful failures. For willful violations, the penalty can be the greater of $100,000 or 50% of the account balance per violation. Since each year is a separate violation, penalties compound quickly.

Example: You have a foreign account worth $200,000. You fail to file FBARs for five years. If the IRS determines the failure was willful, the penalty could be $100,000 per year, for a total of $500,000. That is more than twice the value of the account.

Form 8938 violations: $10,000 per form, with an additional $10,000 for each 30 days of continued failure after IRS notice, up to $50,000 per form.

Example: You fail to file Form 8938. The IRS sends you a notice. You ignore it. After 120 days, you owe $50,000 in penalties, even if you had no tax liability.

Form 5471 violations: $10,000 per form, with additional penalties up to $50,000 for continued failure.

Form 3520 violations: The greater of $10,000 or 35% of the gross value of property transferred to a foreign trust. For failure to report distributions, 35% of the distribution.

Example: You transfer $500,000 to a foreign trust and fail to file Form 3520. The penalty is $175,000 (35% of $500,000). This is in addition to any tax you owe on income from the trust.

These penalties are strict liability in many cases. That means intent does not always matter. Even if you did not know about the requirement, you can still be penalized.

The Difference Between Willful and Non-Willful

The distinction between willful and non-willful violations matters enormously.

Non-willful violations are mistakes. You did not know you had to file, you misunderstood the rules, or you relied on bad advice. The penalties are serious but survivable.

Willful violations are intentional. You knew about the requirement and chose not to comply, or you deliberately ignored information that would have told you about the requirement. Willful penalties are financially devastating.

The IRS defines "willful" broadly. It does not require proof that you intended to break the law. It only requires proof that you knew about the account or asset and chose not to report it. Even reckless disregard for your reporting obligations can be considered willful.

For example, if you checked "no" on your tax return when asked whether you had foreign accounts, and you in fact had foreign accounts, that can be considered willful even if you did not understand the reporting requirements. The IRS will argue that you knew about the accounts and chose to answer dishonestly.

Compounding Over Time

If you fail to file for multiple years, the penalties stack. A person with a $200,000 foreign account who fails to file FBARs for five years could face penalties exceeding the balance of the account itself, even if the failure was unintentional.

This is not theoretical. The IRS has assessed millions of dollars in FBAR penalties against individuals who failed to file for multiple years. In some cases, the penalties exceeded the taxpayer's net worth.

Increased Audit Risk

Non-compliance flags your return for review. Once the IRS starts looking, they often find other issues. What began as a missed form can spiral into a full audit covering multiple years.

An FBAR violation may trigger questions about unreported income. A missing Form 5471 may lead the IRS to examine your foreign business dealings. A late Form 3520 may cause the IRS to scrutinize gifts and transfers. One problem leads to another.

Forced Disclosures Under Pressure

People who fail to report often try to fix the problem later through voluntary disclosure programs. While these programs can reduce penalties, they require you to come forward, pay back taxes, and accept some level of penalty. You lose negotiating leverage and control over the process.

The IRS offers several disclosure programs, including:

- **Streamlined Filing Compliance Procedures:** For taxpayers whose non-compliance was non-willful. Requires filing amended returns and paying a penalty equal to 5% of the highest aggregate balance of foreign accounts (or 0% for certain U.S. residents).
- **Delinquent FBAR Submission Procedures:** For taxpayers who failed to file FBARs but have otherwise been compliant. No penalty if the failure was non-willful and all taxes have been paid.
- **Voluntary Disclosure Practice:** For taxpayers whose non-compliance was willful or who do not qualify for streamlined procedures. Requires full disclosure, payment of all taxes, interest, and penalties, but protects against criminal prosecution.

These programs can help, but they are not a get-out-of-jail-free card. You still pay penalties. You still pay back taxes and interest. And you still face the stress and expense of the disclosure process.

The best approach is not to need these programs in the first place.

Reputational and Legal Risk

In extreme cases, non-compliance can lead to criminal investigations, especially if the IRS believes the failure was willful. Even if criminal charges are never filed, the investigation itself is stressful, expensive, and damaging.

Criminal tax investigations are rare, but they do happen. The IRS Criminal Investigation Division pursues cases involving willful tax evasion, fraudulent returns, and failure to file. If convicted, you face fines and prison time.

Even if the case never becomes criminal, the reputational damage can be severe. Clients, business partners, and lenders all take notice when someone is under IRS investigation. Trust is hard to rebuild.

Importantly, penalties often overshadow the original legal risk the planning was meant to address. You may successfully shield your assets from a lawsuit, only to lose them to IRS penalties for failing to file a form.

Non-Compliance Destroys Protection

Asset protection is not just about legal structure. It is about credibility. When compliance fails, the entire plan can unravel.

Courts become hostile: Judges are less sympathetic to defendants who have hidden assets or failed to disclose foreign holdings. What might have been seen as legitimate asset protection can be reframed as fraud or obstruction.

If you are sued and the opposing lawyer discovers you have unreported foreign accounts, they will argue that you are dishonest, that your asset protection planning was fraudulent, and that the court should disregard it entirely. Judges listen to those arguments, and they often agree.

Trustees become cautious: Professional trustees and custodians distance themselves from clients with compliance problems. If your trustee resigns or your bank closes your account, your plan loses functionality.

Trustees have reputational and regulatory concerns. If they believe you are non-compliant or engaged in tax evasion, they will terminate the relationship to protect themselves. Finding a new trustee after being dropped by the previous one is difficult and expensive.

Banks freeze accounts: Financial institutions are required to report suspicious activity. If they believe you are engaged in tax evasion, they may freeze your funds and report you to authorities.

Under anti-money laundering (AML) rules, banks must file Suspicious Activity Reports (SARs) when they detect potentially illegal behavior. Once a SAR is filed, your accounts may be frozen, and you may be locked out of the banking system entirely.

Advisors withdraw: Lawyers and accountants have ethical obligations. If they discover you have not been compliant, they may terminate the relationship, leaving you without professional support when you need it most.

Lawyers cannot assist clients in ongoing fraud. Accountants cannot prepare returns they know to be false. If your advisors discover that you have been non-compliant, they must either terminate the relationship or insist that you correct the problem immediately.

Losing your advisors at a critical moment, such as during an audit or investigation, is devastating. It leaves you without guidance at the exact time you need it most.

Asset Protection Depends on Credibility

Asset protection depends on credibility. Non-compliance undermines it instantly. A plan built on secrecy and evasion is not a plan at all. It is a ticking time bomb.

The strongest asset protection structures are the ones that can withstand scrutiny. They are properly documented, fully disclosed, and maintained in compliance with all applicable laws. When a creditor challenges them, they hold up in court because there is nothing to hide.

Structures built on secrecy collapse the moment they are exposed. And they always get exposed, eventually.

Transparency Is a Strategic Advantage

Transparency does not mean publicity. It means accurate reporting to authorities, honest disclosure to advisors, and clean documentation.

Why Transparency Protects You

Transparent structures are:

More defensible in court: Judges distinguish between legitimate planning and deceit. A fully disclosed, properly maintained structure is far more likely to withstand a fraudulent transfer challenge or a veil-piercing claim.

When a creditor sues you and tries to set aside your asset protection planning, the court will examine your conduct. Did you disclose the structure on your financial statements? Did you report it to the IRS? Did you maintain proper documentation? If the answer is yes, the court is far more likely to respect the structure.

If the answer is no, if it appears you were hiding assets or evading obligations, the court will view your planning as an attempt to defraud creditors. The structure will be disregarded, and you will lose the protection you thought you had.

More durable over time: Structures that rely on secrecy fall apart when exposed. Transparent structures survive scrutiny because they were designed to.

Life changes. You get divorced. You get sued. You face an audit. Your business partner turns on you. Whatever the trigger, your financial life will eventually be examined. Transparent planning survives that examination. Secret planning does not.

Less likely to unravel under pressure: Audits, litigation, and regulatory inquiries are stressful. Transparent planning means you have nothing to hide and nothing to fear.

Stress makes people make mistakes. When you know your planning is clean and compliant, you can focus on defending yourself, not covering up past errors. When you know you have cut corners, that anxiety affects every decision you make.

Judges and regulators respond differently to planning that is disclosed and maintained properly versus planning that appears deceptive. Even if two structures are legally identical, the one with clean reporting and honest documentation will fare better.

The Psychology of Transparency

There is a psychological component as well. When you know your planning is compliant, you act with confidence. You make decisions clearly. You sleep better.

When you know you have cut corners, hidden assets, or failed to file required forms, that anxiety affects everything. You hesitate. You second-guess. You make mistakes.

Transparency is not a weakness. It is a foundation for clear thinking and effective action.

Confidence matters in asset protection. When you are confident in your planning, you act decisively. You do not panic when a lawsuit is filed. You do not rush into bad settlements. You trust the structure because you know it was built correctly.

When you lack confidence because you know the planning is non-compliant, you make poor decisions. You settle cases you should fight. You give up assets you could have protected. Fear drives the process instead of strategy.

Transparency Does Not Mean Advertising

Transparency to the IRS and other authorities is not the same as broadcasting your financial affairs to the world.

You do not need to publish your asset protection planning on social media. You do not need to tell your friends, your neighbors, or your competitors. You do not need to make your financial life public.

What you do need to do is comply with legal reporting requirements, provide accurate information to professionals who are helping you, and maintain proper documentation.

Transparency is about honesty with those who have a legal right to the information. It is not about volunteering information to those who do not.

Working With Professionals Responsibly

Asset protection is multidisciplinary. It touches law, tax, accounting, and banking. No single professional covers all areas.

Choosing Advisors Wisely

Responsible professionals:

Acknowledge their limits: A good attorney will tell you when a question is outside their expertise and refer you to a tax professional. A good accountant will defer to a lawyer on legal strategy.

No one knows everything. The best advisors are the ones who recognize the boundaries of their expertise and bring in others when needed.

Coordinate with others: The best results come from collaboration. Your lawyer, accountant, and financial advisor should communicate and work toward the same goals.

Asset protection planning requires input from multiple disciplines. Your lawyer designs the legal structure. Your accountant ensures tax compliance. Your financial advisor helps you fund and maintain the plan. If these professionals do not communicate, gaps and mistakes occur.

Emphasize compliance: Advisors who prioritize compliance over clever tricks are the ones you want. Compliance is not exciting, but it is what keeps you out of trouble.

The flashy advisor who promises secrets and loopholes is often the one who gets clients in trouble. The boring advisor who insists on filing every form and following every rule is the one who keeps clients safe.

Avoid guarantees: No one can guarantee outcomes in asset protection. The law is too fact-specific and judges have too much discretion. Professionals who promise certainty are either inexperienced or dishonest.

Be wary of advisors who say things like, "This structure is bulletproof," or "No creditor will ever reach these assets." Asset protection is about reducing risk, not eliminating it. Any advisor who promises absolute certainty is either lying or does not understand how the law works.

Red Flags to Watch For

Be wary of advisors who:

Promise secrecy: Any advisor who tells you that foreign structures will hide your assets from the IRS or that you do not need to report certain accounts is either misinformed or unethical.

The IRS requires disclosure. Period. Anyone who tells you otherwise is wrong.

Dismiss reporting requirements: Phrases like "no one will ever know" or "the IRS doesn't enforce that" are warning signs. The IRS does enforce reporting rules, and the penalties are real.

This is a common tactic used by unscrupulous promoters. They downplay the risks to make their services more attractive. The result is clients who end up facing massive penalties for non-compliance.

Offer one-size-fits-all solutions: Asset protection is personal. Your plan should reflect your specific risks, goals, and circumstances. If an advisor is pushing the same structure on everyone, they are not doing their job.

Cookie-cutter planning fails because everyone's situation is different. What works for a real estate investor may not work for a business owner. What works for someone with $500,000 in assets may not work for someone with $5 million.

Use pressure tactics: Good advisors educate and advise. They do not pressure you into decisions or create artificial urgency.

Phrases like "You need to do this today" or "This opportunity won't last" are red flags. Legitimate asset protection planning takes time. It requires careful analysis, thoughtful design, and proper implementation. Advisors who rush you are often more interested in closing a sale than protecting your assets.

If something feels wrong, trust your instincts. Get a second opinion. Ask questions. Do not move forward until you are comfortable.

Your Role Matters

Even the best advisors cannot protect you from yourself. They cannot compensate for:

Withholding information: If you do not tell your advisors the full picture, they cannot give you accurate advice. Incomplete information leads to incomplete planning.

If you fail to mention a foreign account, a business interest, or a potential liability, your advisors cannot address it. They can only work with the information you provide.

Ignoring instructions: If your lawyer tells you to file a form and you do not, the blame falls on you, not them.

Advisors can guide you, but they cannot force you to comply. If they tell you what to do and you choose not to do it, the consequences are yours.

Failing to file reports: Your advisors can prepare forms and explain requirements, but you are responsible for signing and filing them.

Some people assume that hiring an accountant means they no longer have to think about tax filings. That is not true. You are legally responsible for your tax returns, even if someone else prepares them. If a form is not filed, you face the penalty, not your accountant.

Acting inconsistently: If you tell the IRS one thing and a court another, you create credibility problems that no amount of legal skill can fix.

Consistency matters. If your financial disclosures do not match across different contexts, it raises questions about your honesty. Courts and regulators notice inconsistencies, and they use them against you.

Asset protection is a partnership. It requires discipline, honesty, and follow-through. Your advisors provide expertise and strategy. You provide commitment and execution.

Questions to Ask Your Advisors

Before you commit to any asset protection plan, ask your advisors:

- What reporting requirements will this structure create?
- What forms will I need to file each year?
- What are the penalties for failing to file those forms?
- How will this structure be taxed?
- Will this create any additional tax liability?
- How will this structure be disclosed to the IRS?
- What happens if I am audited?
- What happens if I am sued and the creditor discovers this structure?
- What are the ongoing maintenance requirements?
- What happens if I need to change or dissolve the structure?

Good advisors will answer these questions clearly and completely. If an advisor evades the questions, gives vague answers, or tells you not to worry about compliance, walk away.

The Long View

Asset protection is not about avoiding obligations. It is about surviving worst-case scenarios without creating new ones.

Tax Compliance Preserves Your Options

When you are compliant, you have flexibility. You can move assets, change structures, and respond to new risks without fear that past mistakes will catch up with you.

Compliance gives you freedom. You can adapt your plan as your life changes. You can respond to new threats. You can take advantage of new opportunities.

Non-compliance locks you in. You cannot change structures without exposing past failures. You cannot move assets without triggering questions. You become trapped by your own mistakes.

Tax Compliance Reduces Stress

Knowing you have filed everything correctly and disclosed everything required allows you to focus on your life and your business, not on looking over your shoulder.

Asset protection should reduce anxiety, not create it. When you know your planning is compliant, you can live your life without constant worry.

When you know you have cut corners, every phone call from an unknown number feels like a threat. Every letter from the IRS creates panic. That is no way to live.

Tax Compliance Maintains Credibility

Compliance builds trust with courts, regulators, advisors, and financial institutions. That trust is invaluable when challenges arise.

When you are compliant, people take you seriously. Courts respect your planning. Banks work with you. Advisors are willing to represent you. Regulators give you the benefit of the doubt.

When you are non-compliant, all of that disappears. No one trusts you. No one wants to work with you. Your credibility is gone, and credibility is one of the most valuable assets you have.

When Done Correctly, Compliance Fades Into the Background

When done correctly, compliance fades into the background, and that is exactly where it belongs. You should not spend your days worrying about whether you filed the right form or disclosed the right account. You should spend them building your wealth, protecting your family, and living your life.

Asset protection that creates constant anxiety is not protection at all. It is a burden. True protection is invisible, effortless, and sustainable.

The goal is to build a structure that works, file the necessary forms, maintain proper documentation, and then move on with your life. Compliance becomes routine, not a source of stress.

Looking Ahead

In the next chapter, we will examine when asset protection fails, not in theory, but in practice. We will look at the mistakes that cause well-intentioned plans to collapse and the warning signs that a plan is heading toward failure.

Transparency is not the enemy of protection. It is the price of making protection last. The structures that survive are the ones built on honesty, maintained with discipline, and designed to withstand scrutiny.

If you take nothing else from this chapter, remember this: the goal is not to hide. The goal is to protect what matters while living openly and confidently. That requires compliance, transparency, and a long-term perspective.

Done right, asset protection is not a secret. It is a strategy.

13

When Asset Protection Fails

Asset protection rarely fails because the law suddenly changes or because courts become unpredictable. It fails because of human behavior.

Most failed asset protection plans share a common trait: they were built on assumptions rather than principles. People believed something would work without understanding why it worked, or when it wouldn't.

This chapter examines the most common reasons asset protection fails in the real world. Understanding these failure points is just as important as understanding successful strategies, because mistakes are far easier to repeat than they are to fix.

Poor Timing: The Most Unforgiving Element

Timing is the single most unforgiving element of asset protection. No matter how sophisticated your plan, if you implement it at the wrong time, it can be completely undone.

Planning After Trouble Appears

The most common failure occurs when planning begins after trouble is already visible on the horizon. This includes situations where planning starts:

- After a lawsuit is filed against you
- After a demand letter arrives in the mail
- After a debt becomes unmanageable
- After a business dispute escalates
- After an accident occurs
- After a claim becomes foreseeable

At that point, many of your best options simply disappear.

Courts are deeply skeptical of last-minute transfers. They have seen every trick in the book, and they know the difference between legitimate planning and panic. Laws exist specifically to unwind transfers made with improper intent. Even technically legal actions may be recharacterized as fraudulent if the timing suggests you were trying to hide assets from a creditor.

Here's a real-world example of how this plays out. Imagine you own a rental property worth $500,000 with no mortgage. One of your tenants falls down a staircase and suffers serious injuries. Three weeks later, you receive a letter from an attorney indicating that your tenant intends to file a lawsuit seeking damages of $2 million. Your insurance policy covers only $1 million.

You panic. You immediately transfer the rental property to your brother, telling him you'll transfer it back once this "blows over." You think you've protected the property from the lawsuit.

What you've actually done is committed a fraudulent transfer. The timing alone proves your intent. You knew about the claim. You moved an asset specifically to put it beyond the reach of a creditor. The court will reverse this transfer, and you may face additional penalties for attempting to defraud the injured party.

The same property, transferred to a properly structured LLC five years earlier as part of your regular business planning, would likely have been protected. The difference is not what you did. The difference is when you did it.

When Asset Protection Works Best

Asset protection is strongest when it happens in calm waters:

- No claim exists against you

- No claim is anticipated or foreseeable
- Transfers are part of your normal financial planning
- You have time to establish a track record of proper conduct
- The structures you create can season and develop substance

Think of it like wearing a seatbelt. You put it on before the accident, not during. Late planning is not asset protection. It is damage control, and courts treat it accordingly.

The concept of "seasoning" is critical and often misunderstood. Seasoning means allowing time to pass between when you implement your asset protection strategy and when a claim arises. The longer the seasoning period, the stronger your position.

For example, if you transfer assets to an irrevocable trust and a creditor sues you seven years later, the court will have a much harder time arguing that you made the transfer to defraud that specific creditor. You couldn't have known about them seven years ago. The transfer looks like legitimate estate planning, not asset hiding.

But if you transfer assets to the same trust and get sued six months later, the court will scrutinize your intent much more carefully. Six months is not enough time to establish that this was legitimate planning rather than a response to a foreseeable claim.

Different types of transfers require different seasoning periods. Some states have specific lookback periods for fraudulent transfers, often ranging from four to six years. During these lookback periods, creditors have the right to challenge transfers and potentially reverse them. Beyond these periods, transfers become much harder to attack.

This is why the best time to implement asset protection is always now, assuming you have no current claims against you. The sooner you start, the longer your seasoning period, and the stronger your protection becomes.

The Fraudulent Transfer Problem

When you transfer assets after a claim arises or becomes foreseeable, you trigger fraudulent transfer laws. These laws give creditors the power to reverse your transfers and pull assets back into your name.

Courts will ask:

- When did you know about the problem?
- What did you do with your assets after learning about it?
- Were you trying to put assets beyond the reach of creditors?

If the answers suggest improper intent, your planning will fail regardless of how well it was executed.

Understanding fraudulent transfer laws is essential because they represent the primary weapon creditors use to attack asset protection planning. Every state has fraudulent transfer laws, and they generally follow similar principles.

A transfer is considered fraudulent if you made it with the intent to hinder, delay, or defraud a creditor. Intent is hard to prove directly, so courts look at "badges of fraud." These are circumstances that suggest fraudulent intent even without direct evidence.

Common badges of fraud include:

- The transfer was made to a family member or insider
- You retained possession or control of the property after the transfer
- The transfer was concealed or not disclosed
- You were sued or threatened with suit before the transfer
- The transfer included substantially all of your assets
- You became insolvent as a result of the transfer
- The transfer occurred shortly before or after a substantial debt was incurred
- You received less than reasonably equivalent value for the asset

The more badges of fraud present, the more likely a court will find the transfer fraudulent and reverse it.

Here's what makes this particularly dangerous: you don't need to have actual intent to defraud for a transfer to be fraudulent. Courts also recognize "constructive fraud," which occurs when you make a transfer for less than reasonably equivalent value while you are insolvent or will become insolvent as a result.

For example, if you gift your $300,000 home to your adult children while you owe $500,000 in credit card debt and have no other significant assets, that transfer is constructively fraudulent even if you had no specific intent to defraud your credit card companies. The law presumes that an insolvent person who gives away assets for nothing in return is hindering creditors, regardless of subjective intent.

The consequences of a fraudulent transfer go beyond simply reversing the transfer. You may face:

- Creditor claims against the person who received the asset
- Personal liability for attempting to defraud creditors
- Denial of bankruptcy discharge
- Criminal charges in extreme cases
- Awards of attorneys' fees and costs to the creditor
- Damage to your credibility in court

This is why timing matters so profoundly. The same transfer that is legitimate planning when done early becomes fraudulent when done late. The action is identical. The intent is completely different.

DIY Mistakes: When Simplicity Backfires

The second major cause of failure is do-it-yourself planning. The internet has made it easier than ever to create legal structures, but easier does not mean safer.

The Illusion of Simplicity

Online forms and templates create the illusion that asset protection is simple. The marketing messages are everywhere:

- "Just form an LLC and you're protected"
- "Put everything in a trust"
- "Move it offshore and creditors can't touch it"
- "File these forms and you're done"

What these shortcuts omit is context. They omit the why behind the what. They omit the nuances that determine whether something actually works in your state, for your situation, against your particular risks.

The promise of simplicity is seductive because asset protection seems like it should be simple. You form an entity, transfer some property, file some paperwork, and you're protected. What could be complicated about that?

Everything, as it turns out.

Consider a common scenario. You own a small business and you're worried about liability. You go online, pay $99 to form an LLC, and transfer your business assets to the LLC. You feel protected.

But here's what you probably didn't do:

- Properly value the assets you transferred
- Document the consideration for the transfer
- Update title documents, deeds, and registrations
- Open a separate bank account for the LLC
- Obtain a new employer identification number
- File the necessary tax elections
- Create an operating agreement
- Maintain corporate formalities going forward
- Keep separate books and records
- Avoid commingling personal and business funds

Without these steps, your LLC exists only on paper. When a creditor challenges it, the structure will collapse because it has no substance. The court will treat the LLC as your alter ego and hold you personally liable for its obligations.

This is called "piercing the corporate veil," and it happens regularly to DIY entities. The protection you thought you had was never really there.

Why DIY Planning Often Fails

DIY planning typically fails for predictable reasons:

State law nuances are ignored. An LLC strategy that works in Wyoming may not work the same way in California. Community property rules, exemption laws, and charging order protections vary significantly from state to state. If you don't know the specific rules where you live, you may be building on sand.

For example, some states provide strong charging order protection for LLCs, meaning that a creditor who obtains a judgment against you personally can only get a charging order against your LLC interest. The creditor cannot force the sale of LLC assets or take over management. This makes the LLC interest relatively unattractive to creditors.

Other states provide much weaker protection. In these states, a creditor can foreclose on your LLC interest, taking ownership and control of the entity. If you formed your LLC assuming strong charging order protection, but you live in a state that doesn't provide it, your planning fails.

Similarly, some states recognize tenancy by the entirety for real property owned by married couples, which can protect the property from creditors of only one spouse. Other states do not recognize this form of ownership, or limit it to primary residences. If you rely on tenancy by the entirety protection in a state that doesn't provide it, you have no protection at all.

Entities are improperly used. Forming an LLC is easy. Operating it correctly is harder. If you don't maintain corporate formalities, keep separate books, hold meetings, and treat the entity as truly separate from yourself, a court may disregard it entirely. This is called "piercing the corporate veil," and it happens regularly to improperly maintained entities.

Courts pierce the veil when the entity is merely the alter ego of its owner. Factors that lead to piercing include:

- Commingling of personal and business funds
- Undercapitalization of the entity
- Failure to maintain separate books and records
- Failure to observe corporate formalities
- Using entity assets for personal purposes
- Holding the entity out as merely a department of yourself
- Failure to maintain arms-length relationships in transactions

The standard is whether you treated the entity as truly separate or merely as an extension of yourself. If you used the business bank account to pay your personal mortgage, or you signed contracts in your personal name rather than as manager of the LLC, or you never held meetings or kept minutes, you've demonstrated that the entity was not truly separate.

When a court pierces the veil, it treats the entity's actions as your actions and the entity's debts as your debts. All the protection you thought you had evaporates.

Documentation is incomplete. Asset protection requires a paper trail that tells a coherent story. Without proper documentation of transfers, valuations, consideration, and intent, courts will fill in the blanks against you.

When you transfer assets to an entity or trust, you need to document:

- What was transferred and when
- The fair market value of what was transferred
- What consideration you received in return
- Your intent in making the transfer
- Whether the transfer was made for reasonably equivalent value
- Your solvency before and after the transfer

Without this documentation, a creditor attacking the transfer will present the worst possible interpretation of events, and you'll have no records to refute their claims.

For example, if you transferred your $500,000 home to your LLC five years ago but you have no documentation of the transfer, no record of what membership interest you received in exchange, and no appraisal showing the value at the time, a creditor can argue that:

The transfer was actually made recently, not five years ago

You received nothing of value in exchange (fraudulent transfer)

You remained in control and ownership (the LLC is your alter ego)

You made the transfer specifically to defraud them

Without documents, you have no way to prove otherwise. The court may accept the creditor's version of events because you have nothing to contradict it.

Maintenance is neglected. Asset protection is not a one-time filing. It requires ongoing attention. Annual reports must be filed. Registered agents must be maintained. Bank accounts must be kept separate. Records must be updated. When these details slip, protection erodes.

Many people form entities with good intentions but fail to maintain them over time. They forget to file annual reports and the entity falls into bad standing with the state. They stop keeping separate bank accounts and begin commingling funds. They neglect to update operating agreements when circumstances change. They fail to document major transactions.

These failures accumulate quietly. You may not realize anything is wrong until years later when a creditor challenges your structure. By then, the damage is done and cannot be undone.

For example, if your LLC falls into bad standing because you forgot to file annual reports for three years, a court may find that the entity ceased to exist during those years. Any protection you thought you had during that period is gone.

Asset protection is not filing paperwork and walking away. It is behavior over time.

Paper Protection vs. Real Protection

Here is what many people miss: courts do not protect paperwork. They protect substance.

- When an entity or trust exists only on paper, without the following elements, it provides little to no protection:
- Separate bank accounts and financial records
- Proper capitalization (adequate funds to operate)
- Consistent treatment as a separate entity
- Real business purpose beyond asset protection
- Arms-length transactions
- Independent decision-making

A DIY plan collapses under scrutiny because it cannot withstand basic questions about purpose and conduct. The judge will ask: "Did you really treat this as a separate entity, or was it just a shell you controlled for your own benefit?" If you cannot answer convincingly, your protection vanishes.

Courts are looking for substance over form. They want to see that you treated the entity as a real, separate legal person, not just a piece of paper you created to shield yourself from liability.

Consider two scenarios:

Scenario A: You form an LLC to hold rental properties. You open a separate bank account in the LLC's name. Rent payments go into the LLC account. Expenses are paid from the LLC account. You maintain detailed records of all transactions. You never use LLC funds for personal purposes. You file separate tax returns for the LLC. You sign all lease agreements and contracts in your capacity as manager of the LLC, not in your personal name. You hold annual meetings and keep minutes. You maintain adequate insurance. The LLC has real economic substance and operates as a legitimate business entity.

Scenario B: You form an LLC to hold rental properties. You never open a separate bank account. Rent checks are deposited to your personal account. You pay expenses from your personal account. You sign lease agreements in your personal name. You never hold meetings or keep minutes. You think of the LLC as "just paperwork" for liability protection. The LLC has no economic substance and operates as your alter ego.

In Scenario A, the LLC will likely provide meaningful protection. In Scenario B, the LLC will be disregarded entirely. The difference is not the formation of the LLC. The difference is how you treated it after formation.

This is why DIY planning is so dangerous. The hard part is not creating the entity. The hard part is operating it correctly over time, in a way that respects its separate legal identity. Most people never learn this distinction, and their protection fails when they need it most.

Overconfidence in Single Strategies

Another common failure is reliance on a single tool. People put all their faith in one strategy and assume it will cover everything.

Common Examples of Overconfidence

You hear statements like these all the time:

- "My LLC protects everything I own."
- "I have insurance, so I'm fully covered."
- "My trust is bulletproof."
- "Offshore means untouchable."
- "The homestead exemption covers me."

Each of these beliefs contains partial truth and total risk. Yes, each tool provides some protection. No, none of them provides complete protection.

Let's examine why each of these statements represents dangerous overconfidence:

"My LLC protects everything I own." This fundamentally misunderstands how LLCs work. An LLC provides inside-out protection, meaning it protects you personally from liabilities that arise from the LLC's activities. If your LLC is sued for a business debt or tort, your personal assets are generally protected.

But an LLC does not provide outside-in protection. If you are sued personally for something unrelated to the LLC (a car accident, a personal guarantee, a divorce, a malpractice claim), your ownership interest in the LLC is a personal asset that can be reached by your personal creditors. Depending on your state's laws, a creditor may be able to seize your LLC interest, take control of the entity, or force liquidation of LLC assets.

So the LLC protects you from the LLC's liabilities, but it does not protect the LLC from your personal liabilities. This is a critical distinction that many people miss.

"I have insurance, so I'm fully covered." Insurance is essential, but it is not complete protection. Insurance policies have:

- Coverage limits (the maximum the insurer will pay)
- Exclusions (types of claims not covered at all)
- Deductibles (amounts you pay before coverage begins)
- Conditions (requirements you must meet for coverage to apply)

A $1 million liability policy seems like a lot until you face a $3 million judgment. Then you're personally liable for the $2 million difference. Similarly, your homeowner's insurance may not cover business activities conducted from your home, or your auto insurance may not cover you if you were using your vehicle for business purposes.

Insurance companies also deny claims, sometimes in bad faith. They may argue that your actions violated a policy condition, or that the claim falls under an exclusion, or that you failed to provide timely notice. Even when you believe you're covered, you may find yourself in litigation against your own insurance company while the underlying claim proceeds.

Insurance is a critical first layer of protection, but it should never be your only layer.

"My trust is bulletproof." This depends entirely on what type of trust you have and what you're trying to protect against. A revocable living trust provides zero asset protection because you retain full control over the trust assets. You can dissolve the trust at any time and take the assets back. If you can reach the assets, so can your creditors.

An irrevocable trust can provide meaningful asset protection, but only if you truly give up control. If you retain too many powers (the ability to remove and replace trustees, the ability to direct investments, the ability to receive distributions), courts may find that you still effectively own the trust assets and allow creditors to reach them.

Even a properly structured irrevocable trust has limitations. It may protect against future creditors but not against existing claims. It may trigger gift tax consequences. It may limit your access to the assets when you need them. And if structured incorrectly or at the wrong time, it can be set aside as a fraudulent transfer.

"Offshore means untouchable." This is perhaps the most dangerous misconception. Moving assets offshore does not place them beyond the reach of U.S. courts. If you are subject to the court's jurisdiction (which you are if you're a U.S. person), the court can order you to repatriate assets. If you refuse, you can be held in contempt and jailed until you comply.

Offshore structures also require extensive reporting to the IRS and FinCEN. Failure to report foreign accounts and entities can result in massive penalties, including criminal charges. Promoters who tell you that offshore planning avoids reporting requirements are setting you up for serious legal trouble.

Offshore planning has legitimate uses, particularly for international business operations and estate planning for non-U.S. beneficiaries. But it is not a magic shield against U.S. creditors, and it is certainly not a way to hide assets from the IRS.

"The homestead exemption covers me." Homestead exemptions vary dramatically by state. Some states (like Florida and Texas) provide unlimited homestead protection, meaning your primary residence cannot be taken by creditors no matter its value. Other states provide very limited protection, sometimes as little as $5,000 to $50,000 in equity.

Even in states with generous homestead exemptions, there are important limitations:

- The exemption usually applies only to your primary residence, not to vacation homes or rental properties
- You may need to have lived in the state for a certain period before the full exemption applies
- The exemption may not apply in bankruptcy if you acquired the property within a certain lookback period
- The exemption doesn't protect against foreclosure for failure to pay your mortgage or property taxes
- Some types of claims (IRS tax liens, domestic support obligations) can override the homestead exemption

Relying solely on the homestead exemption leaves all your other assets exposed and may not even fully protect your home depending on your state's specific rules.

Why Single Strategies Fail

Every tool in asset protection has three characteristics:

Limits. An LLC protects you from business liabilities but does not protect the LLC's assets from your personal liabilities. Insurance covers what the policy says it covers, and nothing more. A trust protects against probate but may not protect against creditors if you retain too much control.

Exceptions. Homestead exemptions have dollar limits and may not apply if you moved to the state recently. Retirement accounts are protected in bankruptcy but not always in state court judgments. Every protection has exceptions, and those exceptions matter.

Failure points. Insurance companies deny claims. LLCs can be pierced. Trusts can be set aside. Offshore structures can be ordered repatriated. When your single strategy hits its failure point, you have nothing left to absorb the impact.

Think of asset protection like the security system for your home. You don't rely solely on door locks. You also have window locks, motion sensors, cameras, an alarm system, and perhaps a safe for valuables. Each layer provides protection, and each layer compensates for the weaknesses of the others.

If your only security is a lock on the front door, a burglar who defeats that lock has access to everything. If you have multiple layers, defeating one layer still leaves others in place. The burglar may succeed in picking the door lock, but the motion sensor triggers the alarm before they can reach your valuables in the safe.

Asset protection works the same way. Relying on a single strategy creates a single point of failure. When that point fails, and it often does, you have no backup protection.

The Power of Layering

Asset protection works through layering. Multiple strategies, properly coordinated, create redundancy. If one layer fails, others remain. If one tool reaches its limit, another tool picks up where it left off.

Effective layering means:

- Insurance provides the first layer of protection
- Legal entities (LLCs, corporations) provide the second layer
- Trusts provide protection for specific assets
- Exemption planning protects retirement accounts and homesteads
- Proper titling and ownership structures add another layer
- Geographic diversification may add protection against local courts
- Liquidity planning ensures you can settle claims if necessary

For example, consider a physician who faces malpractice risk:

- Layer 1: Professional liability insurance with adequate limits
- Layer 2: Medical practice operated through a professional corporation
- Layer 3: Real estate holdings in separate LLCs, not owned by the practice
- Layer 4: Investment accounts held in tenancy by the entirety with spouse
- Layer 5: Retirement accounts maximized to benefit from exemption protection
- Layer 6: Primary residence protected by homestead exemption
- Layer 7: Irrevocable trust for benefit of children, removing assets from physician's estate
- Layer 8: Umbrella liability policy for additional coverage beyond primary insurance

If this physician faces a malpractice claim:

- The insurance covers up to its policy limits
- The corporation protects personal assets from practice liabilities
- The real estate holdings are separated from the practice, not available to satisfy a malpractice judgment
- The investment accounts may be protected if held as tenancy by the entirety
- Retirement accounts are protected by federal and state exemptions
- The home is protected by the homestead exemption
- Trust assets are beyond the physician's ownership and control
- The umbrella policy provides additional coverage if the malpractice insurance is exhausted

Notice how each layer protects different assets or provides protection in different circumstances. If one layer fails (insurance coverage is inadequate, or the corporation is pierced), other layers remain. This is the power of layering.

Removing layers creates single points of failure. Single points fail. That is why relying on one strategy, no matter how good it seems, is fundamentally risky.

Aggressive Promoters and Red Flags

Perhaps the most dangerous failures come from trusting the wrong people. Asset protection attracts its share of promoters who prey on fear and confusion.

The Business of Fear

Some promoters build their business model around fear. They:

- Exploit your anxiety about lawsuits, taxes, or economic collapse
- Promise absolute certainty in an uncertain world
- Oversell complexity to justify high fees
- Position themselves as having secret knowledge

This approach is effective marketing. It is also a warning sign.

The asset protection industry, unfortunately, includes many bad actors who profit from fear and misinformation. They understand that people make poor decisions when they're afraid, and they exploit that fear systematically.

Their typical approach follows a pattern:

First, they amplify your fears. They paint a picture of a legal system that is out to get you, of creditors lurking around every corner, of the government waiting to seize your assets. They tell stories (often exaggerated or fabricated) of people who lost everything because they didn't act soon enough. They present worst-case scenarios as typical outcomes.

Second, they position themselves as the solution. They claim to have special knowledge, secret strategies, or unique access to protective structures that others don't know about. They suggest that conventional attorneys don't understand "real" asset protection. They imply that they can provide certainty and absolute protection if you just follow their advice.

Third, they create urgency. They warn that time is running out, that laws are changing, that you must act immediately or face dire consequences. They use high-pressure sales tactics designed to prevent you from thinking clearly or seeking second opinions.

Finally, they charge substantial fees for services that may have little to no actual value. They sell offshore trusts to people who don't need them. They create complex entity structures that provide no additional protection. They promote strategies that are legally questionable or outright fraudulent.

These promoters thrive because asset protection is genuinely complicated, and most people don't have the legal knowledge to evaluate their claims. The average person cannot distinguish between legitimate advanced planning and expensive nonsense.

Common Red Flags

Be immediately skeptical when you encounter these red flags:

Guarantees of protection. No honest professional guarantees that a court can never reach your assets. The law is too complex and fact-specific for guarantees. Anyone promising absolute protection is either ignorant or dishonest.

Asset protection is always about probability and risk reduction, never about certainty. A competent attorney will explain what protection a particular strategy provides, what its limitations are, and what risks remain. They will never guarantee an outcome because too many variables are beyond anyone's control.

When someone guarantees that your assets will be "100% protected" or that creditors "cannot possibly" reach them, they are either lying or they don't understand the law. Courts have enormous power, and determined creditors with skilled attorneys can often find ways to reach assets that seem protected. The goal is to make yourself a difficult enough target that creditors look elsewhere or settle for less. It is not to achieve perfect invulnerability.

Claims that courts "can't touch" your assets. Courts have tremendous power, especially when they believe you are hiding assets. Promoters who claim otherwise are setting you up for failure.

U.S. courts have jurisdiction over U.S. persons regardless of where their assets are located. If you're ordered to repatriate offshore assets and you refuse, you can be jailed for contempt. If you're ordered to turn over assets held in a trust and you refuse, you can face severe sanctions. If the court believes you're deliberately hiding assets, it has numerous tools to compel disclosure and cooperation.

Statements like "move your assets to [country] and creditors can't touch them" or "put everything in [type of trust] and you're judgment-proof" are red flags. They reflect either ignorance of how courts actually work or deliberate misrepresentation.

Dismissal of reporting or compliance. Legitimate structures require reporting. Offshore accounts must be disclosed. Entities must file returns. Anyone who tells you otherwise is either wrong or encouraging you to break the law.

U.S. taxpayers must report foreign bank accounts exceeding $10,000 at any time during the year (FBAR reporting). They must report ownership interests in foreign entities and trusts (Form 5471, Form 8938, Form 3520). Failure to file these reports can result in penalties of $10,000 per violation or more, and repeated willful failure can result in criminal charges.

Any promoter who suggests you don't need to report foreign accounts or entities, or who minimizes the reporting requirements, is steering you toward serious legal trouble. The IRS has become increasingly aggressive in pursuing foreign account violations, and the penalties can be financially devastating.

Similarly, domestic entities require annual reports, tax filings, and maintenance of good standing. Anyone who suggests you can just "file and forget" an entity without ongoing compliance is giving you dangerously incomplete advice.

Urgency tactics. "Do this now or lose everything." "The window is closing." "They're coming for people like you." These are sales tactics designed to shut down your critical thinking. Legitimate planning does not require panic.

High-pressure sales tactics are a hallmark of scams. Legitimate professionals give you time to think, encourage you to seek second opinions, and answer your questions patiently. They don't pressure you to sign contracts immediately or wire funds to offshore accounts before you've had time to verify their credentials.

If someone is pushing you to make a decision right now, without time for due diligence or consultation with your existing advisors, walk away. Asset protection done hastily is usually asset protection done poorly. The planning that works is the planning that is implemented thoughtfully, with proper advice, over adequate time.

Secret structures or loopholes. There are no secret structures that the IRS doesn't know about. There are no magic loopholes that courts haven't seen. If it sounds too good to be true, it is.

The IRS has seen every offshore strategy, every trust gimmick, every entity structure. Courts have heard every argument about why a particular arrangement should shield assets from creditors. There are no secrets in this field, only variations on known themes.

When a promoter claims to have a "secret" strategy or a "little-known loophole," they are either misleading you or promoting a strategy that doesn't actually work. The IRS and courts are not stupid. They have extensive resources and experience. What seems like a clever strategy to you is probably something they've encountered and defeated many times before.

Legitimate asset protection uses well-established tools in ways that are appropriate to your circumstances. It doesn't rely on secrets, tricks, or loopholes. It relies on proper planning, documentation, and maintenance over time.

These promises appeal emotionally. They offer certainty in an uncertain world. They fail legally because courts are not impressed by hype.

One-Size-Fits-All Solutions

No legitimate asset protection plan looks the same for everyone. Your risks, assets, family situation, business interests, and goals are unique. A plan that works for a real estate investor in Florida will not work the same way for a doctor in California or a business owner in Texas.

Promoters who sell prepackaged structures, jurisdiction-only solutions, or cookie-cutter offshore setups are selling convenience, not protection. They are selling the same plan to everyone because it is easy and profitable for them, not because it fits your situation.

For example, some promoters sell Nevada corporations to everyone, claiming that Nevada's corporate laws provide superior asset protection. While Nevada does have some favorable corporate laws, simply forming a Nevada corporation provides no meaningful protection for most people. If you live and operate your business in California, forming a Nevada corporation may actually create additional costs and complications without any real benefit.

Similarly, some promoters sell Nevis or Cook Islands trusts as the ultimate asset protection solution, regardless of the client's circumstances. While foreign asset protection trusts can be useful in certain high-risk, high-net-worth situations, they are expensive to establish and maintain, require extensive reporting, and are often unnecessary for people with more typical risk profiles.

A real estate investor's risks are completely different from a physician's risks. A business owner's asset protection needs are different from a retiree's needs. A married person's planning options are different from a single person's options. State law variations mean that strategies available in one state may not work in another.

Real asset protection requires customization. It requires understanding your specific risks and building a plan around them. Anything else is theater.

Prepackaged solutions fail because they cannot account for:

- Your specific state's laws on exemptions, charging orders, and creditor rights
- Your unique risk profile based on your profession and activities
- Your family situation, including marriage, children, and estate planning goals
- Your tax situation and the tax consequences of various strategies
- Your liquidity needs and access requirements
- Your existing assets and how they are currently titled
- Your future plans for acquiring or disposing of assets
- Your tolerance for complexity and administrative burden
- Your budget for implementation and ongoing maintenance

A surgeon in California facing malpractice risk needs a completely different plan than a real estate developer in Texas facing construction liability. The surgeon might focus on maximum liability insurance, professional corporations, and protecting exempt assets. The developer might focus on separate LLCs for each project, contractual risk allocation, and bankruptcy planning.

Neither should be sold the same offshore trust package just because it's what the promoter has available.

How Failure Usually Unfolds

Asset protection rarely fails all at once. It erodes gradually, often invisibly, until one day you discover it was never really there.

Here is how it typically unfolds:

First, a claim arises. Something happens. An accident, a lawsuit, a business dispute, a divorce. The event that you hoped would never happen has happened.

This is the moment when you discover whether your planning actually works. Up until now, your asset protection structures have existed in theory. Now they face real-world testing.

Many people don't recognize this moment for what it is. They receive a demand letter or a complaint and they think it's a minor issue that will go away. They don't immediately connect the claim to their asset protection planning. By the time they realize the seriousness of the situation, valuable time has been lost.

Then, a structure is challenged. The creditor's attorney looks at your LLC, your trust, your offshore account. They start asking questions. They request documents. They depose you.

This is where most DIY planning falls apart. The creditor's attorney is experienced in attacking asset protection structures. They know what questions to ask. They know what documents to request. They know what inconsistencies to look for.

They will ask:

- When did you form this entity?
- What assets did you transfer to it and when?
- What consideration did you receive?
- Who controls the entity?

- Where are the bank accounts?
- Have you kept separate records?
- Did you file annual reports?
- Have you maintained corporate formalities?
- What was your intent in creating this structure?

If you cannot answer these questions convincingly, with supporting documentation, your structure is in serious trouble.

Next, documentation gaps appear. You cannot find the operating agreement. You never actually transferred title to the LLC. You commingled funds. You signed documents as both trustee and beneficiary. The paperwork does not support the story you are trying to tell.

These gaps are fatal. Without documentation, you have no proof of what you did, when you did it, or why you did it. The court will accept the creditor's version of events because you have nothing to contradict it.

Common documentation failures include:

- No written operating agreement or trust document
- No transfer documents showing assets actually moved to the entity
- No appraisals or valuations supporting transfer values
- No records of meetings or resolutions
- No separate books showing the entity's financial activity
- No documentation of arms-length transactions
- Commingled bank accounts with no clear separation
- Contracts signed in your personal capacity instead of as an entity representative

Each gap weakens your position. Multiple gaps together destroy it.

Finally, courts apply equitable principles. The judge looks at the totality of circumstances. They see through the form to the substance. They conclude you never really gave up control, or you set this up to defraud creditors, or the entity was your alter ego all along.

Courts are not bound by formalities when they believe you are using legal structures to achieve an unjust result. They apply equitable principles to look past the form of what you did to the substance of what you intended.

Equitable principles that work against poorly executed asset protection include:

- Alter ego doctrine: The entity is merely your alter ego and should be disregarded
- Substance over form: What you actually did matters more than what the paperwork says
- Fraudulent transfer: You moved assets to hinder creditors
- Unjust enrichment: You kept the benefit of assets while shielding them from creditors
- Contempt power: You can be jailed for refusing to comply with court orders
- These principles give courts tremendous flexibility to reach assets that appear protected on paper but lack true substance.

By the time the failure becomes visible, it is usually irreversible. The court issues an order. The assets are reached. The protection you thought you had evaporates.

And here's the worst part: by this point, you've often made your situation worse. You've spent money on structures that don't work. You've potentially committed fraudulent transfers that subject you to additional liability. You've damaged your credibility with the court by attempting strategies that appeared designed to evade legitimate obligations. You may have triggered tax consequences from unwinding the failed structures.

The failure cascade is complete.

Avoiding Failure Requires Humility

Successful asset protection requires a mindset that many people find difficult. It requires:

Realistic expectations. Asset protection is about reducing risk, not eliminating it. It works within the law, not around it. It is one piece of a larger financial plan, not a magic shield.

You cannot make yourself completely judgment-proof. You cannot guarantee that no creditor will ever reach any of your assets. What you can do is structure your affairs to reduce the likelihood of catastrophic loss, make yourself a less attractive target, and preserve some assets for your family even if you face significant liability.

Think of asset protection like insurance. Insurance doesn't prevent bad things from happening. It just reduces the financial impact when they do happen. Similarly, asset protection doesn't prevent lawsuits or claims. It reduces your exposure when they occur.

People who approach asset protection with realistic expectations are more likely to implement effective strategies because they're not looking for magic bullets or guaranteed solutions. They're looking for reasonable risk reduction, and that's what asset protection can actually deliver.

Willingness to plan early. This means planning before you need it, when it feels abstract and unnecessary. It means spending money and time on something that may never be tested.

This is perhaps the hardest mental shift for most people. Spending thousands of dollars on asset protection when you have no current claims feels wasteful. You're solving a problem that doesn't exist yet and may never exist.

But that's exactly when asset protection works best. Planning early means:

- You avoid fraudulent transfer concerns
- You establish a seasoning period
- You demonstrate legitimate intent
- You have time to properly implement and maintain structures
- You can make rational decisions without the pressure of an imminent claim

The people who resist early planning are usually the same people who desperately wish they had planned when they later face a claim. The time to build the levee is before the flood, not during it.

Respect for complexity. Asset protection involves multiple areas of law: business entities, trusts, taxes, bankruptcy, family law, and more. Respecting this complexity means working with professionals who understand it.

Asset protection sits at the intersection of numerous legal disciplines. An effective plan requires understanding:

- Entity law: How corporations, LLCs, partnerships, and other entities work
- Trust law: How different types of trusts are created and administered
- Tax law: The tax consequences of various structures and transfers
- Bankruptcy law: What assets are exempt and what strategies survive bankruptcy
- Family law: How divorce affects asset ownership and protection strategies
- Contract law: How to structure agreements to allocate risk
- Real property law: How title and ownership affect creditor rights
- Exemption law: What assets your state protects from creditors
- Fraudulent transfer law: What transfers can be attacked and reversed
- Civil procedure: How courts exercise jurisdiction and enforce judgments

No single professional masters all these areas. Effective asset protection usually requires a team approach, involving your attorney, your CPA, your financial advisor, and sometimes specialists in particular areas.

Respecting this complexity means acknowledging that you cannot do this yourself with internet research and form documents. It means investing in professional advice. It means recognizing that cheap and simple rarely works in this context.

Acceptance of trade-offs. Every strategy has costs. Some are financial. Some involve giving up control. Some create administrative burden. Some limit flexibility. You cannot have perfect protection with zero cost.

Common trade-offs in asset protection include:

- *Cost vs. protection:* More sophisticated structures provide better protection but cost more to implement and maintain
- *Protection vs. access:* Assets that are well-protected are often harder for you to access when you need them

- *Simplicity vs. effectiveness:* Simple structures are easy to maintain but provide limited protection; complex structures provide better protection but require ongoing attention

- *Control vs. protection:* The more control you retain, the less protection you have; truly protected assets usually require giving up some degree of control

- *Privacy vs. transparency:* Some protective structures require public filings and disclosures

- *Flexibility vs. security:* Structures that are easy to change are also easier for creditors to penetrate

- *Current access vs. future protection:* Protecting assets for your family may mean limiting your current access to them

Understanding and accepting these trade-offs allows you to make informed decisions about which strategies fit your situation. People who expect perfect solutions with no downsides inevitably become disappointed or fall victim to promoters who promise exactly that.

Overconfidence is more dangerous than ignorance. The person who knows nothing may seek help. The person who thinks they know everything will not.

This is worth emphasizing because overconfidence is epidemic in asset protection. People read a few articles, form an LLC online, and believe they're protected. They understand 10% of what they need to know but feel 100% confident.

True expertise recognizes nuance, limitations, and areas of uncertainty. The most knowledgeable professionals are usually the most cautious in their advice because they understand how much can go wrong.

If you find yourself feeling completely confident that you've solved your asset protection needs after a few hours of internet research, that's a red flag. It suggests you haven't yet discovered everything you don't know.

Learning From Failure

The value of understanding failure is prevention. Every mistake described in this chapter is avoidable:

Plan early. Start when the sky is clear, not when the storm is visible.

This is the single most important lesson from studying asset protection failures. Early planning eliminates fraudulent transfer concerns, establishes seasoning periods, and allows you to implement strategies properly without time pressure.

If you currently have no claims against you and no foreseeable claims on the horizon, now is the perfect time to plan. Not next year. Not when you have more assets. Not when you feel more at risk. Now.

The protection you establish today may not be tested for years or decades. That's exactly what you want. The longer the time between implementation and testing, the stronger your protection becomes.

Use professionals appropriately. Get competent legal and tax advice. Pay for expertise. Verify credentials. Ask hard questions.

This doesn't mean you need to hire the most expensive attorney in your city or spend $50,000 on your asset protection plan. It means working with qualified professionals who have specific experience in asset protection, who can explain strategies in terms you understand, who will customize a plan to your situation rather than selling you a package, and who will warn you about risks and trade-offs rather than promising guaranteed protection.

Red flags when evaluating professionals:

- They guarantee outcomes
- They have no verifiable experience in asset protection
- They sell only one type of structure to everyone
- They cannot clearly explain how their strategies work
- They discourage you from seeking second opinions
- They use high-pressure sales tactics
- They dismiss compliance and reporting requirements
- Their fees seem either unreasonably low or unreasonably high

Green flags when evaluating professionals:

- They ask detailed questions about your specific situation
- They explain both benefits and limitations of strategies

- They discuss trade-offs openly
- They coordinate with your other advisors
- They have verifiable credentials and experience
- They explain clearly how their fee structure works
- They provide references or examples of their work
- They encourage you to take time to consider your options

Remember that the cheapest option usually costs more in the long run when it fails. Asset protection done poorly is worse than asset protection not done at all because it creates a false sense of security.

Layer protections. Use multiple strategies that complement each other. Create redundancy.

Never rely on a single strategy. Even the best single strategy has limits, exceptions, and potential failure points. Layering means building multiple protections so that if one fails, others remain.

Your layers should be complementary, not redundant. Each layer should protect different assets or protect against different types of claims. Together, they should create comprehensive coverage with minimal gaps.

A well-layered plan might include:

- Adequate insurance for foreseeable risks
- Business entities to separate business and personal assets
- Trusts for estate planning and creditor protection
- Proper titling of assets (individual, joint, entity, trust)
- Maximized contributions to protected retirement accounts
- Utilization of available exemptions (homestead, insurance cash value, annuities)
- Prenuptial or postnuptial agreements if appropriate
- Contractual risk allocation in business dealings
- Geographic diversification if warranted by risk level

The exact combination depends on your situation, but the principle remains: multiple layers working together provide far better protection than any single strategy alone.

Ignore hype. Be skeptical of guarantees, urgency, and secret strategies. If something sounds too good to be true, walk away.

The asset protection field is full of hype, misinformation, and outright fraud. Protecting yourself from bad advice is just as important as protecting yourself from creditors.

When you encounter guarantees, secrets, or urgency, recognize these as marketing tactics designed to manipulate you. Slow down. Seek second opinions. Verify claims independently. Ask for references. Check credentials.

Trust your instincts. If something feels wrong, it probably is. If a strategy sounds too good to be true, it probably doesn't work. If you're being pressured to act immediately, that's a reason to slow down, not speed up.

Maintain what you build. Asset protection requires ongoing attention. File annual reports. Keep records. Maintain separation. Treat structures with respect.

Implementation is just the beginning. Asset protection is an ongoing commitment to proper maintenance and conduct.

Set up systems to ensure:

- Annual reports are filed on time
- Tax returns are prepared and filed
- Registered agents remain current
- Bank accounts stay separate
- Corporate formalities are observed
- Records are kept up to date
- Insurance policies are renewed
- Structures are reviewed periodically for continued effectiveness

Consider putting these items on your calendar or working with a service provider who will remind you when actions are due. The cost of forgetting an annual report or commingling funds for convenience can be the complete loss of your protection.

Document everything. Create a paper trail that tells a coherent, truthful story about your intent and conduct.

Documentation serves multiple purposes:

- It proves what you did and when you did it
- It demonstrates your intent was legitimate
- It shows you maintained formalities
- It establishes the value of transfers
- It provides evidence if your structures are challenged

Maintain organized files that include:

- Formation documents for all entities and trusts
- Operating agreements, bylaws, and trust instruments
- Transfer documents showing movement of assets
- Valuations and appraisals
- Meeting minutes and resolutions
- Tax returns and financial statements
- Bank statements and transaction records
- Insurance policies
- Correspondence related to asset protection planning

Organize these documents in a way that allows you to quickly locate what you need if your planning is ever challenged. Consider keeping copies in multiple locations and ensuring your family knows where to find critical documents.

Act with integrity. Do not try to defraud creditors. Do not hide assets dishonestly. Do not perjure yourself. Courts have powerful tools to punish bad behavior, and they use them.

This may be the most important principle of all. Asset protection must be built on a foundation of honesty and integrity. The moment you cross the line into fraud, you lose not only your protection but potentially your freedom.

Courts have seen every trick. They know when someone is hiding assets. They know when transfers were made to defraud creditors. They know when testimony is false. And they have powerful tools to punish dishonesty:

- Contempt citations and imprisonment
- Denial of bankruptcy discharge
- Punitive damages
- Attorneys' fees and costs
- Criminal charges for perjury or fraud
- Adverse inferences against you in litigation

More importantly, acting with integrity means you can live with your choices. Asset protection should reduce stress, not create it. If you're constantly worried about being discovered or having to lie under oath, you've built your protection on the wrong foundation.

Asset protection does not fail because it is ineffective. It fails because it is misunderstood, poorly executed, or built on a foundation of wishful thinking.

The Cost of Failure

When asset protection fails, the consequences extend beyond the immediate loss of assets.

You may face:

- Personal liability you thought was protected
- Loss of business assets
- Damage to credit and reputation
- Legal fees fighting a losing battle
- Potential claims of fraudulent transfer
- Tax consequences from unwinding structures

- Family conflict over failed plans
- Loss of retirement security

Let's examine what each of these costs actually means:

Personal liability you thought was protected. You believed your LLC protected you from business liabilities, but the veil was pierced and now you're personally liable for a $500,000 judgment. You lose not just the business assets but your personal savings, your home equity, and your peace of mind.

Loss of business assets. Your business is what generates income for your family. When business assets are taken to satisfy a judgment, you lose not just the current value but all future earning potential. A business that took years to build can be destroyed in months.

Damage to credit and reputation. Judgments appear on your credit report. Liens become public record. Business disputes become known in your industry. The reputational damage can affect your ability to get financing, attract customers, form partnerships, or find employment. Some reputational damage is permanent.

Legal fees fighting a losing battle. When your asset protection strategy fails, you often spend tens or hundreds of thousands of dollars fighting the inevitable. You hire attorneys to defend the LLC structure, contest the fraudulent transfer claim, or argue for exemptions. You ultimately lose anyway, but you've depleted your resources fighting.

Potential claims of fraudulent transfer. If your asset protection planning is found to be a fraudulent transfer, you face liability beyond the original claim. The creditor can recover the value of the transferred assets, potentially with interest and penalties. In some cases, fraudulent transfer claims create liability for the people who received the assets, destroying family relationships.

Tax consequences from unwinding structures. When entities are dissolved or trusts are terminated because they failed to provide protection, you may face immediate tax consequences. Capital gains may be recognized. Step-up in basis may be lost. Gift tax returns may need to be amended. The tax costs of unwinding failed structures can be substantial.

Family conflict over failed plans. When you transferred assets to family members as part of your asset protection strategy, and those assets are now being clawed back by creditors, family relationships suffer. Your children may face lawsuits to recover assets you gave them. Your spouse may face claims against jointly held property. The stress of financial loss combined with legal disputes tears families apart.

Loss of retirement security. Perhaps the most devastating cost is the loss of assets you were counting on for retirement. You're 60 years old and you just lost the investment portfolio you spent 30 years building. You have 10 or 15 years of working life left to rebuild, and it will never be enough. Your retirement plans are destroyed, and you may face working well into your 70s or depending on family for support.

Worse, you may face these consequences with no remaining resources to address them, because the very assets you were trying to protect are now gone.

Failed asset protection doesn't just fail to protect. It often makes things worse by:

- Creating fraudulent transfer liability where none existed before
- Depleting resources on ineffective strategies
- Damaging credibility with courts
- Generating tax problems
- Destroying family relationships
- Creating a false sense of security that prevented you from settling claims while settlement was still possible

This is why getting it right matters. The cost of failure is not just the money you lose. It is the opportunity cost of having done nothing, or having done something poorly, when you could have built real protection.

Looking Ahead

Asset protection done right is not complicated, but it does require knowledge, planning, and ongoing attention. It requires understanding your specific risks, implementing appropriate strategies at the right time, maintaining those strategies properly, and acting with integrity throughout the process.

The failures described in this chapter are all preventable. Every mistake is avoidable with proper planning and professional guidance. Every false promise can be recognized if you know the warning signs. Every pitfall can be navigated if you understand the territory.

In the next chapter, we will shift from mistakes to decision-making. We will explore how to choose the right strategy for your situation, based on your specific risks, net worth, and lifestyle.

You will learn how to match tools to problems, how to evaluate trade-offs, and how to build a plan that actually fits your life.

Failure is expensive. Understanding why it happens is the first step in avoiding it. Understanding how to plan correctly is the next.

The goal is not perfect protection. The goal is meaningful protection, properly implemented, maintained over time, and built on a foundation of realistic expectations and honest conduct.

That is what the rest of this book will teach you to build.

14

Choosing the Right Strategy for Your Situation

Asset protection is not about finding the strongest tool available. It is about finding the right tool for you.

One of the most common mistakes people make is copying strategies that are inappropriate for their risk level, net worth, or lifestyle. What works well for a surgeon with seven figures of exposure may be unnecessary or even counterproductive for a small business owner with modest assets. Likewise, minimal planning that works for one person may be dangerously inadequate for another.

This chapter provides a framework for choosing asset protection strategies that fit your reality rather than someone else's.

Understanding Your Starting Point

Before you can choose the right protection strategy, you need to understand where you stand today. This means taking an honest look at three key factors: your level of risk, your current net worth, and how you actually live your life.

Many people start by looking at what their friends or colleagues have done. This is natural, but it's also backwards. Your neighbor might have a complex trust structure because they own multiple medical practices with significant malpractice exposure. You might work a steady job with good insurance. Copying their approach would be like wearing someone else's prescription glasses. The lenses might be high quality, but they won't help you see clearly.

The right strategy is personal. It should fit you like a custom suit, not an off-the-rack option sized for someone else.

Matching Strategies to Risk Levels

Risk, not wealth, is the starting point for asset protection planning.

You might have substantial savings but face very little risk of being sued. Or you might have modest assets but operate in a high-risk profession. These two situations call for completely different approaches.

Low Risk Profiles

Individuals with low exposure typically include:

- Salaried employees with limited public interaction
- Individuals without businesses or rental properties
- Those with strong insurance and limited personal guarantees
- People who work in office environments without physical liability exposure
- Remote workers in non-customer-facing roles

If you work a standard job, don't own rental properties, don't run a business, and don't engage in high-risk activities, your risk profile is probably low. You're unlikely to face a major lawsuit. Your employer carries insurance for work-related issues. You have no business partners who might sue you. You don't have tenants who might slip and fall on your property.

In this situation, appropriate strategies often include:

- Adequate insurance (auto, homeowners, renters)
- Retirement account maximization (401k, IRA contributions)
- Basic estate planning (a simple will, healthcare directive, power of

attorney)

- Properly titled assets (making sure your home and accounts are in your name correctly)

What you don't need: offshore trusts, multiple LLCs, or complex holding company structures. These tools would cost you thousands of dollars annually in setup and maintenance fees. They would require ongoing paperwork and compliance. They would add complexity to your financial life without providing meaningful additional protection.

Over-structuring at this level increases cost without meaningful benefit. It's like buying a bulletproof vest to walk to your mailbox. The protection exists, but the threat doesn't justify it.

Think of it this way: if you're spending more than a few hundred dollars per year on asset protection beyond basic insurance and retirement savings, you're probably overdoing it.

Moderate Risk Profiles

Moderate risk often includes:

- Small business owners with one to three employees
- Professionals with insurance-backed exposure (therapists, accountants, consultants)
- Single-property landlords
- Independent contractors who work directly with clients
- Side business owners who sell products or services
- Anyone who has signed personal guarantees on business loans or leases
- This is where things get more interesting. You have enough risk that someone might actually sue you, but not so much that you need fortress-level protection. You're running a business, which means you have customers or clients. You might have a rental property with tenants. You've probably signed your name to a few agreements that make you personally responsible for certain obligations.

A lawsuit is no longer a distant possibility. It's something that could actually happen. A customer could claim your product injured them. A tenant could sue over a maintenance issue. A client could claim you gave bad advice that cost them money.

Common strategies at this level may include:

- Proper entity use (forming an LLC for your business or rental property)
- Umbrella insurance (an extra $1-2 million of liability coverage beyond your basic policies)
- Risk separation (keeping your business assets separate from your personal assets)
- Thoughtful ownership structure (making sure your LLC actually owns the business assets, not you personally)
- Regular reviews of insurance coverage to match your growing exposure

This is where asset protection begins to pay real dividends. The cost is still reasonable, perhaps a few thousand dollars to set up and a few hundred per year to maintain. But the protection is meaningful. An LLC can shield your personal savings from a business lawsuit. Umbrella insurance can cover damages that would otherwise wipe you out.

Let's look at a real example. Sarah runs a small graphic design business. She has two employees and works with about 30 clients per year. She formed an LLC for her business and pays $800 per year for business liability insurance plus $400 per year for a $2 million umbrella policy. Her total annual cost is about $1,200 for insurance, plus the initial $500 to form the LLC and about $200 per year in state filing fees.

For that modest investment, Sarah has created a meaningful barrier between her business and her personal assets. If a client sues claiming she missed a deadline that cost them money, the lawsuit would target the LLC, not Sarah personally. If the claim exceeds her business insurance, the umbrella policy provides additional coverage. Sarah's home, retirement accounts, and personal savings remain protected.

Without this structure, Sarah would be operating as a sole proprietor. Every business liability would be a personal liability. A single lawsuit could threaten everything she has worked to build.

That's the value of moderate protection. It's not perfect, and it's not impenetrable, but it's appropriate for the level of risk.

High Risk Profiles

High-risk individuals often include:

- Professionals with uncapped liability (doctors, lawyers, architects, engineers)
- Multi-property real estate investors (five or more rental units)
- Entrepreneurs with significant public exposure or high-profile businesses
- High-visibility or high-income individuals (professional athletes, executives, public figures)
- Anyone with substantial wealth and exposure to frequent public interaction
- Business owners in litigation-prone industries (construction, healthcare, financial services)

If you fall into this category, you face serious litigation risk. Not the occasional small claim, but the potential for lawsuits that could reach into the millions of dollars. Your professional license, your reputation, and your entire net worth could be at stake.

A surgeon performs thousands of procedures. A single complication, even one handled properly, could result in a multimillion-dollar lawsuit. A real estate investor with ten rental properties has ten times the exposure of someone with one property. A business owner who has built a $5 million company has created an attractive target for litigation.

At this level, layered planning becomes essential:

- Multiple entities (separate LLCs for different properties or business lines)
- Jurisdictional planning (using entities in states with favorable laws)
- Trust-based strategies (asset protection trusts, family limited partnerships)
- Conservative behavior (avoiding risky business practices, maintaining excellent documentation)

- Professional advisors (a team including attorneys, accountants, and insurance specialists)
- Regular planning reviews (annual check-ins to adjust as circumstances change)

Complexity serves a purpose here. You're not over-engineering for the sake of it. You're building multiple layers of defense because the threats are real and substantial.

Consider Dr. Martinez, an orthopedic surgeon. He earns $750,000 per year and has accumulated $3 million in net worth. He also faces constant malpractice exposure. Even with excellent malpractice insurance, he could face claims that exceed his coverage or situations where insurance doesn't fully protect him.

Dr. Martinez works with an estate planning attorney to create:

- A family limited partnership that owns his investment accounts
- A separate LLC for a medical office building he owns
- A trust structure for his primary residence in a jurisdiction with strong homestead protections
- Maximum contributions to protected retirement accounts
- An umbrella policy with $5 million in coverage
- Careful documentation and insurance review every two years

This structure costs Dr. Martinez about $15,000 to establish and roughly $5,000 per year to maintain (legal reviews, accounting, state fees, and insurance). It's expensive, but it's appropriate. His risk is real, his assets are substantial, and the cost of being unprotected would be catastrophic.

Without this planning, a single lawsuit exceeding his malpractice coverage could wipe out decades of savings. With proper planning, his assets are positioned in ways that make them difficult for creditors to reach while remaining fully accessible to him for legitimate purposes.

Net Worth Tiers and Appropriate Tools

While net worth alone is not the deciding factor, it does influence what makes sense from a cost-benefit perspective.

Emerging Wealth (Net Worth Under $500,000)

For individuals building wealth, priorities should focus on:

- Insurance as the primary protection tool (it's cost-effective at this stage)
- Avoiding premature complexity (don't spend $10,000 on structures to protect $200,000)
- Preserving flexibility (don't lock assets into structures that limit your options)
- Building properly from the start (using retirement accounts correctly, titling assets appropriately)
- Focusing on wealth accumulation rather than wealth protection

At this stage, you're still building. Your biggest asset might be your earning potential, not your current savings. The goal is to protect what you have without slowing down your ability to accumulate more.

Entity misuse at this stage can slow progress. If you spend thousands of dollars setting up complex structures when you have modest assets, that's money that could have been invested for growth. If you create entities you don't maintain properly, you might actually increase your risk rather than decrease it.

Think of someone just starting a side business. They have $50,000 in savings, earn $80,000 from their day job, and make $20,000 from their side business. Should they form an LLC? Probably yes, if the side business involves any meaningful liability risk. It costs a few hundred dollars and provides real protection.

Should they also create an offshore trust, a family limited partnership, and multiple holding companies? Absolutely not. The cost would be $15,000 or more, and the protection would be unnecessary given their current asset level.

Established Wealth (Net Worth $500,000 to $5 Million)

As assets accumulate, the calculation changes:

- Protection becomes more valuable (there's more to lose)
- Litigation leverage increases (you become a more attractive lawsuit

target)

- Planning mistakes become more costly (the stakes are higher)
- Structure can be cost-justified (the math works at this level)

This is often the appropriate time for:

- Advanced entity planning (multiple LLCs if you own multiple properties or businesses)
- Selective trust use (domestic asset protection trusts in appropriate situations)
- Formalized governance (operating agreements, buy-sell agreements, documented procedures)
- Regular professional review (annual or biennial check-ins with your attorney)
- Insurance layering (combining multiple policies for comprehensive coverage)

At this level, you have enough assets that a successful lawsuit could seriously damage your financial security. But you also have enough resources to invest in proper protection without undermining your lifestyle or financial goals.

Consider a couple in their late 40s. Combined income of $300,000. Net worth of $2.5 million, including a paid-off home worth $800,000, retirement accounts with $1.2 million, and taxable investments of $500,000. They own two rental properties worth a combined $600,000 with $200,000 in equity.

This is exactly the point where planning starts to make real sense:

- Each rental property should be in its own LLC
- They should have a $2-3 million umbrella insurance policy
- They might consider a trust for their primary residence if their state allows it
- Their estate plan should be more sophisticated than a simple will
- Total annual cost might be $3,000-5,000, which is reasonable given their net worth

Significant Wealth (Net Worth Above $5 Million)

For high net worth individuals, the priorities shift:

- Tail risk dominates (you're protecting against rare but catastrophic events)
- Reputation and privacy matter (keeping information private becomes important)
- Generational considerations emerge (thinking about children and grandchildren)
- Tax planning and asset protection overlap (structures serve multiple purposes)
- International planning may be relevant (if you have global business interests)

Advanced planning may be justified, but only when aligned with risk and lifestyle. This might include:

- Sophisticated trust structures
- Family limited partnerships or family LLCs
- International planning if appropriate for your circumstances
- Private investment entities
- Comprehensive insurance programs
- Coordinated teams of advisors

Someone with $10 million in net worth faces different considerations than someone with $1 million. The costs are higher, but the benefits are proportionally greater. A comprehensive plan might cost $30,000 to establish and $10,000 per year to maintain. That sounds expensive until you realize it's protecting $10 million of assets from potential litigation or creditor claims.

Lifestyle Considerations

Asset protection does not exist in isolation. It exists within the context of your actual life.

The most sophisticated plan in the world is worthless if it doesn't fit how you live. Consider:

Daily Management: How involved do you want to be in maintaining your asset protection structures? Some strategies require active management. You need to move money between accounts, file annual reports, maintain separate books, and document transactions. Other strategies are more passive once established.

If you hate paperwork and avoid administrative tasks, you need simple structures that require minimal ongoing attention. If you're detail-oriented and enjoy managing your financial affairs, you can handle more complexity.

Travel and Residency: Do you travel frequently? Do you live part-time in multiple locations? Do you have international business interests? These factors affect what structures make sense. Some states have more favorable laws than others. Some strategies require you to be a resident of a particular jurisdiction. International planning opens up options but also adds complexity and reporting requirements.

Administration Tolerance: Every asset protection strategy involves some paperwork. State filing fees. Tax returns. Documentation requirements. The question is how much you're willing to tolerate. A single LLC requires minimal work. A structure with five LLCs, two trusts, and a family limited partnership requires substantial ongoing administration.

Family Dynamics: Who needs access to assets? Are you married? Do you have children? Are you planning for aging parents? Will assets need to be distributed during your lifetime or only after death? Do you have concerns about a child's spending habits or a family member with creditor problems?

A strategy that works beautifully for a single person might be completely impractical for someone with a spouse and three children who need flexible access to resources.

Succession Plans: What happens when you die or become incapacitated? Who takes over management? How smoothly can assets transfer? Some structures make succession easy. Others create complications that burden your heirs.

Your Personality: Are you conservative or aggressive? Do you prefer certainty or are you comfortable with ambiguity? Do you like to be in control or are you comfortable delegating? Your personality should influence your planning.

A strategy that interferes with how you live is unlikely to be maintained. And an unmaintained plan will fail.

Here's a real example: Robert is a successful consultant with $3 million in net worth. His attorney recommends a complex structure involving multiple LLCs and a trust. It provides excellent protection, but it requires Robert to route all personal expenses through the trust, maintain detailed records of every transaction, and file three additional tax returns each year.

Robert tries it for one year and hates it. He finds the paperwork tedious. He forgets to document transactions properly. He resents the time it takes away from his work and family. After 18 months, he abandons most of the structure and goes back to a simpler approach.

The "better" plan failed because it didn't fit Robert's life. A simpler structure that he would actually maintain would have served him far better.

Cost-Benefit Analysis

Every asset protection strategy has costs. Not just financial costs, but time costs and cognitive costs.

Financial Costs:

- Setup fees (attorney fees, filing fees, initial costs)
- Ongoing fees (annual state fees, registered agent fees, accounting fees)
- Insurance premiums
- Professional reviews and updates

Time Costs:

- Learning how structures work
- Maintaining records
- Filing reports
- Coordinating with advisors
- Managing multiple accounts or entities

Cognitive Costs:

- Mental energy to understand the plan
- Stress of keeping track of requirements

- Complexity in decision-making
- Burden on family members who need to understand the structure

The question is not "Is this effective?" The real question is: **Is this effective enough to justify its cost?**

Evaluating Value

Ask yourself:

- What specific risk does this strategy reduce?
- How likely is that risk to actually occur?
- What is the worst-case outcome without this protection?
- How much complexity does this strategy add to my life?
- Could I achieve similar protection with a simpler approach?
- Will I actually maintain this over time?

Good planning balances downside protection with simplicity. The goal is not to eliminate every possible risk. That's impossible and impractical. The goal is to address the risks most likely to occur and most likely to cause serious harm, while keeping your life manageable.

Consider two approaches to protecting rental properties:

- **Approach A:** Put all three rental properties in a single LLC. Cost: $500 setup, $200 per year maintenance. Simple to manage. One tax return. Provides protection against rental property claims reaching your personal assets.
- **Approach B:** Create a separate LLC for each property, plus a holding company LLC, plus a land trust for each property. Cost: $5,000 setup, $2,000 per year maintenance. Complex to manage. Multiple tax returns. Provides marginally better protection by isolating properties from each other.

For most people with three rental properties and moderate net worth, Approach A is better. The additional protection from Approach B exists, but it's small, and the added cost and complexity aren't justified unless you have substantial assets at risk or operate in a particularly litigious area.

Avoiding Over- and Under-Protection

Both extremes are harmful.

Over-Protection

Creates these problems:

- Wastes financial resources that could be invested or used for other purposes
- Creates false confidence (you feel protected but the structures might not work as intended if not maintained)
- Attracts scrutiny (overly complex structures can actually draw attention from courts or creditors)
- Increases the chance of mistakes (complex structures are harder to maintain correctly)
- Makes life unnecessarily complicated

Over-protection often stems from anxiety or from copying what wealthier individuals do. You see someone with $50 million using sophisticated international structures and think you should do the same with your $1 million. But their situation is fundamentally different from yours.

Under-Protection

Under-protection creates these problems:

- Leaves assets exposed to creditors and lawsuits
- Reduces negotiating leverage if a claim does arise (you have nothing to negotiate with)
- Increases stress and anxiety about potential claims
- Creates unnecessary risk that could be easily addressed
- May force you to settle claims you could otherwise defend

Under-protection often stems from denial (thinking "it won't happen to me") or from procrastination (knowing you should do something but never getting around to it).

Finding the Middle Ground

The right strategy lives between these extremes. It provides meaningful protection against realistic risks without turning your financial life into a full-time administrative job.

Here are some guidelines:

- If your asset protection costs more than 1% of your net worth annually, you might be over-protected (unless you have extraordinarily high risk)
- If you have a business or rental property and have no entity protection at all, you're probably under-protected
- If you can't explain your asset protection strategy in a few sentences, it might be too complex
- If the thought of a lawsuit keeps you up at night despite having protection, your plan isn't giving you peace of mind (which is part of its purpose)

Planning Is Iterative

Asset protection is not a one-time decision. It's an ongoing process that evolves with your life.

Your plan should change as:

- Assets grow (what made sense at $500,000 might not make sense at $2 million)
- Risks change (starting a business, buying rental properties, or entering a high-risk profession)
- Laws shift (states change their asset protection laws, tax rules evolve)
- Life circumstances evolve (marriage, divorce, children, retirement)
- Your goals change (early in your career you focus on building wealth; later you focus on preserving it)

The best plans are reviewed periodically and adjusted conservatively. A good schedule might be:

- Annual review of insurance coverage
- Every 2-3 years review of entity structures

- Every 5 years comprehensive planning review with your attorney
- Immediate review after major life changes (marriage, divorce, inheritance, business sale)

This doesn't mean constantly tinkering or chasing the latest planning trend. It means staying current and making thoughtful adjustments when circumstances warrant them.

Think of it like maintaining a car. You don't redesign the engine every year, but you do change the oil, rotate the tires, and address issues before they becomc problems.

The Principle of Sufficiency

The goal of asset protection is not perfection. It is sufficiency.

You want enough protection to:

- Contain foreseeable risks (address the threats most likely to occur)
- Preserve core assets (protect what matters most to your financial security)
- Maintain flexibility (keep options open as life changes)
- Sleep at night (achieve peace of mind)

Beyond that point, complexity becomes vanity. You're not protecting assets anymore; you're building monuments to your own cleverness or anxiety.

Perfect protection doesn't exist. Courts can challenge any structure. Laws can change. New risks can emerge that you never anticipated. The person who tries to achieve perfect protection will spend enormous sums, create unbearable complexity, and still not achieve their goal.

Sufficient protection, on the other hand, is achievable. It's protection that is good enough for your situation. It addresses your real risks without consuming your life or your resources.

Ask yourself: "If I face a lawsuit tomorrow, will this plan meaningfully improve my outcome?" If yes, you have sufficient protection. If no, you need to adjust. If you're not sure, you need to better understand your plan.

Bringing It All Together

Choosing the right asset protection strategy requires honest self-assessment:

- **Assess your risk:** What is your actual likelihood of being sued? What would typical claims involve? What's your worst-case scenario?
- **Know your net worth:** What are you protecting? Not what you hope to have someday, but what you have now.
- **Understand your lifestyle:** What level of complexity can you actually maintain? What fits your personality and daily life?
- **Calculate true costs:** Factor in all costs (setup, maintenance, time, mental energy) and compare to the protection provided.
- **Seek appropriate advice:** Work with professionals, but don't outsource your judgment. Understand what you're implementing and why.
- **Build iteratively:** Start with basics (insurance, simple entities) and add complexity only as needed.
- **Review and adjust:** Set a schedule for periodic reviews and stick to it.

The best asset protection plan is one you'll actually implement and maintain. It should feel proportionate to your situation. You shouldn't be constantly worried it's not enough, nor should you feel burdened by unnecessary complexity.

Looking Ahead

In the next chapter, we will bring everything together with layered asset protection models. You'll see practical examples showing how strategies combine at different risk and wealth levels. You'll see what planning looks like for a small business owner, a mid-career professional, and a high-net-worth individual.

These examples will help you visualize what appropriate protection looks like for someone in a situation similar to yours.

Final Thoughts

Choosing the right strategy is an act of judgment, not ambition. When judgment leads, protection follows.

The person with modest assets who implements appropriate, sustainable protection is better positioned than the person with substantial wealth who creates a complex structure they don't understand or maintain.

Start where you are. Address your real risks. Build structures you can maintain. Review and adjust as needed.

That is sufficient. And sufficient is the goal.

PART V: Putting It All Together

15

Working With Lawyers, Accountants, and Advisors

Asset protection is not a do-it-yourself project, but it is also not something you should delegate blindly.

The quality of your advisors often matters more than the specific strategies they recommend. Well-designed plans fail when poorly implemented or maintained. Poor plans succeed temporarily when managed by disciplined professionals, but eventually unravel.

This chapter explains how to work effectively with lawyers, accountants, and other advisors so that asset protection becomes a coordinated, durable process, not a one-time transaction.

Understanding the Role of Professional Advisors

Asset protection sits at the intersection of law, tax, finance, and risk management. No single professional can master all these domains equally. This is why successful asset protection requires a team approach.

Why You Cannot Do This Alone

The tools of asset protection (trusts, entities, insurance, offshore structures) are legal instruments with tax consequences, reporting requirements, and operational demands. Getting any one element wrong can undermine the entire plan.

You might understand your business better than any advisor. You might even understand legal concepts at a high level. But the details matter enormously, and the details are where non-experts make costly mistakes.

Common DIY mistakes include:

- **Forming entities without proper formalities.** You create an LLC but never fund it, never hold meetings, and commingle personal and business funds. A court may disregard the entity entirely.
- **Transferring assets at the wrong time.** You move property into a trust while a lawsuit is pending or imminent. The transfer is reversed as a fraudulent conveyance.
- **Ignoring tax implications.** You set up an offshore trust without understanding reporting requirements, triggering penalties that dwarf any protection benefit.
- **Using templates without customization.** You download a trust document online, but it doesn't comply with your state's laws or reflect your actual situation.

Professional advisors exist to prevent these errors. But hiring them is only the first step. You must also know how to evaluate, coordinate, and work with them effectively.

What to Ask Before Hiring and Advisor

Before hiring any advisor for asset protection planning, your goal is not to assess how impressive they sound. Your goal is to assess how they think.

Advisors who speak confidently but lack depth will cost you money and create risk. Advisors who think clearly and communicate honestly will save you from mistakes you didn't know existed.

Questions That Reveal Competence

Consider asking:

What risks do you see as most relevant to my situation?

A good advisor will ask about your profession, assets, family, business activities, and potential exposure before answering. If they jump immediately to solutions without understanding your facts, that is a red flag.

What strategies would not make sense for me, and why?

This question tests whether the advisor thinks critically. If everything they recommend sounds perfect, they are either inexperienced or trying to sell you something. Good advisors know what doesn't work and can explain why.

How do you coordinate with other professionals?

Asset protection is a team sport. If the advisor works in isolation, you will end up with fragmented advice that creates gaps or contradictions. Ask whether they regularly collaborate with accountants, financial advisors, and other attorneys.

How do you approach compliance and reporting?

Asset protection that ignores compliance is a ticking time bomb. Ask specifically about IRS reporting (Form 3520, 3520-A, FBAR, Form 8938), state-level requirements, and ongoing administrative obligations.

What are the limits of what you're recommending?

No strategy is bulletproof. A good advisor will tell you what their plan does not protect against. They will explain scenarios where the plan could fail or be challenged. If they cannot articulate limits, they do not understand the plan well enough to implement it.

What Their Answers Tell You

Good advisors are comfortable explaining trade-offs. They are cautious with certainty and clear about boundaries.

Poor advisors make promises they cannot keep, speak in absolutes, and avoid discussing downsides. They may sound confident, but that confidence is often covering for a lack of real expertise.

Experience Matters, But So Does Judgment

Asset protection is fact-specific. What works for a surgeon in California may not work for a real estate developer in Florida. What makes sense for someone with $2 million in exposed assets may be excessive for someone with $500,000.

An advisor with deep experience but poor judgment may over-engineer your plan, adding complexity and cost without corresponding benefit. An advisor with limited experience but strong discipline may underreach, leaving you with protection that feels safe but is actually insufficient.

What to Look For

Look for advisors who demonstrate:

- **Understanding of both domestic and offshore planning (if relevant).** Even if you do not need offshore structures, an advisor who understands them will better appreciate the domestic alternatives and their limitations.
- **Willingness to say "no."** A good advisor will turn down work that doesn't fit. They will tell you when a strategy is overkill, when timing is wrong, or when your request crosses ethical or legal lines.
- **Respect for timing and intent.** Asset protection is deeply sensitive to when and why transfers occur. Advisors who rush you into action or downplay timing concerns do not grasp the legal risks involved.

Specialization vs. Generalization

Some advisors specialize exclusively in asset protection. Others practice broadly but include asset protection as one area of focus.

Specialists often have deeper technical knowledge and more experience with unusual scenarios. Generalists may have a better sense of how asset protection fits into your overall financial and estate plan.

Neither is inherently better. What matters is that the advisor has handled situations similar to yours and can point to specific outcomes and lessons learned.

Understanding Incentives and Conflicts

Every advisor operates within incentives. Understanding them helps you interpret advice and ask better follow-up questions.

Common Incentives

Attorneys are paid to draft and structure. They earn fees by creating legal documents and entities. This does not make their advice wrong, but it does mean they may favor solutions that involve more legal work.

Accountants are paid to report and defend. They earn fees by preparing returns, handling audits, and managing compliance. They may favor simpler structures that are easier to report and defend.

Financial advisors are often paid to manage assets. If they earn a percentage of assets under management, they may resist strategies that move assets out of their control (such as into irrevocable trusts or offshore structures).

These incentives are not inherently bad. They reflect the reality of how professionals are compensated. But they shape perspective, and you need to be aware of that.

How Incentives Affect Recommendations

For example:

An attorney may favor creating multiple LLCs and a domestic asset protection trust because it involves drafting formation documents, operating agreements, and trust instruments. The complexity generates billable work.

A financial advisor may resist moving assets into an irrevocable trust because those assets leave their management and reduce their compensation. They may emphasize the loss of control or liquidity without equally emphasizing the protection benefits.

An accountant may prioritize simplicity because complex structures create ongoing reporting obligations and increase audit risk, both of which generate work for them and stress for you.

No one sees the whole picture alone. This is why coordination is essential.

The Value of Coordination

The strongest asset protection plans emerge when lawyers design structure, accountants manage compliance, and financial advisors align investments.

When these professionals work together, they catch problems before they become crises. The attorney designs a trust structure that the accountant can report cleanly. The financial advisor selects investments that fit within the trust's terms. The accountant alerts the attorney when a reporting issue reveals a structural flaw.

What Coordination Prevents

Coordination prevents:

- **Conflicting advice.** Your attorney tells you to transfer assets into an LLC. Your accountant says the transfer will trigger a taxable event. Your financial advisor says moving the assets will disrupt your investment strategy. Without coordination, you are stuck choosing between bad options or doing nothing.
- **Reporting gaps.** Your attorney sets up an offshore trust but doesn't tell your accountant about the reporting requirements. You miss Form 3520 and face penalties of $10,000 or more.
- **Structural contradictions.** Your estate plan distributes assets through a revocable trust, but your asset protection plan holds the same assets in an LLC owned by an irrevocable trust. At your death, no one knows which document controls, and your family faces litigation to sort it out.

Your Role When Advisors Don't Communicate

If your advisors do not communicate with each other, you become the bridge. You carry information from one to the other, and that is a risky role.

You may misunderstand technical details. You may forget to mention something important. You may inadvertently create liability by relaying advice incorrectly.

Good advisors understand this risk. They will ask for your permission to speak directly with your other professionals and will initiate that contact themselves.

If your advisors refuse to coordinate, consider whether they are the right team for you.

Red Flags and Unrealistic Promises

Asset protection attracts hype. The field is filled with advisors who promise more than they can deliver, either because they are inexperienced or because they prioritize sales over service.

Knowing the warning signs can save you years of trouble and tens of thousands of dollars.

Major Red Flags

Be cautious if an advisor:

- **Guarantees protection.** No structure guarantees protection. Courts have broad equitable powers, and judges are suspicious of asset protection. An advisor who guarantees results either does not understand the law or is lying to you.
- **Promises secrecy or invisibility.** Secrecy is increasingly difficult and often illegal. Offshore privacy has been gutted by international reporting agreements. Domestic privacy is limited by public records, discovery rules, and regulatory requirements. Anyone promising invisibility is selling a fantasy.
- **Dismisses reporting requirements.** Reporting is not optional. It is legally mandated and heavily enforced. Advisors who downplay reporting obligations are setting you up for penalties, audits, or criminal liability.
- **Minimizes timing concerns.** Timing is everything in asset protection. Transfers made after a claim arises or while under financial distress can be reversed as fraudulent conveyances. Advisors who say "don't worry about timing" do not understand the law.
- **Pushes urgency without context.** Legitimate asset protection requires careful planning and cannot be rushed. Advisors who pressure you into signing documents quickly, without adequate time to review and ask questions, are more interested in closing the sale than protecting you.

How Good Advisors Communicate

Real asset protection professionals speak in probabilities, not absolutes.

They say things like:

- "This structure will make it significantly harder for a creditor to reach your assets, but it's not bulletproof."
- "If implemented properly and maintained over time, this plan should provide strong protection in most scenarios, but there are

exceptions."

- "We can never guarantee an outcome in litigation, but we can shift the odds heavily in your favor."
- This kind of language reflects reality. It shows respect for legal complexity and judicial discretion. It demonstrates maturity and experience.

Beware of Product-Driven Advice

Some advisors sell prepackaged trusts, jurisdiction-specific solutions, or turnkey offshore setups.

These products are marketed as one-size-fits-all solutions. You pay a flat fee, receive template documents, and walk away thinking you are protected.

Why This Is Dangerous

Asset protection is not a product. It is a process. It requires analysis of your specific facts, customization to your jurisdiction, and integration with your broader financial and estate plan.

If the solution is the same regardless of your facts, the advice is suspect.

Ask yourself:

- Did the advisor spend significant time learning about my situation before recommending a solution?
- Does the plan reflect my unique assets, risks, and goals?
- Are the documents customized, or do they look like templates with my name inserted?
- If the advisor jumped straight to selling a specific structure without a detailed consultation, they are selling a product, not providing advice.

The Offshore Package Problem

Offshore asset protection is a common area for product-driven sales. You will see advertisements for "Cook Islands trusts" or "Nevis LLCs" that promise bulletproof protection for a fixed fee.

While these jurisdictions offer strong legal frameworks, the structures only work if properly implemented and suitable for your situation. A Cook Islands trust may be excellent for a high-net-worth individual with significant liability exposure, but it may be overkill (and a compliance nightmare) for someone with moderate assets and low risk.

The problem is not the tool itself. The problem is advisors who sell the tool without first determining whether you need it.

Ongoing Maintenance and Reviews

Asset protection is not static. It is a living system that requires attention, adjustment, and periodic review.

Structures that work today may weaken over time due to law changes, asset growth, lifestyle changes, or shifts in risk exposure.

Why Maintenance Matters

Consider what can happen without maintenance:

- **Law changes.** Your state passes a new statute that strengthens or weakens certain exemptions. Your domestic asset protection trust, once effective, is now vulnerable. If you are not reviewing your plan regularly, you will not know until it is too late.
- **Asset growth.** Ten years ago, you had $1 million in exposed assets and set up a single LLC and an umbrella insurance policy. Today, you have $5 million in exposed assets, but your plan has not evolved. You are significantly underprotected.
- **Lifestyle changes.** You move to a new state with different homestead exemptions, community property rules, or trust laws. Your old plan no longer fits the new legal landscape.
- **Shifts in risk exposure.** You start a new business, take on investors, or expand into a higher-risk industry. Your liability exposure increases, but your asset protection plan was designed for your old risk profile.

What Maintenance Involves

Maintenance may include:

- **Updating insurance coverage.** Your umbrella policy has not increased in years, but your net worth has doubled. You review and increase coverage.

- **Reviewing entity compliance.** Your LLCs need annual reports filed, operating agreements updated, and ownership records confirmed. Missing these formalities can lead to loss of liability protection.

- **Refreshing trust administration.** Your trustee has not distributed income as required by the trust terms. Your accountant has not filed the necessary trust tax returns. These lapses can trigger tax penalties or put the trust's validity at risk.

- **Confirming reporting accuracy.** Your offshore structure requires annual Form 3520-A. Your accountant has been filing it, but you have never verified the details. A missed or incorrect filing can result in severe penalties.

- **Revisiting beneficiary designations.** You named your children as beneficiaries of your retirement accounts years ago. One child is now in a high-risk profession and vulnerable to lawsuits. You update the designation to direct that child's share into a protective trust.

Neglect is one of the most common reasons asset protection fails. Plans decay over time, and decay is invisible until a crisis forces you to test the structure.

Review Triggers

You should revisit your plan when:

- **You start or exit a business.** New business ventures bring new liability risks. Selling a business may leave you with liquid assets that need repositioning.

- **You acquire or sell significant assets.** Buying real estate, receiving an inheritance, or selling investments changes your asset profile and may require structural adjustments.

- **You relocate or spend time abroad.** Moving states or spending significant time in another country introduces new legal considerations, tax implications, and jurisdictional issues.

- **Your income or visibility increases.** As you become wealthier or more publicly known, you become a more attractive target for lawsuits and creditor claims.

- **Your family situation changes.** Marriage, divorce, birth of children, or death of a spouse all require plan updates to reflect new realities.

Periodic reviews are far less costly than crisis-driven fixes. Schedule a review every two to three years, even if nothing major has changed. That discipline alone will keep your plan functional.

Your Role in the Process

Even the best advisors cannot protect you from:

- **Ignoring advice.** Your attorney tells you to fund the LLC, but you never transfer the assets. The LLC exists on paper but provides no protection.
- **Cutting corners.** Your accountant says you need to file Form 3520. You decide to skip it and hope the IRS doesn't notice. When they do notice, the penalties are catastrophic.
- **Withholding information.** You don't tell your advisor about a pending lawsuit because you are embarrassed or hope it will go away. They design a plan that is invalidated the moment the court discovers the timing.
- **Failing to follow through.** Your advisor gives you a detailed list of steps to implement the plan. You complete the first two and forget the rest. The plan is incomplete and largely ineffective.

Asset protection rewards discipline and consistency. You hired professionals to design and guide, but you are responsible for execution and follow-through.

The Cost of Passivity

Some clients treat asset protection like they treat insurance. They buy the policy, file it away, and assume they are covered.

But asset protection is not a policy. It is a set of legal structures and financial arrangements that require active management. Entities need to be maintained. Trusts need to be administered. Insurance needs to be reviewed and renewed. Reporting needs to be filed.

If you approach asset protection passively, you are wasting your money. The structures will be there, but they will not function when tested.

The Advisor Relationship as a Long-Term Partnership

The most effective asset protection relationships are ongoing, not transactional.

You do not hire an advisor once, receive documents, and never speak to them again. You build a relationship over years, during which the advisor learns your situation deeply and adjusts as your life evolves.

What Long-Term Relationships Provide

Over time, good advisors:

- **Understand your risk tolerance.** They know whether you prefer conservative or aggressive strategies, and they tailor recommendations accordingly.
- **Anticipate changes.** They watch for legal developments, tax law changes, and shifts in your situation that could affect your plan. They reach out proactively, not just when you call them.
- **Adjust conservatively.** They resist the temptation to over-engineer or make changes for the sake of change. They recommend adjustments only when genuinely beneficial.
- **Protect you from yourself.** They push back when you want to cut corners, skip steps, or make impulsive decisions that undermine protection. They serve as a check on your worst instincts.

This kind of relationship is built on trust, but verified through clarity. You trust your advisor's expertise, but you also understand the reasoning behind their recommendations. You are not a passive recipient of advice. You are an informed partner.

How to Build This Relationship

Building a long-term advisory relationship requires:

- **Transparency.** Share information openly, even when uncomfortable. Your advisor cannot help you if they do not know the full picture.
- **Communication.** Stay in touch. Update your advisor when your situation changes. Do not wait for a crisis to reach out.
- **Respect for expertise.** Trust that your advisor knows more about asset protection law than you do. You can ask questions and seek clarification, but do not second-guess every recommendation based on something you read online.

- **Accountability.** Follow through on what you commit to do. If your advisor gives you a task, complete it promptly. If you cannot, communicate that and work together to find another approach.

When both sides hold up their end, the relationship becomes a true partnership. You bring the facts and the discipline. They bring the expertise and the judgment. Together, you build protection that lasts.

Looking Ahead

In the final chapter, we will step back and reflect on asset protection as a long-term mindset, not a checklist or a fear-driven exercise, but a form of financial hygiene that evolves with your life.

Your advisors are tools. Choosing and using them wisely determines whether those tools build protection or false confidence.

Asset protection is not about perfection. It is about consistency, realism, and the humility to recognize that you cannot do this alone. The professionals you choose, and how you work with them, will matter more than the strategies they recommend.

Choose carefully. Coordinate deliberately. Maintain consistently. And remember that the relationship is not a transaction. It is a partnership that protects what you have built and what you hope to build.

16

Layered Asset Protection Models

Asset protection is most effective when it is layered.

No single tool provides complete protection, and no two people require the same structure. What works is the intelligent combination of strategies, with each addressing a different type of risk, so that if one layer fails, others remain.

This chapter brings the concepts from earlier chapters together through practical, real-world models. These are not templates to copy blindly. They are illustrations of how layered planning adapts to different risk profiles and life circumstances.

Understanding the Layered Approach

Think of asset protection like security for your home. You don't rely on just a lock, or just an alarm, or just exterior lighting. You use all three because they address different vulnerabilities. A lock stops the opportunist trying door handles. An alarm deters someone who defeats the lock. Lighting prevents both by making your home a less attractive target in the first place.

Asset protection works the same way. Insurance handles the routine claims. Legal structures contain the risks that insurance won't cover. Statutory protections preserve certain assets even when other defenses fail. Behavioral discipline prevents problems from arising in the first place.

When you layer these tools properly, you create what engineers call "redundancy." If one system fails, others are still working. A lawsuit that pierces one defense must still overcome the next. A creditor who reaches one asset finds others out of reach.

This redundancy is what separates effective planning from false security.

Model 1: Low-Risk Profile

Profile

- Salaried employee
- No business ownership
- No rental properties
- Limited public exposure
- Stable income with predictable tax situation
- Few if any employees or contractors under your supervision

Primary Risks

- Auto accidents
- Personal injury claims (slip and fall at your home, recreational accidents)
- Contract disputes (disputes with contractors, service providers)
- Basic liability exposure from daily life

Layered Strategy

Layer 1: Insurance

Your first and most important layer is comprehensive insurance coverage.

Strong auto coverage means carrying liability limits well above your state's minimum requirements. If your state requires only $25,000 in liability coverage but you have $300,000 in net worth, you are catastrophically underinsured. A serious accident could wipe out everything you own.

Homeowners or renters insurance protects you from claims arising on your property. Someone slips on your front steps during winter. Your dog bites a neighbor. A contractor is injured while working on your house. These are not exotic scenarios. They happen every day.

An umbrella liability policy sits on top of your auto and homeowners coverage, providing an additional $1 million to $5 million in protection. Umbrella policies are remarkably inexpensive, often costing just a few hundred dollars per year, because they only pay out after your underlying policies are exhausted. For most people in this risk category, a $1 million umbrella policy is sufficient. If your net worth exceeds $1 million, consider $2 million or more.

Layer 2: Statutory Protections

Federal and state law already protect certain assets from creditors. Use these protections fully before spending money on entities or trusts.

Maximize contributions to retirement accounts. In most states, 401(k) plans, 403(b) plans, and defined benefit pension plans are fully protected from creditors. Traditional and Roth IRAs are protected up to a certain dollar amount, which is adjusted periodically for inflation. As of recent updates, the exemption for IRAs is over $1 million per person. But even beyond that threshold, most states provide strong protection.

If you own your home, understand your state's homestead exemption. Some states, like Florida and Texas, provide unlimited homestead protection. Others, like New Jersey and Pennsylvania, provide very little. If you live in a state with a strong homestead exemption, owning your home outright (or with manageable debt) can be one of your most powerful asset protection tools.

Tenancy by the entirety, where available, is another statutory protection. If you and your spouse own property as tenants by the entirety, creditors of only one spouse generally cannot reach that property. This protection is automatic in some states and unavailable in others, so check your local law.

Layer 3: Behavioral Discipline

Even with good insurance and statutory protections, you can undo your planning through careless behavior.

Avoid signing personal guarantees whenever possible. If you cosign a loan for a friend or family member, you are personally liable if they default. If you guarantee a lease for a business you are involved in, even informally, you have created personal exposure.

Keep your finances clean and simple. Pay your taxes on time. Avoid legal disputes over minor matters. Don't lend money to people unless you are comfortable never seeing it again. Litigation often arises not from bad luck but from unnecessary complexity or poor judgment.

Why This Works

At this risk level, insurance and statutory protections absorb nearly all realistic exposure. Your risks are predictable and insurable. Your assets are modest enough that statutory exemptions cover a meaningful percentage of your wealth.

Adding entities or trusts would increase cost without meaningful benefit. An LLC costs money to set up and maintain. It requires separate accounting, annual filings, and ongoing compliance. For someone with no business and no investment properties, these costs buy nothing.

If your risk profile changes, your planning should change with it. But until then, simplicity is both cheaper and more effective.

Model 2: Business Owner

Profile

- Actively operating business (retail, services, consulting, trades)
- Employees, contractors, or both
- Regular customer or client interaction
- Moderate net worth, with much of it tied to the business
- Personal income dependent on business performance

Primary Risks

- Business litigation (customer disputes, contract claims, vendor conflicts)
- Employment claims (wrongful termination, discrimination, harassment, wage disputes)
- Professional liability (errors and omissions, negligence)
- Premises liability (injuries occurring at your business location)

- Product or service defects causing harm

Layered Strategy

Layer 1: Insurance

Insurance is still your primary defense, but your needs are more complex than an employee's.

General liability insurance covers injuries or property damage caused by your business operations. A customer slips in your store. Your product causes property damage. Your work creates an unexpected problem. General liability handles these routine claims and provides a lawyer to defend you.

Employment practices liability insurance (EPLI) covers claims from current, former, or prospective employees. Wrongful termination, discrimination, harassment, retaliation, and wage-hour disputes are all covered. Even baseless claims are expensive to defend. EPLI pays defense costs and settlements.

Professional liability insurance (also called errors and omissions insurance) is essential for service-based businesses. If your advice, services, or professional work cause financial loss to a client, professional liability insurance responds.

Workers' compensation insurance is generally required by law if you have employees. It covers medical costs and lost wages for employees injured on the job and protects you from most employee lawsuits over workplace injuries.

An umbrella policy extends your liability coverage across all your policies. For business owners, this often means $2 million to $5 million in additional coverage.

Layer 2: Entity Structure

Operating your business as a sole proprietorship is a critical mistake. Every dollar you earn and every asset you own becomes exposed to business liabilities.

Form a separate legal entity for your operating company. In most cases, this will be a limited liability company (LLC) or a corporation. The entity owns the business assets, hires the employees, signs the contracts, and generates the liabilities.

If the business is sued, the plaintiff's claim is generally limited to the assets inside the entity. Your personal home, personal bank accounts, and personal investments are not part of the lawsuit. This is the core concept of "limited liability."

But limited liability only works if you respect the separation between yourself and the entity. That means separate bank accounts, separate records, adequate capitalization, and no commingling of funds. If you treat the business as an extension of your personal finances, courts will do the same. This is called "piercing the corporate veil," and it destroys your liability protection.

For businesses with significant risk, consider separating your operating company from your asset-holding entities. The operating company runs the business, generates revenue, and holds minimal assets. A separate entity (often another LLC) holds valuable equipment, real estate, or intellectual property and leases it to the operating company.

If the operating company is sued, the plaintiff can only reach the assets inside that company. The valuable assets are held elsewhere, insulated from the operating risk.

Layer 3: Personal Asset Isolation

Do not hold business assets personally. If you own the business's delivery van in your own name, a lawsuit involving that van can reach all your personal assets. The vehicle should be titled in the business entity's name.

Similarly, do not hold personal investments inside your business entity. If your operating company owns your brokerage account or rental property, a business lawsuit can reach those assets. Keep business assets in the business and personal assets outside of it.

Layer 4: Retirement Planning

Business owners often neglect retirement planning because they view the business as their retirement asset. This is a dangerous assumption. Businesses fail, get sued, and lose value. Your retirement should not depend entirely on the business's survival.

Employer-sponsored retirement plans, such as a solo 401(k), SEP IRA, or defined benefit plan, receive strong creditor protection in most states. Contributions are also tax-deductible, making them one of the most efficient ways to build protected wealth.

Even a small business owner can contribute significant amounts to retirement accounts each year. The money is protected from business creditors, grows tax-deferred, and builds a financial cushion outside the business.

Why This Works

Risk is generated by the business but contained within it. Personal assets are buffered by insurance, entity structures, and statutory protections.

If a customer sues the business, the lawsuit is directed at the entity, not at you personally. Insurance handles the defense and most claims. If a judgment exceeds insurance, the plaintiff can reach business assets but not personal assets (assuming you've maintained proper separation).

If the business fails, creditors can pursue the assets inside the business entity, but your home, retirement accounts, and personal savings remain protected.

This structure allows you to take business risks without betting everything you own on the business's success.

Model 3: Real Estate Investor

Profile

- Multiple rental properties (single-family homes, duplexes, small apartment buildings)
- Direct tenant interaction and management responsibilities
- Growing equity across a portfolio
- Active acquisition and disposition of properties

Primary Risks

- Property-related injuries (tenant or visitor slips and falls, structural failures, maintenance accidents)
- Habitability claims (mold, pest infestations, heating or plumbing failures, building code violations)
- Fair housing and discrimination claim
- Lease disputes and eviction conflicts

- Environmental allegations (lead paint, asbestos, contaminated soil)
- Contractor and vendor disputes

Layered Strategy

Layer 1: Insurance

Each rental property should have its own landlord insurance policy, also called "dwelling fire" or "rental property" insurance. This covers property damage, liability claims arising on the property, and loss of rental income.

Landlord policies are different from homeowners policies. They are designed for rental use and cover risks that a standard homeowner policy excludes, such as tenant-caused damage or injuries to tenants and their guests.

An umbrella liability policy is essential for real estate investors. You are managing multiple properties, each of which generates independent liability exposure. A serious injury at one property can result in a multi-million-dollar judgment. An umbrella policy provides an additional layer of coverage across your entire portfolio.

For investors with larger portfolios, consider separate umbrella policies for different entities (discussed below). This prevents a single large claim from exhausting coverage for all properties.

Layer 2: Entity Segmentation

This is where real estate investors often differ from business owners.

A business owner typically operates one business and can use one operating entity. A real estate investor owns multiple properties, each of which generates independent liability. If you own five rental properties in one LLC, a lawsuit involving one property can expose the equity in all five properties.

The solution is entity segmentation. Higher-risk properties are held in separate single-property LLCs. Lower-risk properties, or properties with little equity, can be grouped together in portfolio LLCs.

What makes a property "higher-risk"? Properties with significant equity, properties with many tenants, properties in litigious areas, properties with known defects or hazards, and properties involving short-term rentals or commercial tenants are all higher-risk.

Single-family homes with little equity and stable long-term tenants are generally lower-risk and can often be grouped together.

Entity segmentation does add complexity and cost. Each LLC must file an annual report, maintain a separate bank account, and comply with state formalities. But the protection it provides is real. A claim involving Property A stays inside the LLC that holds Property A. Properties B, C, D, and E are held in separate entities and remain untouchable.

Layer 3: Capital Management

One of the biggest mistakes real estate investors make is building up excessive cash reserves inside their LLCs.

An LLC that holds $500,000 in property equity and $200,000 in cash is a more attractive target than an LLC that holds $500,000 in property equity and $10,000 in cash. If the LLC is sued, the plaintiff can reach everything inside the entity.

Keep cash reserves outside of your property-holding LLCs. Hold them personally, in separate LLCs, or in protected accounts like retirement plans. Transfer only the minimum operating cash needed to cover expenses for each property.

This concept is sometimes called "equity stripping," though that term is often misunderstood. You're not hiding assets or defrauding creditors. You're simply managing where your liquid assets are held so that they are not unnecessarily exposed to property-specific risks.

Layer 4: Financing Discipline

Minimize personal guarantees on mortgages and loans where possible. If you personally guarantee a loan for a rental property and the property value drops, you are personally liable for the deficiency.

Many lenders require personal guarantees, especially for smaller investors. But as your portfolio grows, you gain negotiating leverage. Commercial lenders, portfolio lenders, and private lenders are often willing to lend on a non-recourse basis or with limited guarantees.

When personal guarantees are unavoidable, try to limit them. A "bad boy carve-out" guarantees only specific acts like fraud or failure to pay property taxes, rather than the full loan balance.

Avoid cross-collateralizing your properties. If you pledge multiple properties as collateral for a single loan, a default on one property can trigger foreclosure on all of them.

Why This Works

Each property's risk is contained. A claim at one location does not threaten the entire portfolio or personal wealth.

If a tenant is injured at Property A, the lawsuit is directed at the LLC that owns Property A. Insurance covers the claim. If the judgment exceeds insurance, the plaintiff can reach the equity and assets inside that LLC but cannot reach Property B, Property C, or your personal assets.

If Property A's value collapses and you walk away from a non-recourse loan, the lender can foreclose on Property A but cannot pursue you personally or reach your other properties.

This structure allows you to grow a real estate portfolio without concentrating all your risk in one place.

Model 4: High-Net-Worth / High-Liability Individual

Profile

- Significant net worth (multiple millions or more)
- High public visibility (media presence, public-facing business, professional prominence)
- Professional exposure to uncapped liability (doctors, lawyers, architects, executives)
- Wealth concentrated in liquid or accessible assets
- Family or personal circumstances that attract legal claims

Primary Risks

- Catastrophic lawsuits (malpractice, major accidents, high-value contract disputes)
- Reputation-driven claims (defamation, public disputes, targeted litigation)
- Excess verdicts beyond insurance limits (multimillion-dollar judgments)
- Frivolous but expensive litigation from opportunistic plaintiffs

- Family law claims (divorce, inheritance disputes)
- Regulatory or government actions

Layered Strategy

Layer 1: Insurance

Insurance is still your first line of defense, but the stakes are higher.

Maximize your coverage across all activities. For professionals, this means high limits on malpractice or errors and omissions insurance. For business owners, this means comprehensive general liability, product liability, and employment practices coverage.

Personal umbrella policies at this level often start at $5 million and can extend to $10 million or more. Some insurers offer even higher limits through excess liability policies.

But insurance has limits. No policy will cover every claim. Policies have exclusions, coverage gaps, and aggregate limits. If you're sued for $20 million and your insurance covers $5 million, you're exposed for $15 million.

That's where advanced planning becomes necessary.

Layer 2: Advanced Entity Planning

At this level, entity planning is no longer just about separating business risk from personal assets. It's about creating multiple barriers between potential claims and concentrated wealth.

Separate operating risk from asset holding. If you run a high-risk business, the operating company should hold minimal assets. Valuable assets, real estate, intellectual property, and equipment should be held in separate entities and leased or licensed to the operating company. If the operating company is sued, there's little to take.

Management companies can provide an additional layer. If you are a professional (doctor, lawyer, executive), a management company can employ you and provide your services to the operating entity. This creates distance between you personally and the entity generating liability.

Domestic LLCs and limited partnerships provide charging order protection in many states. This means that if you are sued personally, a creditor who wins a judgment generally cannot seize your ownership interest in the LLC or partnership. Instead, they receive a "charging order," which entitles them to distributions from the entity but gives them no control and no access to the entity's assets.

Charging order protection is powerful but not absolute. Some states provide weak protection, and courts sometimes allow exceptions. But in strong charging order states like Nevada, Wyoming, and Delaware, this protection can be a significant deterrent.

Layer 3: Trust Planning

Trusts add a new dimension to asset protection by separating legal ownership from beneficial enjoyment.

Domestic asset protection trusts (DAPTs) are allowed in about 20 states. These are irrevocable trusts where you transfer assets into the trust, give up direct control, but retain the ability to receive distributions. If you're sued, creditors generally cannot reach assets held in a properly structured DAPT (though exceptions exist for fraudulent transfers and certain types of claims).

DAPTs work best for long-term planning. If you transfer assets into a DAPT and get sued the next month, the transfer will likely be unwound as fraudulent. But if you fund a DAPT years before any claim arises, and the trust is managed properly, the assets are generally protected.

Offshore asset protection trusts (OAPTs) take this concept further. These are irrevocable trusts established in foreign jurisdictions with strong asset protection laws, such as the Cook Islands, Nevis, or Belize.

The key advantage of an OAPT is jurisdictional resistance. If a U.S. creditor wants to reach assets in the trust, they must sue in the foreign jurisdiction, under foreign law, often within a very short statute of limitations. Most jurisdictions do not recognize U.S. judgments, so the creditor must re-litigate the entire case. The burden of proof is often on the creditor to prove fraudulent intent beyond a reasonable doubt, a much higher standard than in U.S. courts.

OAPTs are expensive and complex. Setup costs often start at $50,000, with annual maintenance costs of $10,000 or more. They require detailed compliance with U.S. tax and reporting rules. They are not suitable for everyone.

But for someone facing catastrophic liability exposure, or someone with wealth that far exceeds what insurance can protect, an OAPT provides leverage that no domestic tool can match. It doesn't make you judgment-proof, but it makes collecting on a judgment so difficult and expensive that many creditors settle for far less than the judgment amount.

Layer 4: Jurisdictional Diversification

Don't keep all your assets in one legal system.

If you live in California and hold all your assets in California entities under California law, a California court can reach all of them with a single order. If you hold assets in multiple states, or in foreign jurisdictions, a creditor must pursue multiple lawsuits in multiple jurisdictions, dramatically increasing their cost and effort.

This doesn't mean hiding assets. It means thoughtful placement. Real estate in different states. Bank accounts in stable foreign jurisdictions. Entities formed in states with strong asset protection laws.

Jurisdictional diversification is not about secrecy. It's about increasing the friction and cost of collection, which in turn increases your negotiating power.

Why This Works

This structure accepts that not all risk can be insured or predicted. Insurance covers most claims, but not all. Entities provide separation and charging order protection. Trusts move assets beyond the reach of future creditors. Jurisdictional diversification increases the cost and complexity of enforcement.

No single tool is foolproof. But the combination creates a system where a creditor must overcome multiple barriers, each governed by different laws, to reach meaningful assets. In practice, this often forces settlement or abandonment of the claim.

Offshore elements are not for everyone. They are specialized tools for specialized risks. But for someone with significant wealth and significant exposure, they provide leverage and resilience where domestic tools reach their limits.

Domestic-Only vs. Hybrid Offshore Structures

Not every high-net-worth individual needs an offshore trust. The decision depends on your risk profile, asset level, and tolerance for complexity.

Domestic-Only Structures

Best suited for:

- Moderate to high net worth ($1 million to $10 million)
- Predictable and insurable risk
- Individuals seeking simplicity and lower cost
- Those uncomfortable with offshore structures
- Lower administrative tolerance

Advantages:

Lower cost. Domestic structures are significantly cheaper to set up and maintain. A domestic LLC might cost $1,000 to $3,000 to establish, with annual maintenance costs of a few hundred dollars. A domestic asset protection trust might cost $5,000 to $15,000 to set up, with ongoing costs of $2,000 to $5,000 per year.

Familiar legal environment. You and your advisors understand U.S. law. Disputes are resolved in U.S. courts. Compliance is straightforward.

Easier maintenance. Domestic structures require less ongoing attention, less paperwork, and less coordination with foreign trustees and advisors.

Limitations:

Exposure to U.S. court enforcement. A U.S. court can order you to repatriate assets, dissolve entities, or turn over property. If you refuse, you can be held in contempt. Domestic asset protection trusts provide meaningful protection, but they are not immune from U.S. court orders.

Limited leverage in extreme cases. If you're facing a $50 million judgment and all your assets are domestic, your negotiating power is limited. The creditor knows they can eventually reach your assets through U.S. legal processes.

Hybrid Offshore Structures

Best suited for:

- Very high net worth ($10 million or more)
- High or unpredictable liability exposure

- Professionals with uncapped risk (surgeons, business owners in volatile industries)
- Individuals willing to invest in long-term planning
- Those with significant liquid assets that can be transferred to foreign trusts

Advantages:

Jurisdictional resistance. A foreign trust in a non-U.S. jurisdiction is not subject to U.S. court orders. A creditor must sue in the trust's jurisdiction, under foreign law, and often cannot rely on a U.S. judgment.

Increased litigation friction. The cost, delay, and uncertainty of pursuing assets offshore often makes collection economically impractical. Creditors frequently settle for a fraction of the judgment amount.

Stronger catastrophic protection. For risks that exceed insurance limits and domestic protections, offshore trusts provide a final layer of defense.

Tradeoffs:

Higher cost. Offshore trusts are expensive. Setup costs typically range from $50,000 to $100,000, with annual maintenance costs of $10,000 to $25,000 or more. This includes trustee fees, legal fees, accounting fees, and compliance costs.

Increased compliance. Offshore trusts must comply with detailed U.S. tax and reporting requirements, including Form 3520 (for trust transactions) and FinCEN Form 114 (for foreign bank accounts). Errors can result in severe penalties.

Greater complexity. You'll work with foreign trustees, foreign banks, and foreign legal systems. Communication and coordination take more time and effort. You must plan carefully to avoid triggering adverse tax consequences.

Potential reputational concerns. Some people view offshore structures with suspicion, even when they are fully legal and compliant. This may matter if you're a public figure or operate in a highly regulated industry.

Hybrid structures are not upgrades. They are specialized tools.

A domestic structure is not inferior to a hybrid offshore structure. It is appropriate for a different risk profile. Many high-net-worth individuals are well-protected with purely domestic planning. Offshore structures should be considered only when the risk justifies the cost and complexity.

What These Models Have in Common

Despite their differences, all effective asset protection models share certain characteristics.

Early planning. Asset protection must be implemented before a claim arises. Transferring assets after you're sued is fraudulent and ineffective. The time to build protections is when you don't need them yet.

Multiple layers. No single tool provides complete protection. Effective planning uses insurance, entities, statutory protections, trusts, and behavioral discipline in combination.

Conservative assumptions. Assume your insurance won't cover everything. Assume your entities will be challenged. Assume your trusts will be tested. Plan accordingly.

Respect for compliance. Every tool requires maintenance. Entities need annual filings. Trusts need proper administration. Insurance policies need regular review. Cutting corners destroys protection.

Alignment with lifestyle. Asset protection should fit your life, not the other way around. If a structure is too complex or burdensome, you won't maintain it, and it will fail when you need it most.

No effective model relies on secrecy or a single point of failure. Good planning is defensible, documented, and built to withstand scrutiny.

Models Are Starting Points

These examples illustrate principles, not instructions.

Your ideal structure depends on factors these models can't capture:

- **Risk tolerance.** Some people are comfortable with higher exposure in exchange for simplicity. Others want maximum protection despite the cost.
- **Net worth.** A $500,000 net worth suggests one approach. A $50 million net worth suggests another.

- **Family dynamics.** Are you married? Do you have children? Are there creditor concerns among family members? Family structure influences planning.

- **Professional exposure.** A surgeon faces different risks than a software engineer. A public figure faces different risks than a private investor.

- **Geographic location.** State laws vary dramatically. Some states provide strong protections with minimal planning. Others require aggressive structuring.

- **Time horizon.** Are you building wealth or preserving it? Are you starting a business or selling one? Your stage of life affects your planning.

The purpose of these models is understanding, not imitation. They show how different people with different risks might layer protections. They demonstrate the logic behind each choice.

But your situation is unique. What works for someone else might be excessive or insufficient for you.

Common Mistakes in Applying Models

Even when people understand these models intellectually, they often make mistakes in application:

- **Mistake 1: Copying a structure without understanding it.** You hear that a successful investor uses a Wyoming LLC, so you form one too, without understanding why Wyoming law mattered for their situation and whether it matters for yours.

- **Mistake 2: Over-engineering for low risk.** You're a salaried employee with no business, but you set up multiple LLCs and a trust because you read that high-net-worth individuals use them. You've added cost and complexity without addressing any real risk.

- **Mistake 3: Under-protecting high risk.** You own a business with significant liability exposure, but you operate as a sole proprietor because forming an LLC seems like too much paperwork. You're saving a few hundred dollars while risking everything you own.

- **Mistake 4: Ignoring maintenance.** You set up an LLC five years ago but haven't filed an annual report, kept separate books, or maintained a separate bank account. When you're sued, the court pierces the veil, and your protection evaporates.

- **Mistake 5: Assuming one size fits all.** You have three rental properties, so you put them all in one LLC because that's simpler. When a tenant is seriously injured at one property, all three properties are exposed to the judgment.

The models in this chapter are not formulas. They're frameworks for thinking about risk and protection in context.

When to Update Your Model

Asset protection is not static. Your structure should evolve as your life changes.

Update your planning when:

- Your net worth increases significantly
- You start or sell a business
- You acquire or dispose of major assets
- Your professional role changes
- You move to a different state
- Your family situation changes (marriage, divorce, children)
- You face new risks or liabilities
- Laws change in ways that affect your structure

A structure that was perfect five years ago may be inadequate or excessive today. Regular review, at least every two to three years, ensures your planning remains aligned with your life.

Working with Advisors to Build Your Model

Don't try to implement these models alone. Asset protection involves law, tax, insurance, and financial planning. Mistakes are costly and often irreversible.

Work with advisors who understand your specific situation and can customize a structure for you. Avoid advisors who promote a single solution for everyone. Be skeptical of anyone who promises complete protection or claims their approach is "bulletproof."

The next chapter will cover how to work effectively with lawyers, accountants, and other advisors: how to evaluate their guidance, ask the right questions, and avoid conflicts of interest.

Conclusion: Systems That Adapt

Layered asset protection is not about building walls. It is about designing systems that fail gracefully instead of catastrophically.

A single wall, no matter how strong, will eventually break under enough pressure. But a series of walls, each built differently and each addressing different weaknesses, creates resilience.

Insurance handles the routine. Entities contain the major. Trusts absorb the catastrophic. Statutory protections catch what falls through. Behavioral discipline prevents breaches in the first place.

When one layer fails, the others hold. When pressure increases, the system adapts. When you face the unexpected, you have options.

That is what layered planning provides: not invincibility, but resilience. Not perfection, but protection.

And in the unpredictable world of legal liability, resilience is the only realistic goal.

17

Final Thoughts: Protection Without Paranoia

Asset protection is easiest to misunderstand after certain events have occurred.

After learning about lawsuits, creditors, structures, and worst-case scenarios, it's tempting to see risk everywhere. You might start believing that more layers, more entities, and more distance must always be better. You may find yourself lying awake at night, wondering if you've done enough, or if there's some vulnerability you haven't considered.

But that mindset doesn't lead to safety. It leads to anxiety, expense, and unnecessary complexity.

Effective asset protection does the opposite. It reduces worry. It helps you sleep better at night. It allows you to focus on building your life rather than constantly defending it.

This final chapter steps back from the technical tools and tactical strategies to focus on something equally important: perspective. We'll explore how to think about asset protection as a normal, healthy part of financial life rather than a reaction to fear or paranoia. We'll discuss how to know when you've done enough, how to maintain what you've built, and how to move forward with confidence.

Asset Protection as Financial Hygiene

Asset protection works best when it's treated like financial hygiene. It's a routine part of responsible financial management, not a dramatic response to crisis.

Think about the routine financial tasks you already do without much drama:

- You carry insurance on your car, home, and health
- You save for retirement through a 401(k) or IRA
- You maintain legal documents like a will or power of attorney
- You keep financial records organized
- You file your taxes on time
- You review your credit report periodically
- You update beneficiaries on your accounts when life changes
- You back up important documents
- You review your budget or spending occasionally

None of these activities are glamorous. They don't make for exciting dinner conversation. You don't obsess over them daily or lose sleep worrying about whether you're doing them perfectly.

But you do them because they're part of being financially responsible. They're the boring, unglamorous work of taking care of yourself and your family.

Asset protection belongs in the same category.

The Three Characteristics of Good Financial Hygiene

Financial hygiene is:

- **Boring:** It's routine maintenance, not high-stakes drama. You set up your smoke detectors once and check them periodically. You don't rebuild them from scratch every month or stay up at night wondering if they're positioned optimally.

- **Preventive:** You do it before problems arise, not after. You don't wait until your house is on fire to buy smoke detectors. You don't wait until you're in an accident to buy car insurance. You don't wait until you're sued to think about asset protection.
- **Routine:** It becomes a normal part of how you manage money. Just as you review your insurance coverage every few years, you review your asset protection strategies. Just as you update your will when you have children, you update your structures when your assets or risks change.

Why This Perspective Matters

You don't check your smoke detector every day. You don't reorganize your filing cabinet weekly. You don't rewrite your will every month. You don't call your insurance agent constantly to ask if you have enough coverage.

You set these things up properly, maintain them when needed, and then move on with your life.

The same applies to asset protection.

You take the time to understand your risks. You implement reasonable protections. You maintain them appropriately. And then you get back to living your life and building your wealth.

When asset protection is framed this way, as boring financial hygiene rather than dramatic crisis management, it becomes far less intimidating and far more effective.

You're not preparing for battle. You're just being responsible.

Planning for Peace of Mind, Not Fear

Fear is a poor financial planner. It clouds judgment, drives expensive decisions, and often leads to strategies that create more problems than they solve.

What Fear-Driven Planning Looks Like

Fear-driven asset protection often looks like this:

- **Overly complex structures:** Multiple entities layered on top of each other with no clear purpose. Three LLCs feeding into two trusts managed by a holding company, when one LLC would have been sufficient. The complexity itself becomes a source of stress and confusion.

- **Secrecy-focused decisions:** Choosing strategies based on hiding assets rather than protecting them. Obsessing over privacy to the point where you can't even explain your structure to your own attorney or accountant. Worrying constantly about who knows what.
- **Aggressive tactics:** Pushing legal boundaries in ways that invite scrutiny. Transferring assets immediately after being sued. Using offshore structures without legitimate business purpose. Creating arrangements that look designed to defraud creditors.
- **Constant second-guessing:** Wondering if you've done enough, changing plans frequently, adding "just one more layer" of protection. Calling your attorney every few months with new worries. Spending more time managing your protection than building your wealth.
- **Expensive overkill:** Spending thousands or tens of thousands on protections you don't actually need. Creating elaborate offshore trusts when you have modest assets and no international business. Hiring specialists for problems you don't have.
- **Paralysis by analysis:** Becoming so worried about making the wrong choice that you make no choice at all. Spending years "researching" while remaining completely exposed because you haven't implemented anything.

These approaches rarely hold up well under legal scrutiny. Judges and creditors can often see through fear-driven strategies, especially those that seem designed primarily to hide assets or frustrate legitimate claims.

More importantly, they often create more stress than they remove. You end up worrying about maintaining your structures, explaining them to professionals, keeping track of multiple entities, filing multiple tax returns, and wondering if they'll actually work when tested.

Instead of feeling protected, you feel burdened.

The Better Question

Good asset protection planning asks a calmer, more grounded question:

What would allow me to live my life knowing that one bad event is unlikely to undo everything I've built?

Notice what this question doesn't ask:

- It doesn't ask "How can I become completely invulnerable?"
- It doesn't ask "How can I hide everything from everyone?"
- It doesn't ask "What's the most aggressive strategy I can implement?"
- It doesn't ask "How can I avoid all possible risks?"

Instead, it focuses on a reasonable goal: preventing disproportionate outcomes. Making sure one mistake, one lawsuit, one bad business deal, or one unexpected event doesn't destroy decades of responsible work and saving.

The answer is rarely "maximum protection at all costs."

It's almost always "reasonable protection, properly maintained."

What This Means in Practice

This means:

- **Understanding your actual risks** – Not every worst-case scenario you can imagine, but the risks you actually face based on your profession, assets, activities, and circumstances. A surgeon faces different risks than a software engineer. A landlord faces different risks than an investor in index funds.

- **Implementing proportional protections** – Matching your strategies to your real exposure. If you have $100,000 in assets, you probably don't need the same structures as someone with $10 million. If you run a low-risk online business, you need different protections than someone who operates a manufacturing facility.

- **Maintaining what you create** – Following through on compliance and documentation. A well-maintained simple structure beats a poorly maintained complex one every time. This means filing annual reports, holding meetings when required, keeping corporate formalities, and treating your entities as real.

- **Living your life normally** – Not constantly looking over your shoulder. Not avoiding legitimate business opportunities because you're worried about exposure. Not letting asset protection consume your mental energy or dominate your decision-making.

The Result: Peace of Mind

Peace of mind comes from knowing you've taken sensible steps to protect what matters, not from achieving theoretical perfection.

It comes from being able to say:

- "I've addressed my major risks"
- "I have reasonable protections in place"
- "I understand what's protected and what isn't"
- "I'm comfortable with this level of exposure"
- "I can focus on my work and family now"

This is what good asset protection feels like. Not anxiety. Not obsession. Not constant worry.

Just quiet confidence that you've been responsible and prudent.

When "Enough" Protection Is Enough

One of the most important skills in asset protection is knowing when to stop. When have you done enough? When do additional layers stop adding value and start adding only complexity and cost?

There's a point where additional asset protection delivers diminishing returns. Understanding this point is crucial.

What Happens Past the Point of Diminishing Returns

Past that point:

- **Complexity increases:** More entities mean more paperwork, more filings, more coordination between structures. You need to remember which entity owns what, which bank accounts belong to which LLC, which tax returns need to be filed. Simple questions like "Can I write a check for this?" become complicated.
- **Costs rise:** Legal fees for forming entities, maintenance fees for registered agents, tax preparation costs for multiple returns. A single LLC might cost $800 to set up and $200 per year to maintain. Five LLCs cost $4,000 to set up and $1,000 per year. Complex trusts can cost $5,000 to $15,000 just to create, plus ongoing trustee fees and

tax preparation.

- **Maintenance becomes burdensome:** Annual meetings, corporate resolutions, updated operating agreements, tracking transfers between entities. Each entity needs attention. If you travel for three months, who's handling the compliance? If you forget to file something, does it compromise your protection?

- **Flexibility decreases:** Moving money or making changes becomes complicated. Want to refinance your rental property? Now you need to deal with lenders who don't like lending to LLCs. Want to sell an asset? You may need to transfer it out of a trust first. Need cash quickly? You can't just write a check; you need to follow proper procedures.

- **Tax efficiency suffers:** Extra layers can create unnecessary tax complications. Some structures trigger different tax treatment. You may need more expensive tax preparation. You may have additional reporting requirements. You may inadvertently create situations where you're paying more in taxes or preparation fees than you're saving in protection.

- **Opportunities may be missed:** Some people become so focused on protecting what they have that they pass up legitimate opportunities to grow. They don't buy the rental property because they're worried about liability. They don't start the business because they can't figure out the perfect structure. Protection becomes paralysis.

And here's the critical point: the actual risk reduction may be minimal or even nonexistent.

Going from no protection to basic protection makes a huge difference. Going from basic protection to moderate protection makes a meaningful difference. Going from moderate to elaborate protection often makes little difference at all, while dramatically increasing cost and complexity.

Knowing when to stop adding layers is a mark of good judgment, not insufficient protection. It shows you understand the concept of proportionality and diminishing returns.

What "Enough" Looks Like

Enough protection means:

- **Core assets are insulated:** Your home, retirement accounts, and essential savings have appropriate protection. These are the assets that matter most to your family's security and wellbeing. If something goes wrong, these should be protected.

- **Predictable risks are addressed:** Business liability, professional exposure, and rental property risks are managed. You've identified the most likely sources of problems and put protections in place. You're not protected against every theoretical risk, but you're protected against the ones that actually matter.
- **Catastrophic exposure is reduced:** A single lawsuit can't wipe out everything you've built. One tenant injury, one business mistake, one car accident won't destroy your family's financial security. You might lose the asset that created the problem, but not everything else.
- **You understand remaining risks:** You know what's protected and what isn't, and you're comfortable with that balance. You're not operating under the illusion of perfect protection. You've made informed decisions about acceptable risk.
- **Your life is simplified, not complicated:** Your protection works in the background without requiring constant attention. You're not spending hours every month on maintenance. You're not stressed about compliance. The structures serve you; you don't serve them.

You don't need zero risk. That's impossible anyway. You need acceptable risk.

Examples of "Enough" for Different Situations

For many people, enough protection looks surprisingly simple. Let's walk through some examples:

For a professional (doctor, lawyer, accountant, engineer):

Adequate professional liability insurance is the foundation. This directly addresses your primary risk, which is a claim related to your professional work. Most claims will be covered by insurance.

A homestead exemption protects your primary residence. In many states, this requires nothing more than filing a simple form. In states with automatic homesteads, you already have this protection.

Maxing out protected retirement accounts (401k, IRA, Roth IRA) puts significant wealth beyond the reach of most creditors. This money is often protected by federal and state law, without needing any additional structure.

Adding an LLC for a side business makes sense if you have one. If you run a consulting practice, own rental properties, or have other business activities beyond your primary employment, an LLC provides an additional layer.

Creating offshore trusts? Probably doesn't make sense unless you have substantial assets (multiple millions), international business activities, or very specific risks. The cost and complexity rarely justify the benefit for typical professionals.

For a small business owner:

A properly maintained LLC for the business is essential. This is the fundamental separation between business risks and personal assets. The LLC must be respected, well-maintained, and treated as a real entity.

General liability insurance protects against the most common business risks. Slip and fall, property damage, basic claims. Insurance handles most problems more effectively than any structure.

Keeping personal assets separate from business assets is critical. Don't mix funds. Don't use business accounts for personal expenses. Don't use personal credit cards for business purchases. This separation is what makes the LLC protection work.

An umbrella insurance policy adds extra liability coverage beyond basic policies. This is inexpensive (often just a few hundred dollars per year) and provides substantial additional protection.

Multiple nested holding companies? Usually unnecessary unless you have multiple distinct business lines, significant intellectual property to protect, or are operating at a much larger scale. For most small businesses, one LLC plus insurance is sufficient.

For a rental property owner:

An LLC per property (or per few properties) provides meaningful protection. If a tenant is injured in one property, they can't reach your other properties or personal assets. The specific number of properties per LLC depends on property values, state laws, and your risk tolerance.

Landlord insurance is essential. This covers liability for tenant injuries, property damage, loss of rents, and other common landlord risks. The insurance handles most problems before any LLC protection is even needed.

Proper lease agreements and tenant screening reduce risk in the first place. Many landlord problems are preventable. Good leases, thorough screening, proper maintenance, and responsive management prevent most issues before they become lawsuits.

Adequate liability limits on your umbrella policy add another layer of protection at minimal cost. This is often more cost-effective than creating additional LLCs.

Complex trust structures? These may add cost without meaningful benefit for typical rental property owners. Trusts can make sense for estate planning, but purely for asset protection purposes, they're often unnecessary when you already have LLCs and insurance.

For a high-income professional or executive:

Maxing out protected retirement accounts should be the first priority. Get every dollar possible into 401(k)s, IRAs, defined benefit plans, or other protected accounts. These are often bulletproof against creditors and come with tax benefits.

Maintaining solid insurance coverage is critical. Professional liability, general liability, umbrella coverage. High-income individuals should have high liability limits, often $2-5 million or more on umbrella policies.

Using a trust for estate planning handles both asset protection and wealth transfer goals. A properly structured trust can provide some protection while also achieving tax efficiency and smooth wealth transfer to the next generation.

A homestead exemption or placing your home in tenancy by the entirety (if married) protects your primary residence. These strategies cost little or nothing but provide significant protection.

Elaborate offshore arrangements are rarely justified unless you have substantial assets (think $10 million plus), legitimate international business activities, or very specific risks that domestic strategies don't address. For most high-income professionals, domestic strategies are sufficient, far less expensive, and much simpler to maintain.

The Common Thread

What do all these examples have in common?

- They match the protection to the actual risk, without unnecessary complexity.

- They use insurance as the first line of defense, because insurance is often the most effective and cost-efficient protection.
- They implement structures only where they add meaningful value, not because "more must be better."
- They remain simple enough to maintain properly, because poorly maintained complex structures often fail.
- They allow the person to focus on building wealth, not just protecting it.

This is what "enough" looks like in practice.

Revisit Plans as Life Changes

Asset protection is not a "set it and forget it" endeavor. It's contextual. What works for your current situation may not work for your future situation.

What made sense five years ago might be excessive, insufficient, or simply outdated today.

Life changes. Your assets change. Your risks change. Your responsibilities change. Your protection should change with them.

Why Regular Review Matters

Think about your life five years ago:

- Did you have the same income?
- Did you have the same assets?
- Were you in the same profession?
- Did you have the same family situation?
- Were you living in the same state?

For most people, the answer to several of these questions is "no."

Yet many people set up asset protection structures once and never revisit them. They have an LLC from a business they no longer run. They have protection designed for assets they've since sold. They're following strategies appropriate for a different life stage.

This is like wearing the same shoes you wore five years ago without checking if they still fit. They might fit fine. But they might be too tight, too loose, or worn out.

Regular review ensures your protection still fits your life.

Life Changes That Justify Review

Let's look at specific life changes that warrant reviewing your asset protection strategy:

Family changes:

- **Marriage:** Your spouse's assets and liabilities now affect you, and yours affect them. What happens if your spouse gets sued? What if they have existing debts or legal problems? How do state laws treat marital property in your jurisdiction? Do you need a prenuptial or postnuptial agreement? Should some assets be kept separate? How does joint ownership affect your protection?

- **Divorce:** Previous joint protections may need restructuring. Assets that were jointly owned may be divided. Structures that named your ex-spouse may need updating. Your risk profile may change dramatically. If you're paying alimony or child support, protecting other assets becomes more important.

- **Children:** New considerations around inheritance and responsibility enter the picture. You need to think about estate planning in addition to asset protection. Do you want assets to go directly to children or through trusts? How do you protect assets while ensuring your children are provided for? What happens if you become disabled?

- **Aging parents:**Potential caregiving costs or inheritance planning become relevant. Will you need to help support your parents? Might you inherit assets? Do you need to protect your own assets from potential nursing home costs? How do you plan for long-term care?

Each of these changes can dramatically affect your asset protection needs and strategies.

Career changes:

- **Starting a business:** New liability exposure requires new protection. When you start a business, you're taking on risks you didn't have as an employee. Product liability, customer disputes, employee lawsuits, contract disputes, and many other risks emerge. You need structures to contain these risks.

- **Changing professions:** Different industries carry different risks. Moving from a low-risk office job to a high-risk profession (medical practice, construction, financial services) means dramatically different exposure. Or vice versa: if you retire from a high-risk profession, you may be able to simplify some protections.

- **Retirement:** Some protections become less important; others more so. You're no longer worried about professional liability. But you may have more assets accumulated and need to protect them. You may be more vulnerable to lawsuits because you have more visible wealth. You may need to focus more on estate planning.

- **Increased income:** More assets to protect, possibly different strategies needed. When you were earning $75,000 per year, simple strategies made sense. Now you're earning $300,000 per year, accumulating wealth faster, and may be a more attractive lawsuit target. Higher income often justifies more sophisticated protection.

Each career transition changes your risk profile and may justify adjusting your protection.

Asset changes:

- **Purchasing real estate:** New properties may justify new structures. Each rental property represents a new source of potential liability. Whether to put each property in its own LLC, group properties together, or use other strategies depends on values, locations, and your overall risk tolerance.

- **Selling a business:** Proceeds need appropriate protection. When you sell a business for $2 million, that money needs protection. It may make sense to move it into protected retirement accounts, invest it in protected assets, or use other strategies to ensure you don't lose it to future claims.

- **Inheritance:** Received assets may need different treatment. If you inherit $500,000 from a parent, does it go into joint accounts with your spouse? Do you keep it separate? Does it go into a trust? How do you protect it? The answer depends on your situation and your state's laws.

- **Investment growth:** Significantly increased net worth may warrant review. When your portfolio was $200,000, you needed basic protection. Now it's $2 million. That difference may justify additional strategies or higher insurance coverage.

Asset changes often trigger the need for updated protection because what you're protecting has changed.

Risk profile changes:

Increased public visibility: More exposure to potential claims. If you start appearing in media, speaking publicly, writing books, or becoming known in your field, you become a more attractive target. People who might not have sued you before may now see you as worth pursuing.

Geographic relocation: Different state laws mean different protections. Moving from California to Texas means different homestead protections, different LLC laws, different creditor exemptions. What worked in your old state may not be optimal in your new state.

International activity: Cross-border considerations come into play. If you start doing business internationally, owning foreign property, or having foreign income, you need to consider international asset protection strategies, tax implications, and foreign judgments.

New business ventures: Each venture brings unique risks. Starting a new side business, investing in a different industry, or launching a new product line each comes with distinct risks. Each may justify separate structures or additional insurance.

Risk changes require protection changes. What protected you adequately before may be insufficient now.

How Often Should You Review?

A good rule of thumb:

- **Formal review every 3-5 years:** Sit down with an attorney, accountant, or financial advisor and review your entire asset protection strategy. Make sure everything is still appropriate, properly maintained, and serving your current needs.
- **Informal review annually:** Each year when you're doing tax preparation or year-end financial planning, take a moment to think about whether your protection still makes sense. Have there been

major changes? If so, note them for your next formal review.

- **Immediate review after major life events:** Marriage, divorce, birth of children, starting a business, selling a business, buying significant property, inheriting substantial assets, moving to a new state, or any other major change should trigger an immediate review. Don't wait for your scheduled review if something significant has changed.

This ensures you're never operating with outdated protection that no longer fits your life.

What Review Involves

When you review your asset protection strategy, ask:

- Do I still have the same risk exposures I did when I set this up?
- Have I acquired new assets that need protection?
- Have I disposed of assets that no longer need protection?
- Are my structures still appropriate for my current situation?
- Am I maintaining my structures properly?
- Have relevant laws changed?
- Have my state or jurisdiction changed?
- Are my insurance coverages still adequate?
- Is anything becoming unnecessarily complex?
- Is anything missing?

Plans that were once appropriate can become obsolete or excessive. Life rarely stays static, and your protection shouldn't either.

Regular review keeps your protection aligned with your current reality rather than your past reality.

Avoiding the Trap of Over-Optimization

Asset protection is not a competition. There's no trophy for the most entities, the most complex structure, or the most aggressive strategy. There's no leaderboard ranking you against other people.

Yet many people fall into the trap of trying to optimize every detail, protect against every conceivable risk, and achieve theoretical perfection.

This is a mistake.

Trying to optimize for every conceivable scenario leads to predictable problems:

Decision Paralysis

When you try to protect against every possible risk, you become unable to make any decision.

Should you use an LLC or a trust? Well, it depends on dozens of factors. Which state should you form in? There are arguments for Wyoming, Delaware, Nevada, and your home state. Should you add another layer? Maybe, but then again maybe not. What if circumstances change? Then you might need something different entirely.

These questions spiral endlessly if you're seeking perfection.

You research for months. You read every article. You compare every strategy. You second-guess every decision. You wonder if there's some better approach you haven't discovered yet.

Meanwhile, you remain completely unprotected because you haven't actually implemented anything.

This is the paralysis of optimization. The perfect becomes the enemy of the good. You're so worried about making the wrong choice that you make no choice at all.

The reality is that many different approaches would work reasonably well. You don't need the single optimal strategy. You need a good strategy that you actually implement.

Unnecessary Expense

Every additional entity costs money to form and maintain. Every additional layer of complexity increases professional fees.

Let's talk specific numbers:

- Legal fees for forming entities: A simple LLC might cost $500-$1,500 to set up properly. A complex multi-entity structure might cost $5,000-$15,000. An elaborate trust structure might cost

$10,000-$25,000 or more.

- Annual maintenance: Each LLC needs a registered agent ($100-$300/year), annual report filing ($50-$300/year depending on state), and possibly franchise taxes or other state fees. Trusts may require trustee fees if you use a professional trustee.
- Tax preparation: A simple personal return might cost $300-$500. Add one LLC and it's $800-$1,200. Add multiple LLCs, a trust, and complex investments? Now you're paying $2,000-$5,000 or more annually just for tax preparation.
- Ongoing legal advice: As structures become more complex, you need more attorney time for basic questions. "Can I do this?" "How should I handle that?" These questions cost $200-$400 per hour.

All of this might be worth it if there's a proportional benefit. If you have $10 million in assets and high risk exposure, spending $10,000 on sophisticated structures makes sense. The protection may be worth far more than the cost.

But if you have $300,000 in assets and low risk, spending $10,000 on elaborate structures means you've spent 3% of your net worth on protection that may provide minimal additional benefit beyond simple strategies.

Often, simpler approaches provide 80-90% of the protection at 20-30% of the cost. The last 10-20% of theoretical protection might cost three to five times as much as the basics.

This is the law of diminishing returns in action.

False Confidence

Ironically, the most complex structures can create a false sense of security.

People assume that because they've spent a lot of money and created elaborate arrangements, they must be well protected. They feel invulnerable. They take risks they shouldn't take. They assume their structures will withstand any challenge.

But complexity without purpose is just complexity. It may not hold up when challenged.

A poorly maintained complex structure is often weaker than a well-maintained simple structure. If you don't understand your own protection, can't explain it clearly, haven't maintained corporate formalities, or have mixed assets improperly, your elaborate structure may collapse under scrutiny.

Courts are skeptical of complexity that lacks clear purpose. If a judge reviews your structure and can't understand why you have five entities doing what one could do, they may decide you're just trying to hide assets or frustrate creditors. That's not a good outcome.

False confidence is dangerous because it may lead you to:

Take inappropriate risks because you think you're fully protected

Neglect maintenance because you assume the structure itself is enough

Fail to carry adequate insurance because you think your structures replace it

Ignore warning signs of problems because you feel invulnerable

Simpler structures often provide more real confidence because you understand them, can maintain them, and can explain them clearly if challenged.

The Better Approach

Instead of over-optimizing, aim for:

- **Clarity:** Understand what each protection does and why it exists. If you can't clearly explain the purpose of a structure, you probably don't need it. Each entity, trust, or strategy should have a clear, articulable reason for existing.
- **Proportionality:** Match your strategies to your actual risks. $500,000 in assets doesn't require the same protection as $5 million. A low-risk profession doesn't require the same protection as a high-risk one. Be honest about your actual exposure.
- **Maintainability:** Only implement what you can realistically maintain. A simple structure you maintain properly provides more protection than a complex structure you neglect. Consider your time, attention span, organizational skills, and willingness to deal with compliance.
- **Flexibility:** Leave room to adapt as circumstances change. Structures that are too rigid, too complex, or too intertwined may be difficult to modify when your life changes. Build in flexibility to adjust as needed.

- **Understandability:** If you don't understand your own structure, it's probably too complex. You should be able to explain your asset protection to your spouse, your attorney, your accountant, and potentially to a judge without confusion.

No structure survives all circumstances. No amount of planning eliminates all risk. No strategy provides perfect protection.

The goal is resilience, not invulnerability.

Resilience means you can withstand most reasonable challenges. Invulnerability means you can withstand everything. The first is achievable. The second is impossible.

Focus on being reasonably protected, not perfectly protected. Focus on addressing likely risks, not every theoretical risk. Focus on structures you can maintain, not structures that sound impressive.

This mindset leads to better outcomes at lower cost with less stress.

Asset Protection and Responsibility Are Compatible

One final misconception deserves to be addressed directly and retired permanently.

Protecting your assets does not mean avoiding responsibility. The two ideas are not in conflict. In fact, they're compatible and complementary.

This misconception causes many people unnecessary guilt about pursuing asset protection. They feel like protecting assets means they're trying to cheat people, avoid legitimate obligations, or shirk responsibility.

That's not what asset protection is about.

What Asset Protection Actually Means

Asset protection means:

- **Accepting that risk exists:** You can't eliminate it entirely. Life is uncertain. Accidents happen. People make mistakes. Businesses face unexpected challenges. You're acknowledging this reality rather than pretending you're immune to risk.

- **Managing it lawfully:** Using legitimate legal tools and structures that are recognized and permitted by law. These tools exist precisely because society understands that people need reasonable ways to separate risks and protect their families.

- **Preventing disproportionate outcomes:** Ensuring one mistake doesn't destroy a lifetime of work. Making sure that an isolated event, even if you're partially at fault, doesn't result in your family losing everything including their home and retirement.

Asset protection is about proportionality. It's about preventing outcomes where the punishment far exceeds the offense.

What Asset Protection Does Not Mean

It does not mean:

- **Evading legitimate debts:** Asset protection doesn't help you avoid paying what you truly owe. If you borrow money, you owe it back. If you damage someone's property, you should compensate them. If you make a professional error, you should make it right. Asset protection is about limiting your exposure to reasonable levels, not avoiding all obligations.

- **Acting recklessly:** Protection doesn't give you license to be careless or unethical. You still have every incentive to be responsible, professional, and careful. Insurance and structures provide a safety net, not permission to be negligent.

- **Cheating people:** Proper asset protection is legal and transparent, not fraudulent. You're not hiding assets from people you've wronged. You're separating assets before problems arise so that if something goes wrong in one area of your life, it doesn't destroy everything else.

- **Breaking the law:** Asset protection works within the legal system, using tools the law provides. Fraudulent transfers, hiding assets, lying about ownership, or creating sham entities are not asset protection. They're fraud, and they won't work.

The distinction is critical. Legitimate asset protection is about using legal tools properly and in advance. Fraudulent asset protection is about hiding, lying, or breaking rules after you've harmed someone.

The Positive Role of Asset Protection

Asset protection actually enables responsible behavior. Far from being opposed to responsibility, proper asset protection makes it possible for people to take responsible risks that benefit everyone.

It allows you to take productive risks

Without asset protection, starting a business or investing in real estate might feel too dangerous. Why would you start a business if one lawsuit could cost you your house? Why would you invest in rental property if one tenant injury could destroy your retirement?

With reasonable protection, you can pursue opportunities that create value for yourself and others. You can start the business that employs people. You can invest in the properties that provide housing. You can launch the product that solves problems.

Asset protection doesn't encourage recklessness. It encourages calculated risk-taking that drives economic growth and innovation.

It lets you build businesses

Entrepreneurs create jobs. They serve customers. They drive economic growth and innovation. They solve problems and meet needs.

But entrepreneurship is inherently risky. Most new businesses fail. Even successful businesses face lawsuits, disputes, and unexpected challenges.

Asset protection helps entrepreneurs do their work without risking their family's home and retirement. This doesn't make them less responsible. It makes them more willing to take the entrepreneurial risk that benefits society.

A world where entrepreneurs risked total financial ruin from any business setback would be a world with far fewer entrepreneurs. Society would be poorer for it.

It enables confident investing

Real estate investors provide housing. They maintain properties, find tenants, and make housing available. Without them, many people would have nowhere to rent.

Stock market investors provide capital to companies. This capital funds research, expansion, hiring, and innovation.

But both real estate and stock investing involve risk. Properties can decline in value. Tenants can sue. Companies can fail. Investments can go wrong.

Reasonable protection helps people invest without fear of total ruin from a single mistake or unlucky event. This means more capital available for housing, business growth, and economic activity.

It helps you support families and communities

When you're protected from disproportionate losses, you can be more generous with your time, money, and energy.

You can volunteer knowing that if something goes wrong, you won't lose everything. You can donate to causes knowing you've protected your core assets. You can help others without constant worry about your own exposure.

You can take leadership roles in community organizations. You can serve on boards. You can contribute your expertise to causes you care about.

Asset protection doesn't make you less giving or less involved. It gives you the confidence to engage fully without fear of catastrophic loss.

You can stay involved in your children's activities, coach youth sports, host community events, or help neighbors without constant worry that any mishap could destroy you financially.

The Balance

Yes, it's possible for people to abuse asset protection strategies. Some people do use these tools improperly, trying to cheat creditors or avoid legitimate obligations.

But the vast majority of people using these tools are simply being prudent. They're not trying to cheat anyone or avoid responsibility. They're trying to:

- Protect their family's financial security from disproportionate losses
- Separate business risks from personal assets so one failure doesn't destroy everything
- Prevent one bad event from undoing decades of responsible behavior
- Continue contributing to society without fear of total financial destruction

- Pursue opportunities that create value without risking total ruin
- Engage in their communities and professions with confidence

This is not only legal. It's wise. It's responsible. It's exactly what prudent people should do.

An Analogy

Think about car insurance. You carry car insurance not because you plan to drive recklessly, but precisely because you don't. You're a responsible driver. You follow traffic laws. You're careful.

But you know that even responsible drivers can have accidents. A moment of distraction, an unexpected obstacle, another driver's mistake. The insurance doesn't exist because you're irresponsible. It exists because risk is unavoidable.

Does carrying insurance mean you're planning to hit someone? Does it mean you accept no responsibility for your driving? Of course not.

It means you're being prudent. You're acknowledging that even responsible people face risks. You're protecting yourself and your family from disproportionate consequences.

Asset protection works the same way. It doesn't mean you plan to be irresponsible. It means you're prudent enough to acknowledge that even responsible people face risks.

This is not only legal and ethical. It's smart. It's exactly what financial advisors, attorneys, and other professionals recommend to their clients.

There's no need for guilt, hesitation, or apology about pursuing legitimate asset protection.

A Quiet Success

Here's how to know if your asset protection plan is working effectively:

You rarely think about it.

The best protection sits quietly in the background, properly maintained and periodically updated, while you focus on the things that actually matter in life.

Think about other aspects of your life that work well:

When your health is good, you don't think about it constantly. When your car runs reliably, you don't worry about it every day. When your relationships are solid, you don't obsess over them hourly.

The same should be true of your asset protection.

What You Should Be Thinking About Instead

When your protection is working, you can focus on:

- **Work:** Building your career or business, serving clients, creating value, pursuing opportunities. You're focused on doing good work, not constantly worrying about lawsuits.
- **Family:** Spending time with the people you love, creating memories, being present. You're engaged with your spouse and children, not distracted by financial anxieties.
- **Health:** Taking care of your physical and mental wellbeing, exercising, eating well, managing stress. You have the mental space to focus on your health rather than constant worry about asset protection.
- **Relationships:** Nurturing friendships and community connections, being present for others, contributing to your social circles. You can invest emotionally in relationships rather than being consumed by financial anxiety.
- **Opportunities:** Pursuing new projects and experiences, taking calculated risks, building wealth. You can move forward confidently rather than being paralyzed by fear.
- **Learning and growth:** Developing new skills, pursuing education, expanding your capabilities. You have mental bandwidth for growth rather than constant defensiveness.
- **Enjoyment:** Actually living your life, pursuing hobbies, traveling, experiencing things that matter to you. You're living, not just protecting.
- **Service:** Contributing to causes you care about, helping others, making a difference. You can focus outward on impact rather than inward on protection.

This is what life should look like when your asset protection is working properly. Protection fades into the background. Life comes to the foreground.

Warning Signs Something Is Wrong

If your asset protection plan creates constant stress, requires weekly attention, or makes you anxious about legal compliance, something is wrong.

Warning signs include:

- Spending hours every month on maintenance and compliance
- Constantly worrying about whether you've done enough
- Unable to make financial decisions without consulting your attorney
- Afraid to answer questions about your structures
- Complexity that confuses even your own professionals
- Feeling like you're constantly walking on legal eggshells
- Unable to explain your own structure clearly
- Stress about maintaining the façade
- Fear that someone will discover how your assets are structured

These are signs that your protection has become too complex, too aggressive, or inappropriate for your situation.

Either the plan is too elaborate for your needs, or you've focused too much on worst-case scenarios, or you've implemented strategies that don't quite fit within the law.

What Good Protection Feels Like

Good protection should feel like insurance: you're glad it's there, but you don't think about it every day.

You should feel:

- **Confident:** Knowing you've addressed major risks appropriately
- **Clear:** Understanding what's protected and what's not

- **Calm:** Not worried constantly about lawsuits or creditors
- **Capable:** Able to maintain your structures without heroic effort
- **Free:** Able to focus on building wealth and living your life

If you reach the end of this book feeling calmer and more confident, not more anxious and paranoid, then it has served its purpose.

Asset protection should reduce stress, not create it. It should provide peace of mind, not constant worry.

Final Thought

Asset protection is not about distrust. It's about respect for uncertainty.

Life is unpredictable. This isn't pessimism. It's realism.

Accidents happen. People make mistakes. Businesses face unexpected challenges. Economic conditions change. Legal environments shift. Relationships change. Health changes. Circumstances evolve.

Even the most responsible, careful, ethical people face unexpected events. Even people who do everything right can find themselves in difficult situations through no fault of their own.

You cannot control every outcome. No amount of planning eliminates all risk. No amount of caution prevents all problems. No structure survives every possible challenge.

But you can control how exposed you are to these uncertainties.

What You Can Control

You can take reasonable steps to ensure that:

- **Your family's home is protected:** One lawsuit or business failure won't result in your spouse and children losing the roof over their heads. The place where your family lives, where your children grew up, where your memories are made stays protected even if other things go wrong.
- **Your retirement savings remain intact:** The money you've spent decades accumulating for your later years doesn't disappear because of one bad event. Your future security isn't destroyed by a present

problem.

- **One business failure doesn't destroy your personal wealth:** If a business venture doesn't work out, if a startup fails, if a investment goes bad, you can lose what you put into that venture without losing everything else. You can take entrepreneurial risks without betting your entire financial life.

- **A single lawsuit doesn't undo decades of work:** Years of saving, building, investing, and working don't disappear because of one mistake, one accident, one angry litigant. The lifetime you've spent building wealth isn't destroyed by an isolated event.

- **You can continue living your life with confidence:** You can pursue opportunities, start businesses, invest in real estate, engage in your profession, serve in your community, and live fully without paralyzing fear. You can take the calculated risks that make life meaningful and productive.

What This Requires

This doesn't require paranoia, extreme secrecy, or aggressive tactics. It requires something much simpler and more sustainable:

- **Planning early:** Setting up protection before problems arise. Doing it when you're calm and thinking clearly, not when you're panicked and facing a lawsuit. Asset protection works best when implemented before you need it.

- **Planning reasonably:** Matching your strategies to your actual risks, not every theoretical scenario. Being honest about what you're really exposed to and addressing those risks proportionally. Not overdoing it or underdoing it, but finding the right balance.

- **Maintaining what you build:** Following through on compliance and documentation. Treating your structures as real. Maintaining corporate formalities. Filing required documents. Keeping records. Respecting the protections you've created so they'll be there when you need them.

- **Moving on with your life:** Not obsessing over worst-case scenarios. Not spending every waking hour worried about asset protection. Not letting protection consume your mental energy or dominate your decision-making. Setting it up properly and then getting back to the work of building your life and wealth.

That's asset protection done right.

That's protection without paranoia.

Moving Forward

Now take what you've learned from this book and implement what makes sense for your situation.

You don't need to implement everything. You don't need the most aggressive strategies. You don't need to copy what someone with completely different circumstances has done.

You need to understand your own risks, implement appropriate protections, maintain them properly, and then move on with your life.

Start with the basics:

- Adequate insurance coverage
- Retirement accounts funded properly
- Homestead protection if available in your state
- An LLC if you have business activities
- Separation between personal and business assets

Then, if your situation warrants it, add additional layers:

- Additional LLCs for specific high-risk activities
- Trusts for estate planning and asset protection
- Additional insurance coverage as assets grow
- More sophisticated strategies if risks or assets justify them

But always remember: the goal is not maximum protection. The goal is appropriate protection that allows you to live confidently.

Get back to building the life you want. Get back to doing work that matters. Get back to serving others. Get back to creating value. Get back to enjoying your life.

The protection you've built will be there, quietly working in the background, if you ever need it.

You've got this.

You understand the principles. You know the tools. You can assess your risks. You can implement appropriate strategies. You can maintain what you build.

Now go live your life with confidence, knowing you've taken reasonable steps to protect what matters most.

That's what asset protection is really about. Not fear. Not hiding. Not paranoia.

Just prudent preparation that allows you to live fully, engage completely, and pursue opportunities confidently.

Protection without paranoia.

That's the goal. That's what you can achieve. That's what you deserve.

Appendices

These appendices serve as practical reference tools. They summarize key ideas from the book in a format you can return to over time, especially when reviewing your plan or speaking with professional advisors.

How to Use These Appendices

For initial planning:

- Read Appendix A to understand geographic differences
- Use Appendix B to identify current vulnerabilities
- Bring Appendix C questions to advisor meetings

For annual reviews:

- Re-check Appendix B for new mistakes
- Verify nothing has changed that affects your plan
- Update advisors on life changes

When circumstances change:

- Marriage, divorce, new business, retirement, move to new state
- Revisit all three appendices
- Schedule review with advisors

When facing a threat:

- Understand it's likely too late for major changes
- Focus on insurance and legal defense
- Learn for next time (if there is one)

A Note on Perspective

These appendices are not meant to scare you or make asset protection seem impossibly difficult.

They are meant to:

- Keep you oriented toward what actually matters
- Ground you in reality rather than marketing promises
- Give you control through understanding

Good asset protection should make you feel more secure, not more anxious.

If your planning is creating stress rather than relieving it, something is wrong. Either the plan is too complicated for your situation, poorly designed, or you're working with the wrong advisors.

The goal is reasonable protection proportional to your risks and resources, maintained with reasonable effort over time.

That goal is achievable for most people with the right guidance, realistic expectations, and consistent follow-through.

These appendices are tools to help you get there.

Appendix A: State-by-State High-Level Asset Protection Overview

Asset protection in the United States is highly state-dependent. While federal law governs certain areas (notably retirement accounts and bankruptcy), many of the most important protections vary dramatically from state to state.

This overview is intentionally high-level. It is meant to help you understand patterns and regional differences, not replace state-specific legal advice from a qualified attorney.

1. Homestead Exemptions (Primary Residence)

Your primary residence may be one of your most valuable assets. How well it's protected depends almost entirely on where you live.

States generally fall into three categories:

Strong / Unlimited Protection

These states protect most or all home equity from creditors, making them among the most protective jurisdictions in the country for homeowners.

Key characteristics:

- Protects unlimited or very high amounts of home equity
- Often subject to residency requirements (you may need to live in the state for a certain period before the full exemption applies)
- In these states, even a multi-million dollar home may be fully protected
- Some states require the property to be on a limited amount of acreage

States with unlimited or very strong homestead protection include:

- **Florida:** Unlimited protection on up to half an acre in a municipality or 160 acres outside (subject to caps for those who purchased recently or with intent to defraud creditors)
- **Texas:** Unlimited protection on up to 10 acres in a municipality or 100 acres for a family (200 acres for a single person) in rural areas
- **Oklahoma:** Unlimited on up to one acre in a city or 160 acres in rural areas
- **Kansas:** Unlimited on up to one acre in a city or 160 acres of farming land
- **Iowa:** Unlimited protection (with some recent creditor limitations)
- **South Dakota:** Unlimited on limited acreage

Important considerations for unlimited homestead states:

- Recent residency (often 1,215 days or about 40 months) may cap the exemption at around $170,000 to prevent last-minute "exemption planning"
- Some states have anti-fraud provisions that limit protection if you bought the home specifically to shield assets from known creditors
- Protection typically applies only to your primary residence, not investment properties or vacation homes

- You generally must be living in the home at the time you claim the exemption

Moderate Protection

These states protect a capped amount of equity. The protection can be meaningful but won't shield unlimited value.

Key characteristics:

- Protects a specific dollar amount of equity (commonly ranging from $50,000 to $600,000)
- Cap varies widely by state
- May have different caps for individuals versus married couples
- May have different caps based on age, disability status, or family situation
- Protection applies only up to the dollar limit

Examples of states with moderate homestead protection:

- **California:** Ranges from approximately $30,000 to $600,000 depending on family status, age, and income
- **Massachusetts:** Up to $500,000 for most homeowners
- **Minnesota:** Up to $390,000 (higher in some cases)
- **Arizona:** $150,000 ($250,000 for age 65+ or disabled)
- **Nevada:** $605,000
- **Montana:** $350,000
- **Oregon:** $40,000 ($50,000 for married couples; up to $100,000 if certain conditions are met)
- **Washington:** $125,000
- **Michigan:** $40,500 (adjusted periodically)
- **Colorado:** $75,000 ($105,000 for elderly or disabled)

What moderate protection means in practice:

If you live in a state with a $200,000 homestead exemption and your home is worth $500,000 with a $200,000 mortgage, you have $300,000 in equity. The exemption would protect $200,000 of that equity, but creditors could potentially force a sale to access the remaining $100,000 (minus selling costs and their legal fees).

Minimal Protection

These states offer very limited homestead protection, leaving many homeowners vulnerable.

Key characteristics:

- Low caps (sometimes as little as $5,000 to $25,000)
- Narrow applicability
- May only apply in specific circumstances
- Offers little meaningful protection for most homeowners

States with minimal homestead protection include:

- **New Jersey:** None (no homestead exemption)
- **Pennsylvania:** None (no homestead exemption)
- **Delaware:** None (no homestead exemption)
- **Maryland:** None or very limited protection
- **Virginia:** $5,000 ($10,000 for veterans or those 65+)
- **Georgia:** $21,500
- **Indiana:** $19,300
- **Tennessee:** $5,000 to $7,500 depending on county
- **Kentucky:** $5,000
- **Ohio:** $25,975
- **Illinois:** $15,000
- **Missouri:** $15,000

What minimal protection means:

In states with little to no homestead exemption, your home equity is vulnerable to most judgment creditors. Even if you've built substantial equity in your home, creditors may be able to force a sale to satisfy judgments. This makes other asset protection strategies particularly important in these states.

Key Takeaway

Where you live can determine whether your largest personal asset is well protected or barely protected at all. This is one of the most significant geographic differences in asset protection law.

For many families, the homestead exemption is their single most important asset protection. If you live in a state with weak protection and own significant home equity, you may need to explore other strategies such as equity stripping (placing a lien on the property), holding title in protected forms of ownership, or incorporating the equity into a more comprehensive asset protection plan.

2. LLC Charging Order Protection

When you own an LLC, what happens if a creditor gets a judgment against you personally? The answer depends on your state's charging order laws.

Charging order laws determine what a creditor can do if they obtain a judgment against an LLC owner.

What is a Charging Order?

A charging order is a court order that entitles a creditor to receive distributions that would otherwise go to the debtor/owner. In strong protection states, this is often the creditor's only remedy.

Think of it this way: if you own an LLC that generates income, a charging order says "any money that would have been paid to the debtor must now be paid to the creditor instead." But crucially, in states with strong charging order protection, that's all the creditor gets. They don't get to:

- Control the LLC's operations
- Vote on LLC decisions
- Force the LLC to make distributions
- Access LLC assets directly

- Participate in management

This makes a charging order a relatively weak remedy for creditors, which is exactly why LLCs can be powerful asset protection tools in the right states.

Why Charging Orders Matter

The charging order limitation creates what's known as the "poison pill" effect. Here's how it works:

If a creditor can only receive distributions, but can't force distributions, they're stuck. Meanwhile, if the LLC makes distributions, the creditor may owe income taxes on their share of the LLC's profits (called "phantom income") even if they receive no actual money. This often motivates creditors to settle for much less than the full judgment amount.

States Vary Significantly On:

- Whether charging orders are the **exclusive remedy** (meaning the creditor gets nothing else)
- Whether protection applies to **single-member LLCs** (many states treat these differently)
- Whether **foreclosure** on ownership interests is allowed
- Whether creditors can **force dissolution** of the LLC
- Whether creditors can become **substitute members** with voting rights

Stronger States

These states limit creditors to economic rights only, providing robust LLC protection.

Characteristics of strong charging order states:

- Creditor cannot take control of the LLC
- Creditor cannot force distributions
- Creditor cannot vote or participate in management
- Protection often applies even to single-member LLCs
- Charging order is the exclusive remedy

States with strong LLC charging order protection include:

- **Nevada:** Explicit statutory protection, charging order is exclusive remedy even for single-member LLCs
- **Wyoming:** Strong protection, charging order exclusive, applies to single-member LLCs
- **Delaware:** Generally strong, though case law continues to develop
- **Alaska:** Charging order is exclusive remedy
- **South Dakota:** Strong statutory protections
- **Arizona:** Charging order exclusive for multi-member LLCs
- **Tennessee:** Strong protection under recent statutes

Weaker States

These states allow broader creditor remedies, reducing the protective value of LLCs.

Characteristics of weak charging order states:

- Allow foreclosure on ownership interests
- May permit creditors to become substitute members
- Often provide less protection for single-member LLCs
- May allow creditors to force dissolution or sale

States with weaker LLC protection include:

- **Florida:** Courts have allowed foreclosure remedies for single-member LLCs in some cases
- **Georgia:** Permits broader creditor remedies
- **Colorado:** Has allowed foreclosure in single-member LLC situations
- **Connecticut:** Weaker protections, especially for single-member LLCs

The Single-Member LLC Problem

Many states that provide strong charging order protection for multi-member LLCs (those with two or more owners) provide much weaker protection for single-member LLCs (those with only one owner).

The reasoning: Courts in these states have determined that the charging order protection was designed to protect innocent co-owners from having an unwanted partner (the creditor) forced upon them. When there's only one owner, there are no other members to protect, so courts feel more comfortable allowing creditors additional remedies like foreclosure.

Strategies to address this:

- Add a second member to your LLC (such as a spouse, family member, or trust)
- Form your LLC in a state that explicitly protects single-member LLCs
- Use multiple layers of entities
- Consider a Series LLC structure where appropriate

Key Takeaway

An LLC's protective value depends as much on state law as on how well you operate it. The same LLC structure can offer excellent protection in one state and minimal protection in another.

If you're forming an LLC primarily for asset protection (rather than just for business liability purposes), the state you choose matters enormously. You're not always required to form your LLC in the state where you live, though there may be registration and tax implications for doing business in your home state with an out-of-state LLC.

3. Domestic Asset Protection Trust (DAPT) Availability

A Domestic Asset Protection Trust is a special type of trust where you can be a beneficiary of your own trust while still receiving some creditor protection. This is called a "self-settled" trust.

The Traditional Rule and Why DAPTs Are Special

Traditionally, if you create a trust and name yourself as a beneficiary, creditors can reach the trust assets. The law generally doesn't allow you to shield assets from creditors while still maintaining the right to benefit from those assets. It's considered trying to have your cake and eat it too.

However, certain states have passed laws specifically allowing self-settled asset protection trusts. These states permit you to transfer assets into a trust, retain some beneficial interest, and still gain creditor protection under specific circumstances.

Important Limitation

Only a limited number of states (currently fewer than 20) allow self-settled asset protection trusts. If your state doesn't allow them, you must use a state that does.

Even among states that allow DAPTs, there are significant differences in:

- **Creditor exceptions:** What types of creditors can still reach the assets (such as child support, alimony, or existing creditors)
- **Statutes of limitation:** How long creditors have to challenge transfers into the trust (typically 2 to 4 years)
- **Trustee requirements:** Whether you need an in-state trustee or can serve as your own trustee
- **Fraudulent transfer lookback periods:** How far back courts will examine your transfers
- **Enforceability in other states:** Whether other states will respect the DAPT

States with DAPT Statutes

Leading DAPT jurisdictions include:

- **Alaska (1997):** The first DAPT state; 4-year statute of limitations; requires Alaska trustee
- **Delaware (1997):** Very popular for trusts generally; strong trust laws; requires Delaware trustee
- **Nevada (1999):** 2-year statute of limitations (shortest); strong spendthrift provisions; Nevada trustee required
- **South Dakota (2005):** No state income tax on trusts; strong privacy provisions; perpetual trusts allowed
- **Tennessee (2007):** Competitive statute; requires Tennessee trustee
- **Wyoming (2007):** No state income tax; strong privacy; Wyoming

trustee required

- **Utah (2003):** Competitive provisions
- **Missouri (2003):** DAPT provisions available
- **Oklahoma (2004):** Allows self-settled trusts
- **Rhode Island (2011):** More recent DAPT state
- **Hawaii (2010):** DAPT provisions
- **New Hampshire (2008):** Allows DAPTs
- **Ohio (2013):** More restrictive than some states
- **Virginia (2012):** DAPT available with limitations
- **West Virginia (2011):** Self-settled trust provisions
- **Michigan (2016):** Among the most recent additions

Key Differences Among DAPT States

Statute of Limitations (how long creditors have to challenge the transfer):

- Nevada: 2 years
- Tennessee: 3 years for existing creditors, shorter for future creditors
- Alaska: 4 years
- Most others: 2-4 years depending on creditor type

Exceptions (who can still reach DAPT assets):

All DAPT states provide exceptions for certain creditors, but the specific exceptions vary:

- Child support and alimony obligations (nearly universal exception)
- Pre-existing creditors at the time of transfer (common exception)
- Tort claims that arose before the transfer (varies by state)
- Creditors who can prove fraudulent transfer (universal)
- Tax obligations (federal government can typically reach assets)

Spendthrift Protection Strength:

Some states have stronger spendthrift provisions than others, making it harder for creditors to access trust assets even when exceptions might apply.

Privacy and Confidentiality:

- Nevada and South Dakota offer strong privacy protections
- Some states allow for private trust companies
- Disclosure requirements vary

The Full Faith and Credit Problem

Here's the biggest challenge with DAPTs: constitutional questions about whether one state must honor another state's DAPT protections.

The scenario:

You live in New York. You create a Nevada DAPT. You're sued in New York. Will the New York court respect the Nevada DAPT's protections?

The uncertainty:

- The U.S. Constitution's Full Faith and Credit Clause generally requires states to respect other states' laws
- However, courts may not honor another state's laws if they violate the forum state's strong public policy
- Many states have strong public policies against self-settled trusts
- There's limited case law testing whether states must respect out-of-state DAPTs

What this means for you:

- DAPTs work best when you have a legitimate connection to the DAPT state
- They're stronger if you actually reside in a DAPT state
- They're less certain if you're sued in a non-DAPT state
- They should be one component of a broader strategy, not your only protection

DAPT Requirements and Costs

Typical requirements:

- Must use a qualified trustee in the DAPT state (usually cannot be you alone)
- Must transfer assets irrevocably (you give up direct control)
- Must comply with specific statutory formalities
- Should have some connection to the state (though not always legally required)

Costs to consider:

- Legal fees for trust creation: typically $5,000 to $15,000+
- Trustee fees: often $2,000 to $10,000+ annually depending on asset value
- Administrative costs
- Ongoing legal review and maintenance

Key Takeaway

A DAPT's effectiveness depends on both the jurisdiction you choose and the specific facts of your situation. Protection is not guaranteed, especially if you're sued in a state other than where the trust is established.

DAPTs can be powerful tools, but they're not magic. They work best as part of a comprehensive asset protection strategy, ideally established well before any creditor problems arise.

4. IRA and Retirement Account Exemption Protections

Retirement accounts often receive strong protection, but the level of protection depends on the type of account and where you live.

Federal Protection (Strong)

ERISA-qualified plans receive robust federal protection:

- **401(k) plans**
- **403(b) plans**
- **Defined benefit pensions**

- **Profit-sharing plans**
- **Money purchase plans**

Protection level:

- Protected in bankruptcy up to unlimited amounts
- Strong protection outside bankruptcy under federal law (ERISA's anti-alienation provisions)
- Generally cannot be seized by creditors
- Exceptions: IRS tax liens, certain domestic relations orders (QDROs), and in some cases, criminal fines

Why ERISA plans are so well protected:

Federal law (the Employee Retirement Income Security Act) includes powerful anti-alienation provisions designed to ensure retirement funds are actually used for retirement. These protections preempt state law, meaning they apply regardless of where you live.

State-Level Protection (Variable)

State law governs protection for:

- **Traditional and Roth IRAs**
- **SEP IRAs**
- **SIMPLE IRAs**
- **Non-ERISA retirement accounts**
- **Creditor exemptions outside of bankruptcy**

How States Differ

Some states provide unlimited protection:

- **Arizona:** IRAs fully exempt
- **Texas:** IRAs fully exempt (subject to fraudulent transfer analysis)
- **Florida:** IRAs fully exempt
- **Washington:** IRAs fully exempt

- **Michigan:** IRAs fully exempt
- **Colorado:** IRAs fully exempt

Other states cap protection:

- **California:** Only the amount "necessary for support" (determined case-by-case, no fixed dollar limit)
- **New Mexico:** Limited exemption amounts
- **Connecticut:** Present value of payments exempt
- **Missouri:** Exempts only the amount "reasonably necessary for support"

Some states distinguish by account type:

- Traditional IRA vs. Roth IRA
- Contributory IRA vs. Rollover IRA (from former employer plans)
- Inherited IRA (recent Supreme Court case ruled inherited IRAs are NOT protected in bankruptcy)

Some states apply "reasonably necessary" tests:

Instead of a hard dollar cap, these states require that the protected amount be "reasonably necessary" for retirement support. Factors courts consider include:

- Your age
- Your health
- Your income and expenses
- Other assets available
- Your career prospects
- Your dependents

This creates uncertainty because you won't know exactly how much is protected until a court decides your specific case.

Protection in Bankruptcy vs. Outside Bankruptcy

In bankruptcy (federal law applies):

- ERISA plans: Unlimited protection
- Traditional and Roth IRAs: Protected up to approximately $1.5 million (adjusted periodically for inflation; currently $1,512,350 as of 2022, adjusted every 3 years)
- Rollover IRAs from ERISA plans: Unlimited protection
- Inherited IRAs: NOT protected (per 2014 Supreme Court decision in *Clark v. Rameker*, 573 U.S. 122 (2014))

Outside bankruptcy (state law applies):

Protection varies dramatically by state as described above.

Special Considerations

SEP and SIMPLE IRAs:

- Often treated like traditional IRAs for exemption purposes
- Some states provide the same protection as ERISA plans
- Check your specific state's treatment

Inherited IRAs:

- After the Supreme Court's 2014 ruling, inherited IRAs receive no federal bankruptcy protection
- Some states still protect inherited IRAs outside of bankruptcy
- Dramatically changes estate planning for those concerned about beneficiaries' creditors

Roth Conversions:

- Converting a traditional IRA to a Roth IRA doesn't affect creditor protection in most states
- However, recent conversions may be scrutinized as fraudulent transfers if done to shield assets from known creditors
- The converted funds may be subject to the same exemption limits as any other IRA

Multi-Generational Protection

Strategy consideration:

Because inherited IRAs are generally not protected from beneficiaries' creditors, many planners now recommend:

- Naming a trust as IRA beneficiary instead of individuals
- Using a properly designed "IRA Inheritance Trust"
- Providing creditor protection for beneficiaries within the trust structure
- Balancing tax efficiency with asset protection

Key Takeaway

Retirement accounts are generally strong protective anchors, but the level of protection varies significantly once you leave federal safe harbors. Know your state's specific rules.

For most people, maximizing contributions to ERISA-qualified plans (401(k)s, 403(b)s, defined benefit plans) should be a priority both for retirement savings and asset protection. These accounts provide the strongest protection regardless of where you live.

5. Additional State-Specific Considerations

Beyond the major categories above, states also differ in several other important areas that affect asset protection planning.

Tenancy by the Entirety Protection

Some states recognize a special form of property ownership available only to married couples called "tenancy by the entirety."

How it works:

- Property is owned by the marital unit, not by the individuals
- Creditors of only one spouse generally cannot reach property held as tenants by the entirety
- Both spouses must consent to sell or encumber the property

- Property automatically passes to the surviving spouse upon death
- Provides protection from individual creditors but not joint creditors

States that recognize tenancy by the entirety:

- **Strong protection states:** Alaska, Arkansas, Delaware, Florida, Hawaii, Illinois, Indiana, Kentucky, Maryland, Massachusetts, Michigan, Mississippi, Missouri, New York, North Carolina, Ohio, Oklahoma, Oregon, Pennsylvania, Rhode Island, Tennessee, Vermont, Virginia, Wyoming
- **Limited or unclear:** Some states recognize it for real estate but not personal property
- **Not available:** Arizona, California, Colorado, Georgia, Idaho, Kansas, Louisiana, Maine, Minnesota, Montana, Nebraska, Nevada, New Hampshire, New Mexico, North Dakota, South Carolina, South Dakota, Texas, Utah, Washington, West Virginia, Wisconsin

What can be held as tenancy by the entirety:

- **Most states:** Real estate (primary home, investment property)
- **Some states:** Bank accounts, brokerage accounts, vehicles, other personal property
- **Very few states:** Business interests, partnership interests

Limitations:

- Only protects against individual creditors (creditors of just one spouse)
- Offers no protection against joint creditors (creditors of both spouses)
- May not protect against federal tax liens (IRS)
- Must be properly titled
- Only available to married couples (not available to unmarried partners)
- Divorce terminates the protection (property converts to tenancy in common)

Strategy note:

In states with strong tenancy by the entirety protection, this can be one of the simplest and most effective asset protection strategies for married couples. Simply retitling assets can provide substantial protection at no cost.

Wage Garnishment Limits

Both federal and state laws limit how much of your wages can be garnished by creditors.

Federal law (minimum protection everywhere):

The Consumer Credit Protection Act limits wage garnishment to the lesser of:

- 25% of disposable earnings, or
- The amount by which disposable weekly earnings exceed 30 times the federal minimum wage

Disposable earnings means gross pay minus legally required deductions (taxes, Social Security, etc.).

Enhanced state protections:

Many states provide greater protection than federal law:

- **Texas:** Wages generally exempt except for child support, alimony, taxes, and student loans
- **Pennsylvania:** Wages generally exempt except for specific debts
- **North Carolina:** Wages generally exempt except for specific debts
- **South Carolina:** Strong wage protections
- **New Hampshire:** Strong wage protections
- **Florida:** Head of household wages are exempt

Head of household protection:

Several states provide complete or enhanced wage protection if you qualify as "head of household," meaning you provide more than half the support for a dependent.

Bank Account Exemptions

Many states exempt certain amounts in bank accounts or provide special protections for specific types of funds.

Common exemptions:

- **Social Security benefits:** Protected under federal law when directly deposited
- **Veterans benefits:** Protected under federal law
- **Disability benefits:** Often protected
- **Unemployment benefits:** Usually protected
- **Workers' compensation:** Typically protected

State-specific bank account protections:

- Some states exempt a specific dollar amount in bank accounts (wildcard exemption)
- Some states protect wages deposited in accounts for a certain period
- Some states protect accounts holding exempt funds (like Social Security)
- Head of household protections may extend to bank accounts

Important limitation:

Once exempt funds (like Social Security) are commingled with non-exempt funds in a bank account, tracing can become complicated. Best practice is to maintain separate accounts for exempt income.

Wildcard Exemptions

Some states offer a "wildcard" exemption that can be applied to any property of your choosing.

How wildcard exemptions work:

You get to protect a certain dollar amount of any asset (or combination of assets), regardless of category.

States with significant wildcard exemptions:

- **California (System 2):** Approximately $32,000 wildcard (if you don't claim homestead)
- **New York:** $1,000 wildcard plus additional amounts in certain circumstances
- **Connecticut:** $1,000 wildcard
- **Massachusetts:** $1,250 wildcard plus additional unused homestead exemption

Strategic uses:

- Protecting cash or savings
- Protecting business equipment
- Protecting vehicles beyond standard auto exemption
- Protecting valuable personal items
- Covering assets that don't fit other exemption categories

Tools of the Trade Exemptions

Most states exempt tools, equipment, and materials necessary for your profession or trade.

Typical limits:

Range from $1,000 to $10,000+ depending on state

What qualifies:

- Equipment and tools for your profession
- Books and materials
- Vehicles used for business (sometimes)
- Computer equipment (in some states)

Example state provisions:

- **Texas:** Tools, equipment, books, and apparatus needed for a trade or profession, including farming and ranching tools
- **California:** Tools, implements, materials, uniforms, and furnishings

necessary to carry out your trade, business, or profession (up to certain dollar limits)

Motor Vehicle Exemptions

States vary widely in how much of a vehicle's value they protect.

Range:

- **Minimal:** $1,000 to $3,000 in some states
- **Moderate:** $5,000 to $10,000 in many states
- **Generous:** $15,000 to $25,000 in some states
- **Unlimited:** Texas (one vehicle per licensed driver in the family)

Considerations:

- Some states provide higher exemptions for disabled individuals
- Some states allow separate exemptions for each spouse
- Vehicles necessary for work may receive additional protection

Insurance and Annuity Protections

Many states provide strong protection for certain insurance products and annuities.

Life insurance:

- **Cash value:** Many states exempt cash value from creditors
- **Death benefit:** Generally protected once paid to beneficiaries (unless beneficiary is the debtor's estate)
- **Varies by state:** Some states fully exempt, others cap protection

Annuities:

- Some states fully exempt annuity values
- Others exempt only periodic payments
- Some distinguish between qualified and non-qualified annuities

Disability insurance:

- Benefits typically protected
- Some states protect the underlying policy value

Long-term care insurance:

- Increasingly protected by state laws
- Benefits generally exempt

Strategy note:

In states with strong insurance and annuity protections, these products can serve dual purposes: providing insurance/retirement benefits while also protecting assets from creditors.

College Savings Plans (529 Plans)

Federal bankruptcy protection:

529 plans receive some protection in bankruptcy for contributions made more than 2 years before filing (contributions in the previous 1-2 years have dollar limits).

State protection outside bankruptcy:

Varies significantly:

- Some states fully exempt 529 plans
- Others provide no specific protection
- Some treat them like other financial accounts

Business Property and Inventory

Protection for business assets varies:

- Some states provide exemptions for business inventory
- Some protect business equipment
- Limits vary widely
- Often overlaps with "tools of trade" exemptions

6. Practical Planning Insight

Many people assume: "I'll just form entities in my home state and use local advisors."

In asset protection, default choices are rarely optimal.

Jurisdiction is a Planning Variable

Consider:

- **The state where you form an entity can be different from where you live**
- **For trusts, you can often choose favorable trust jurisdictions**
- **For LLCs holding real estate, you typically need an entity in the state where the property is located** (or at minimum, must register to do business there)
- **For other assets, you may have flexibility**
- **You can have different entities in different states for different purposes**

Multi-State Planning Strategies

Common planning approaches:

- Living in one state while using another state's LLC laws for business entities
- Establishing trusts in trust-favorable jurisdictions while living elsewhere
- Using holding company structures with entities in multiple states
- Segregating different asset types into entities formed in optimal jurisdictions

Examples:

- A Florida resident might form a Wyoming LLC to hold business assets for stronger charging order protection
- A New Jersey resident might establish a Nevada DAPT because New Jersey doesn't permit self-settled trusts

- A real estate investor might use Delaware LLCs to hold properties in multiple states

Warning: Substance Over Form

Simply choosing a "strong" state doesn't guarantee protection. Courts may not respect out-of-state protections if they appear designed primarily to evade creditors, especially if you have no genuine connection to that state.

What courts look for:

- Whether you have a legitimate business purpose for the structure
- Whether you have actual connections to the chosen state
- Whether you're following the formalities required
- The timing of transfers relative to creditor claims
- Whether the structure has substance beyond asset protection

Red flags:

- Forming entities in a state you've never visited
- Having no business operations in the chosen state
- Timing that suggests transfers were made to evade specific known creditors
- Failing to follow formalities or maintain the entity
- Keeping complete control despite apparent transfers

Best Practice Approach

Work with advisors who understand multi-state planning and can help you navigate these choices appropriately.

Key planning steps:

1. **Assess your specific situation:** What assets do you have? What are your primary risks? Where do you live and work?
2. **Understand your home state's protections:** Start by knowing what protection you already have based on where you live.

3. **Identify gaps:** Where is your home state's protection weak?
4. **Evaluate strategic alternatives:** What other states' laws might be beneficial for specific assets or structures?
5. **Ensure legitimate connections:** Make sure chosen jurisdictions have some genuine connection to your situation.
6. **Document legitimate purposes:** Maintain records showing business and tax reasons for your structure, not just asset protection.
7. **Act before problems arise:** Implement strategies when the sky is blue, not when storm clouds are gathering.
8. **Maintain formalities:** Follow all legal requirements for entities and trusts in all relevant states.
9. **Coordinate with tax planning:** Ensure asset protection strategies don't create unnecessary tax problems.
10. **Review regularly:** Laws change, your situation changes, and your planning should adapt accordingly.

The Cost-Benefit Analysis

Not every asset protection strategy makes sense for every person.

Consider:

- **Setup costs:** Legal fees, filing fees, and initial costs
- **Ongoing costs:** Annual fees, registered agent fees, trustee fees, accounting costs
- **Complexity:** Administrative burden, tax return complexity, ongoing maintenance
- **Your actual risk:** Are you in a high-risk profession or situation?
- **Asset value:** Do you have enough assets to justify the cost and complexity?

General principle:

Asset protection is like insurance. You need enough to protect against realistic risks, but you shouldn't spend more on protection than the value of what you're protecting or the likelihood of the risk justifies.

Conclusion

The state-by-state variations in asset protection law create both challenges and opportunities.

Key takeaways:

- Your home state's laws significantly impact your baseline protection
- Strategic use of favorable jurisdictions can enhance protection
- One-size-fits-all solutions don't exist in asset protection
- Planning must be individualized to your situation
- Multi-state planning requires careful coordination
- Substance and legitimacy matter more than clever structures
- Early planning is more effective and less expensive than crisis planning

Final reminder:

This appendix provides general information about state-level asset protection variations. It is not a substitute for specific legal advice from a qualified attorney in your state. Laws change, court interpretations evolve, and individual circumstances vary significantly.

Before implementing any asset protection strategy, consult with an attorney who:

- Is licensed in your state
- Understands multi-jurisdictional planning
- Has specific expertise in asset protection
- Can evaluate your unique situation
- Can coordinate with your tax and estate planning advisors

Asset protection is complex, but with proper planning and professional guidance, you can significantly improve your financial security while remaining compliant with all legal requirements.

Appendix B: Common Asset Protection Mistakes Checklist

Use this checklist as a diagnostic tool. One "yes" doesn't necessarily mean your plan will fail, but patterns of multiple "yes" answers should concern you.

Review this checklist annually and whenever your circumstances change significantly.

Timing Mistakes

☐ **Started planning after a lawsuit or demand letter arrived**

- Planning done after a claim exists is often considered fraudulent
- Courts look very skeptically at transfers made under threat of litigation
- Proper planning happens during peaceful times

☐ **Transferred assets when a claim was reasonably foreseeable**

- You don't need an actual lawsuit for a transfer to be fraudulent
- If you knew or should have known a claim was coming, transfers may be unwound
- "Foreseeable" is broader than you might think

☐ **Assumed late planning would still be effective**

- Asset protection is not a last-minute solution
- Most protective structures require years to season
- Courts have long memories and lookback periods

☐ **Made large transfers shortly before or after a major event**

- Getting divorced, selling a business, or retiring are times of heightened scrutiny
- Sudden changes in asset ownership raise red flags
- Gradual, well-documented planning is safer

Key timing principle: Asset protection works best when implemented well before any threats appear on the horizon.

Structure Mistakes

☐ **Relying on a single LLC or trust for all protection**

- Single point of failure
- One lawsuit can pierce through your entire structure
- No redundancy or backup protection

☐ **Mixing personal and business funds**

- Destroys the corporate veil
- Makes it easy for creditors to argue the entity is your "alter ego"
- One of the most common and fatal mistakes

☐ **Holding risky assets personally**

- Real estate in your personal name

- Business interests without entity protection
- Vehicles used for business purposes owned individually

☐ **Overloading one entity with multiple risks**

- One LLC holding multiple rental properties
- Single entity for multiple business lines
- Creates unnecessary cross-collateralization of risks

☐ **Using entities formed in the wrong jurisdiction**

- Not researching which states offer better protection
- Defaulting to your home state without analysis
- Missing opportunities for stronger legal shields

☐ **Failing to properly title assets in entity names**

- Assets still in personal name despite having entities
- Inconsistent titling
- Deeds, titles, and accounts not properly transferred

☐ **No separation between high-risk and low-risk assets**

- Liquid assets mixed with liability-generating assets
- Safe assets exposed to operational risks
- No firewall between different risk categories

Key structure principle: Proper design includes both vertical layers (entity on entity) and horizontal separation (different risks in different entities).

Behavioral and Operational Mistakes

☐ **Ignoring entity formalities**

- No operating agreements or bylaws
- No annual meetings or minutes
- No documented decision-making

- Treating the entity as if it doesn't exist

☐ **Using business accounts for personal expenses**

- Paying personal credit cards from business accounts
- Using business funds for vacations or personal items
- No clear separation between business and personal spending

☐ **Signing personal guarantees unnecessarily**

- Guaranteeing business debts personally without negotiation
- Not understanding what you're signing
- Giving away protection you worked hard to create

☐ **Commingling assets between entities**

- Moving money between LLCs without documentation
- Blurring lines between different entities
- No clear economic substance to each entity

☐ **Failing to maintain adequate records**

- No bookkeeping or financial statements
- Cannot prove proper operation if challenged
- Missing documentation of legitimate business purposes

☐ **Making decisions without consulting advisors**

- Major transactions done without legal or tax review
- Assuming you understand all implications
- Learning about problems only after they occur

☐ **Not updating plans as life changes**

- Structure designed 10 years ago never reviewed
- New assets not properly integrated
- Changes in family or business not reflected in planning

Key behavioral principle: Asset protection structures only work if you actually operate them as separate legal entities. Discipline matters more than sophistication.

Insurance Mistakes

☐ **Inadequate liability limits**

- Minimum coverage when significant assets are at risk
- Not adjusting limits as wealth grows
- Underinsuring relative to net worth

☐ **No umbrella coverage**

- Relying solely on auto and homeowner's policies
- No additional layer of protection
- Umbrella policies are relatively inexpensive for the protection they provide

☐ **Mismatch between ownership and policy names**

- Property owned by LLC but insured in personal name
- Insurance policy won't pay because named insured is wrong
- Creates gaps in coverage

☐ **Not reviewing policies annually**

- Coverage limits unchanged for years
- New risks not added to policies
- Policy exclusions not understood

☐ **Assuming insurance covers everything**

• Not reading exclusions carefully
• Intentional acts typically not covered
• Some claims (like fraud) are uninsurable

☐ **No directors and officers (D&O) liability coverage**

- If you serve on boards, this coverage is essential
- Personal exposure for management decisions
- Often not covered by general liability policies

☐ **Gaps between when entity protection and insurance protection apply**

- Some risks covered by insurance but not entities
- Other risks covered by entities but not insurance
- Need both working together

Key insurance principle: Insurance should be your first line of defense, with entities and trusts serving as backup layers. Don't over-rely on legal structures when insurance can do the job better.

Offshore-Specific Mistakes

☐ **Believing offshore equals secrecy**

- Modern tax treaties and reporting requirements eliminate secrecy
- Offshore accounts must be disclosed to the IRS
- Criminal penalties for non-disclosure

☐ **Ignoring reporting obligations**

- FBAR (Foreign Bank Account Report) filings
- Form 8938 for foreign assets
- Foreign trust reporting requirements
- Penalties can exceed the account value

☐ **Retaining too much control**

- Serving as trustee of your own offshore trust defeats the purpose
- Courts can order you to repatriate assets if you have control
- Independence of trustee is critical

☐ **Not understanding foreign laws**

- Assuming U.S. legal concepts apply abroad
- Not working with local counsel in the foreign jurisdiction
- Surprises about how the structure actually operates

☐ **Using offshore for tax evasion**

- Confusing asset protection with tax avoidance
- Offshore structures must be tax-compliant
- IRS has become very aggressive in this area

☐ **Choosing jurisdiction based on marketing rather than substance**

- Exotic locations may sound good but lack legal infrastructure
- Established jurisdictions (like Cook Islands, Nevis) have track records
- Political and economic stability matters

☐ **Failing to fund the structure properly**

- Setting up an offshore trust but leaving assets in the U.S.
- Defeating the purpose through incomplete implementation
- Assets must actually move for protection to work

Key offshore principle: Offshore planning is the most complex and regulated form of asset protection. It requires complete transparency with U.S. authorities and expert guidance. It is not a solution for hiding assets.

Advisor-Related Mistakes

☐ **Trusting guarantees or "bulletproof" claims**

- No structure is bulletproof
- Anyone promising guaranteed outcomes is misleading you
- Good advisors discuss weaknesses, not just strengths

☐ **Using one-size-fits-all solutions**

- Template approaches without customization

- No analysis of your specific risks and goals
- Cookie-cutter documents that don't fit your situation

☐ **Advisors who discourage second opinions**

- Legitimate advisors welcome scrutiny
- Pressure tactics are a red flag
- Complex planning benefits from multiple perspectives

☐ **Working with advisors who lack asset protection experience**

- General practice attorneys may not understand nuances
- Need specialists in this area
- Credentials and track record matter

☐ **Advisors who don't coordinate with each other**

- Attorney doesn't talk to CPA
- Insurance agent unaware of entity structure
- Conflicting advice from different professionals

☐ **No ongoing relationship or maintenance plan**

- Set it and forget it approach
- No annual reviews
- Advisor disappears after initial setup

☐ **Cost-driven decision making**

- Choosing cheapest option for critical planning
- Not understanding what you're paying for
- Expensive fixes later due to cheap planning now

☐ **Advisors who promise to hide assets**

- Ethical advisors don't help you conceal assets
- If it sounds illegal, it probably is

- You're responsible even if advisor suggested it

Key advisor principle: Asset protection usually fails because of poor execution, not because of flawed ideas. The quality of your advisors and your relationship with them matters enormously.

Self-Reflection Questions

After completing this checklist, ask yourself:

- How many boxes did I check?
- Are there patterns in my mistakes (all timing, all operational, etc.)?
- Which mistakes pose the greatest risk to my plan?
- What can I fix immediately?
- What requires professional help to address?
- Am I being honest with myself about my discipline and follow-through?

Key takeaway: Asset protection usually fails because of execution errors, not conceptual problems. This checklist helps you identify vulnerabilities before they become disasters.

Appendix C: Questions to Bring to a Professional Advisor

Asset Protection: Questions to Ask Your Advisor

Use these questions to evaluate an advisor's competence, judgment, and fit with your needs. You're assessing their thinking, not just their credentials.

Good advisors welcome tough questions. They see them as signs of an engaged, thoughtful client who will be a good partner in the planning process.

Questions About Risk Assessment

These questions help you understand whether the advisor truly grasps your unique situation:

"What risks concern you most in my situation?"

Listen carefully to the response. You want to hear specific, personal analysis rather than generic risks that apply to everyone. Good advisors identify risks you may not have considered based on your particular circumstances. They should prioritize risks by likelihood and severity, not just list everything that could theoretically go wrong.

"Which risks are not worth planning around?"

This tests whether the advisor can distinguish real threats from theoretical ones. It shows judgment and proportionality in their thinking. Advisors who want to protect against everything often over-engineer solutions, creating unnecessary complexity and expense. You want someone who can tell you what to worry about and what to ignore.

"How does my lifestyle affect my exposure?"

Risks vary dramatically by profession, activities, wealth level, and public profile. Your advisor should ask detailed questions about your daily life, hobbies, travel patterns, social media presence, and public visibility. A one-size-fits-all risk assessment is a major warning sign. The doctor who performs high-risk procedures faces different exposures than the consultant who works from home.

"What would you do if you were in my position?"

This question reveals the advisor's genuine beliefs versus what they're selling. Good advisors can put themselves in your shoes and give you an honest answer. Compare their answer to what they're recommending for you. If there's a significant gap, ask why. Sometimes there are good reasons, but sometimes it reveals that they're recommending what's profitable rather than what's appropriate.

"Am I over-thinking this, or under-thinking it?"

This tests the advisor's objectivity and willingness to give you a reality check. Some clients need to do less planning and worry less. Others need to take their risks more seriously. Your advisor should be able to tell you honestly which category you're in, even if it means talking you out of expensive planning you don't need.

Questions About Strategy and Design

These questions probe the reasoning behind specific recommendations:

"Why is this strategy appropriate for me specifically?"

You should hear your own facts reflected back to you in the answer. If the response could apply to anyone, it's generic thinking. Look for customization based on your assets, your risks, your family situation, and your goals. Template solutions rarely provide optimal protection.

"What are the weaknesses of this approach?"

Every strategy has limitations and vulnerabilities. Advisors who can't articulate the weaknesses of their recommendations either don't fully understand the strategy or aren't being honest with you. This question reveals intellectual honesty and depth of understanding. The best advisors will tell you what could go wrong before you have to ask.

"What alternatives did you consider and reject?"

This shows the breadth of the advisor's analysis. It helps you understand the opportunity costs of the recommended approach. Good advisors can explain why they chose option A over options B, C, and D. They've actually considered multiple paths and can articulate why they settled on this particular one for your situation.

"How does this strategy interact with my existing planning?"

Asset protection doesn't exist in isolation. It must coordinate smoothly with your estate planning, tax planning, business succession planning, and insurance coverage. Conflicts between different plans can be disastrous. For example, an asset protection trust might conflict with your estate tax planning, or a business entity restructuring might trigger unexpected tax consequences.

"What assumptions does this strategy rely on?"

Every plan has embedded assumptions. These might include assumptions about the law remaining stable, courts interpreting structures favorably, your behavior following certain patterns, or family members cooperating. Understanding these assumptions helps you monitor whether the plan remains valid over time. It also alerts you to what could go wrong if assumptions prove incorrect.

"Is this the simplest approach that accomplishes the goal?"

Complexity should serve a clear purpose. Unnecessary complexity creates maintenance burdens, increases costs, and creates more potential failure points. Good advisors can justify each layer of complexity in their recommendations. If they can't explain why something needs to be complicated, it probably doesn't.

"How would you attack this plan if you were a creditor's attorney?"

The best advisors think like the opposition. This question reveals vulnerabilities you should address before implementation. It shows whether the advisor engages in adversarial thinking, which is essential in asset protection. You want someone who can anticipate how a hostile attorney would try to unwind your planning.

Questions About Timing and Intent

These questions address the legitimacy and durability of your planning:

"How does timing affect this plan?"

Understanding timing is critical. Your advisor should explain fraudulent transfer lookback periods in your jurisdiction, seasoning requirements for various structures, and when protection actually becomes effective. Some protection is immediate, while other strategies need years to mature. Timing can be the difference between a plan that works and one that fails.

"What facts would make this strategy inappropriate or risky?"

This is your opportunity to make sure you've disclosed everything relevant. Are there pending lawsuits you haven't mentioned? Foreseeable claims on the horizon? Recent events that create problems? Your advisor needs complete information to give you sound advice. This question also tests whether they're thinking critically about red flags.

"How would a court likely view this structure?"

The subjective element matters enormously in asset protection. Courts assess intent and good faith, not just technical compliance. Your advisor should have a realistic view of how judges are likely to receive the proposed structure. Overly aggressive planning that technically complies with the law but offends judicial sensibilities often fails when tested.

"When should I have started this planning?"

If the honest answer is "years ago," that's sobering but valuable information. It helps you calibrate your expectations about what's achievable now. It may also influence which strategies are still viable and which have become too risky due to timing issues. Better to hear hard truths now than discover them in litigation.

"What can we do now, and what should we wait on?"

Sequencing matters in asset protection planning. Some steps are time-sensitive and should be implemented immediately. Others actually benefit from patience and deliberate pacing. Your advisor should have a clear implementation timeline that explains the order of operations and the reasoning behind it.

"How do we document legitimate purposes?"

This is crucial. Asset protection should be a side benefit of planning done for other legitimate reasons. Tax efficiency, estate planning, business succession, investment management, and creditor protection can all be valid purposes. Courts scrutinize structures created solely to defeat creditors. Your advisor should help you document the multiple legitimate purposes driving your planning.

Questions About Compliance and Reporting

These questions address ongoing obligations that many people underestimate:

"What reporting is required?"

Get a complete picture of reporting obligations. This includes tax returns (Form 1040, 1041 for trusts, 1120 for corporations), information returns (Form 5471 for foreign corporations, Form 3520 for foreign trusts, Form 8938 for foreign assets, FBAR reports), state filings, and other regulatory requirements. The reporting burden can be substantial and expensive.

"Who is responsible for ongoing filings?"

Clarify roles before problems occur. Will your CPA handle tax reporting? Will the attorney manage entity filings? Are you responsible for tracking deadlines? Missed filings can trigger significant penalties or even unwind your protection. Get this in writing.

"What happens if something is missed?"

Understand both the penalties and the consequences for your planning. Can errors be corrected? What's the process and cost? How does a missed filing affect the protective effectiveness of the structure? Some mistakes are easily fixed, others can be catastrophic.

"How much will ongoing compliance cost?"

You need a realistic budget for long-term maintenance. Include annual accounting fees, legal maintenance, filing fees, registered agent costs, and your own time commitment. Many people implement sophisticated planning and then can't afford to maintain it properly. Factor these costs into your decision about whether to proceed.

"Will this structure affect my tax return complexity?"

More sophisticated planning usually means more complex tax reporting. Additional schedules and forms increase preparation fees. Some structures create audit triggers. Understand how your annual tax compliance will change. If you currently do your own taxes, will you now need professional help?

Questions About Maintenance and Longevity

These questions focus on the life cycle of your plan:

"What needs to be reviewed annually?"

Asset protection planning requires ongoing attention. Insurance policies need review to ensure adequate coverage. Entity operating agreements may need updates. Trust terms should be checked against current law. Asset titling must be verified to ensure nothing has slipped out of protection. Get a clear checklist of annual maintenance tasks.

"What life changes should trigger a review?"

Major life events can invalidate planning or create new opportunities. Marriage or divorce changes your family structure and potential claims. Birth of children affects estate planning integration. Starting or selling a business changes your risk profile. Significant wealth increases may justify more sophisticated planning. Retirement or career changes alter your exposure. Moving to a different state can completely change the legal landscape.

"What is the long-term cost of keeping this plan healthy?"

Beyond compliance costs, consider ongoing legal fees for updates and reviews, accounting costs for tax planning and reporting, the administrative burden of maintaining formalities, and your time commitment. These costs accumulate year after year. Make sure you're prepared for the long haul.

"How long does this structure need to remain in place?"

Some planning is designed to be permanent. Other strategies can sunset after specific risks pass. Understanding the expected time horizon helps you evaluate whether the cost and complexity are justified. If you only need protection for five years, permanent structures may be overkill.

"What would cause you to recommend unwinding this?"

Laws change. Your circumstances evolve. Sometimes the cost exceeds the benefit. Better alternatives become available. Your advisor should be able to articulate the conditions under which they'd recommend dismantling what you've built. This shows they're thinking about your interests rather than just creating billable work.

"Who will manage this if something happens to me?"

Consider succession planning for the planning itself. Identify successor trustees or managers who can step in. Make sure family members who need to understand the structure have been educated. Create documentation that ensures continuity. Your carefully constructed protection shouldn't collapse because you become incapacitated or die.

"What happens to this structure when I die?"

Understand how asset protection planning integrates with your estate plan. Some structures create complications or conflicts with estate planning goals. Determine whether protection continues for your heirs or terminates at death. Make sure your estate planning attorney and asset protection advisor are coordinating their work.

Questions About Limitations and Boundaries

These questions define what the plan will NOT accomplish:

"What will this plan NOT protect against?"

Every strategy has limits. Asset protection generally cannot protect against fraud claims, certain types of creditors (IRS, child support, alimony), liability for your own intentional wrongdoing, or claims that arose before you implemented planning. Get a clear picture of the boundaries of your protection.

"What could cause this protection to fail?"

Understand the vulnerabilities. Operational mistakes like commingling funds or ignoring formalities can destroy protection. Fraudulent transfer challenges can unwind planning. Corporate veils can be pierced. Court orders can compel transfers. Know what could go wrong so you can avoid these pitfalls.

"What am I giving up by implementing this plan?"

Asset protection always involves tradeoffs. You may give up direct control over assets. You may sacrifice flexibility to access or sell assets quickly. You may lose simplicity in your financial life. You might give up valuable tax benefits like stepped-up basis at death. Make sure you understand what you're trading for protection.

"Are there any criminal law implications I should understand?"

The line between legal planning and illegal concealment must be crystal clear. Fraudulent conveyance can be criminal in some contexts. Tax fraud exposure is real. Understand exactly where the boundaries are. Legitimate asset protection is always transparent and compliant with disclosure requirements.

"What disclosure am I making by implementing this?"

Some structures require public filings that create a record. Privacy considerations matter to many people. Understand who will know about your planning. Some protection comes at the cost of confidentiality. Make sure you're comfortable with whatever disclosure is required.

Questions About the Advisor Relationship

These questions help you assess fit and establish clear expectations:

"How do you charge for your services?"

Understand the fee structure completely. Do they charge hourly, flat fee, or a percentage of assets? What's included in the quoted fee and what costs extra? Are there ongoing fees or just one-time charges? Get this in writing before you commit.

"Who else on your team will work on this?"

Find out whether you'll work primarily with partners, associates, or paralegals. Will you have the opportunity to interact with team members directly? How much consistency can you expect in personnel over the years? Turnover can be disruptive to complex planning.

"How often will we communicate?"

Set expectations for contact. Will you have annual reviews? As-needed contact only? What's a reasonable timeframe for responses to questions? Some clients want frequent check-ins, others prefer minimal contact. Make sure your expectations align.

"Do you work with my other advisors?"

Asset protection planning requires coordination with your CPA, financial advisor, and insurance agent. Does this advisor have a history of successful collaboration with other professionals? Are they willing to have joint meetings to ensure everyone is aligned? Lack of coordination can create expensive problems.

"Can you provide references from similar clients?"

Speaking with people in comparable situations gives you valuable insight. You can learn from their experience with this advisor. You can verify the track record. Good advisors are happy to connect you with satisfied clients who can speak to their work.

"What happens if we disagree about strategy?"

Disagreements will happen. How does this advisor handle them? Are they willing to explain patiently until you understand their reasoning? Do they respect different perspectives? Can they disagree without being disagreeable? You're entering a long-term relationship, so conflict resolution matters.

"Will you help me if I'm sued?"

Asset protection planning is different from litigation defense. Some advisors do both, others focus on planning and refer litigation to specialists. Clarify the scope of representation. Will they stand by the structures they created if they're challenged in court? Make sure you understand what's included.

Red Flag Questions: What to Watch For

Pay close attention to how advisors respond to your questions. These are warning signs:

Guarantees of outcomes: No one can guarantee you won't be sued or won't lose assets. Promises of absolute protection are either naive or dishonest. Asset protection is about improving your position, not creating invulnerability.

Pressure to act immediately: Legitimate planning doesn't require panic. If an advisor is creating artificial urgency or pressuring you to sign before you're ready, walk away. Good planning benefits from careful thought.

Reluctance to explain: If an advisor can't make their recommendations understandable to you, they may not understand them well themselves. You should be able to explain your own planning to a reasonably intelligent friend. Complexity should be necessary, not obscurantist.

Dismissiveness about risks or costs: Honest advisors acknowledge tradeoffs. They tell you what could go wrong and what the planning will really cost over time. If everything sounds perfect with no downsides, you're not getting the full picture.

Discouraging second opinions: Confidence welcomes scrutiny. Advisors who discourage you from seeking other perspectives may be hiding weaknesses in their recommendations. Good advisors encourage you to do your due diligence.

Focus on secrecy rather than legitimacy: Legal planning doesn't hide assets, it protects them. If the emphasis is on concealment, offshore accounts that "no one will know about," or similar language, you're likely heading into dangerous territory. Legitimate planning is transparent.

Single area of expertise: Asset protection intersects with tax law, estate planning, corporate law, bankruptcy law, and other areas. Advisors who only know one piece of the puzzle often miss important issues. Look for either broad expertise or strong collaboration with other specialists.

Questions to Ask Yourself After the Meeting

After you've met with an advisor, reflect on these questions before making a decision:

"Did I feel heard and understood?"

Were your specific circumstances discussed in detail? Did the advisor ask probing questions about your situation? Do you feel like they genuinely understand what you're facing and what you need? Generic advice suggests you'll get generic service.

"Do I trust this person's judgment?"

This goes beyond technical knowledge. You're looking for wisdom, experience, and the ability to guide you through difficult decisions, not just execute your instructions. Do they have the judgment to tell you things you don't want to hear?

"Was I encouraged to think critically?"

Good advisors educate their clients, they don't just issue recommendations. You should understand the "why" behind the advice, not just the "what." If you left the meeting more confused than when you arrived, that's a problem.

"Am I comfortable with the level of complexity?"

Be honest with yourself. Will you actually maintain what's being proposed? Is it proportional to your risks and assets? Simple plans that get maintained properly often outperform sophisticated plans that get neglected.

"Does this feel right?"

Sometimes instinct matters. If something feels off about the advisor or their recommendations, explore that feeling. You don't need to be able to articulate exactly what's wrong. Trust your gut. You're entering a long-term relationship that requires trust.

The Mindset That Makes Asset Protection Work

Asset protection is as much about mindset and discipline as it is about legal structures. Understanding what behaviors the process rewards and punishes will help you succeed.

Asset Protection Rewards:

Asking thoughtful questions

Curiosity is genuinely protective. The more you understand about your planning, the better you'll maintain it and the fewer mistakes you'll make.

Good questions lead to good answers, which lead to better planning. Never stop asking "why?"

Respecting complexity

Asset protection is genuinely complicated because it sits at the intersection of multiple areas of law. Simple solutions to complex problems rarely work well. This is a field where expertise matters enormously. Recognize what you don't know and get proper help.

Planning early

Time is your most valuable asset protection tool. The earlier you plan, the more options you have and the more effective those options are. Later planning is harder, more expensive, and less effective. If you're reading this before you need protection, you're already ahead.

Maintaining discipline

Following formalities consistently matters. Keeping detailed records protects you. Respecting boundaries between entities prevents piercing. Filing reports on time avoids penalties. Consistent behavior over years builds a track record that courts respect. Shortcuts create vulnerabilities.

Staying humble

No plan is perfect. Every strategy has weaknesses. Overconfidence leads to mistakes and sometimes to catastrophic failures. The willingness to acknowledge what you don't know, adjust as you learn, and take advice seriously is protective.

Thinking long-term

Asset protection is not a transaction you complete and forget. It's a commitment that requires ongoing attention for years or decades. The benefits compound over time as structures season and mature. Patient people who maintain their planning consistently get the best results.

Valuing relationships over transactions

Good advisors become long-term partners in protecting your wealth. Trust is built through multiple interactions over time. Invest in these relationships before you need them urgently. The advisor who knows you and your situation will serve you far better in a crisis.

Asset Protection Punishes:

Taking shortcuts

Cutting corners on structure to save money now creates vulnerabilities that cost far more later. Skipping steps in implementation leaves gaps. Using template solutions without customization fails to address your specific risks. Shortcuts rarely save money in the long run.

Confusing secrecy with protection

Hiding assets is not the same as protecting them. Failing to disclose when legally required can turn legal planning into criminal conduct. Privacy and concealment are completely different concepts. Legitimate planning is always transparent where transparency is required.

Overconfidence

Believing you're smarter than the courts leads to aggressive planning that fails when tested. Thinking the rules don't apply to you invites disaster. Ignoring warnings from advisors because you know better often proves expensive. Humility is protective, overconfidence is dangerous.

Procrastination

Waiting until threats appear before implementing planning usually means it's too late for the most effective strategies. "I'll deal with it later" often becomes "I wish I'd dealt with it earlier." Learning about fraudulent transfer laws only after you've made a questionable transfer doesn't help you.

Being sloppy

Ignoring corporate formalities gives creditors arguments for piercing. Commingling personal and business funds destroys entity protection. Inconsistent behavior creates evidence that can be used against you. Courts punish carelessness.

Making Asset Protection Work for You

Asset protection planning works best when you approach it as a long-term commitment to protecting what you've built. The most successful clients share common characteristics: they plan early, ask good questions, maintain their structures carefully, work with qualified advisors they trust, and stay humble about what they don't know.

If you're considering asset protection planning, start by identifying your real risks. Not theoretical risks, not generic risks, but the actual threats you face based on your profession, your assets, your activities, and your circumstances. Then find advisors who can help you address those specific risks proportionally.

Remember that the goal is not invulnerability. No plan can guarantee complete protection. The goal is to improve your position meaningfully while maintaining legitimacy, staying compliant with all legal requirements, and creating structures you can actually maintain over time.

The questions in this guide will help you find advisors who can deliver that kind of practical, sustainable protection. Use them. Good advisors welcome serious questions because they indicate you'll be a thoughtful, engaged client who takes the planning seriously.

That mindset, combined with well-designed structures and consistent maintenance, is what makes asset protection work.

Glossary of Asset Protection Terms

This glossary provides plain-English definitions of common asset protection terms used throughout this book. The goal is clarity, not technical precision. Legal definitions may vary by jurisdiction and context.

A

Alter Ego / Alter Ego Doctrine A legal theory used by courts to disregard a business entity when the owner treats it as an extension of personal affairs rather than a separate legal entity. Often cited when piercing the corporate veil. Courts look for evidence that no real separation existed between owner and entity.

Asset Protection The lawful organization of assets and activities to reduce unnecessary exposure to legal claims, creditors, and liability, implemented before problems arise. Not about hiding assets, but about using legitimate legal structures to separate risks from wealth.

Asset Protection Trust (APT) A trust designed to protect assets from creditors by separating legal ownership from beneficial use. Can be domestic (DAPT) or offshore (OAPT).

B

Bad Faith Conduct showing dishonest intent, such as creating entities or transferring assets primarily to avoid known or anticipated creditors. Courts closely scrutinize actions taken in bad faith and will often unwind such planning.

Bankruptcy A legal process that addresses insolvency and provides structured relief from debts; certain assets may be protected by exemptions. Federal and state laws determine which assets are protected.

Beneficiary A person or entity entitled to receive benefits from a trust, insurance policy, retirement account, or other arrangement. In asset protection trusts, the grantor may also be a beneficiary.

Beneficial Owner The person who ultimately owns or controls an asset, even if title is held in another name or entity. Courts look to beneficial ownership when determining true control, regardless of how paperwork is structured.

Burden of Proof The obligation to prove one's case in legal proceedings. In asset protection contexts, some jurisdictions require creditors to prove fraudulent transfer by "clear and convincing evidence" (a higher standard) rather than "preponderance of the evidence" (the normal civil standard).

C

C-Corporation A corporation taxed as a separate entity under Subchapter C of the Internal Revenue Code, resulting in potential double taxation (once at the corporate level, once when distributed to shareholders). Used for larger businesses or those planning to raise capital.

Capitalization The amount of money or assets contributed to an entity when it's formed and during operations. Adequate capitalization shows the entity was created for legitimate business purposes. Undercapitalization can lead to veil piercing.

Charging Order A creditor remedy that allows the creditor to receive distributions from an LLC or partnership interest if and when distributions are made, without seizing entity assets or gaining management rights. In strong protection states, this may be the creditor's exclusive remedy.

Civil Liability Legal responsibility arising from lawsuits between private parties (as opposed to criminal prosecution), often involving monetary damages. The primary risk that asset protection planning addresses.

Commingling The improper mixing of personal and business funds or assets, which can undermine liability protection and support veil-piercing claims. One of the most common and fatal mistakes in asset protection planning.

Contempt of Court A finding that someone has disobeyed or disrespected a court's authority. Failing to comply with court orders regarding asset disclosure or repatriation can result in fines or imprisonment.

Contingency Fee A legal fee structure where an attorney is paid only if a claim succeeds, typically as a percentage of recovery. Common in U.S. plaintiff's litigation but prohibited or impractical in many offshore jurisdictions.

Contingent Liability A potential obligation that depends on the occurrence of a future event, such as a lawsuit that has not yet been filed. Asset protection planning should address contingent as well as actual liabilities.

Corporate Formalities The legal requirements for operating a corporation or LLC properly, including holding meetings, keeping minutes, maintaining separate records, and documenting major decisions. Failure to observe formalities can lead to veil piercing.

Corporate Veil The legal separation between an entity and its owners that protects owners from personal liability. Can be "pierced" when courts determine the entity was improperly maintained or used fraudulently.

Creditor A person or entity with a legal right to collect a debt, judgment, or obligation from another party. Includes judgment holders, lenders, government agencies, ex-spouses owed support, and anyone seeking payment for alleged harm.

D

Debtor A person or entity who owes money or is subject to a legal claim. In asset protection planning, you are the debtor seeking to protect assets from potential future creditors.

Deep Pockets / Deep Pockets Doctrine The practical reality that plaintiffs often pursue defendants perceived to have substantial assets or insurance coverage, regardless of actual fault. High-net-worth individuals and visible wealth holders face increased litigation risk for this reason.

Disregarded Entity An entity ignored for federal tax purposes. A single-member LLC is typically treated as a disregarded entity, with all income flowing to the owner's personal tax return. This doesn't affect liability protection.

Domestic Asset Protection Trust (DAPT) A self-settled trust created under the laws of certain U.S. states (Alaska, Delaware, Nevada, South Dakota, Wyoming, Tennessee, and others) that may limit creditor access to trust assets. Effectiveness may vary if challenged in other states.

Duress Clause A trust provision preventing distributions if the trustee is pressured by a court or creditor. Common in offshore trusts to resist court orders compelling repatriation of assets.

E

Entity A legally recognized structure such as an LLC or corporation that exists separately from its owners and can own property, enter contracts, and be sued independently of its owners.

Equity The value of an asset after subtracting liabilities (for example, property value minus mortgage balance). What creditors can potentially reach after secured debts are satisfied.

ERISA (Employee Retirement Income Security Act) A federal law governing most employer-sponsored retirement plans (401(k), 403(b), pension plans), providing strong creditor protection both in and outside bankruptcy.

Errors and Omissions Insurance (E&O) Professional liability insurance covering claims arising from alleged mistakes, negligence, or failures in professional services. Also called malpractice insurance.

Estate Planning The process of arranging for management and distribution of assets after death. Related to but distinct from asset protection, which focuses on creditor protection during life.

Exemption / Exempt Assets Assets protected by law from certain creditors, such as retirement accounts or homestead-protected residences, depending on jurisdiction. Statutory protections that don't require special planning structures.

F

FATCA (Foreign Account Tax Compliance Act) U.S. law requiring foreign financial institutions to report accounts held by U.S. persons to the IRS. Also requires U.S. taxpayers to report foreign assets on Form 8938. Severe penalties for non-compliance.

FBAR (Foreign Bank Account Report) FinCEN Form 114, required when U.S. persons have foreign financial accounts exceeding $10,000 in aggregate at any point during the year. Filed separately from tax returns with severe penalties for non-compliance.

Foreclosure Legal process by which a creditor takes possession of property used as collateral. In asset protection contexts, some states allow creditors to foreclose on LLC ownership interests; others limit creditors to charging orders.

Fraudulent Transfer (Fraudulent Conveyance) A transfer of assets made to hinder, delay, or defraud creditors, or made for less than fair value while a claim exists or is foreseeable. Such transfers can be undone by courts. The single most important concept in understanding timing requirements.

G

Garnishment / Wage Garnishment A court-ordered seizure of a portion of future income or bank account funds to satisfy a judgment. Federal law limits wage garnishment to 25% of disposable earnings; many states provide greater protection.

General Liability Insurance Insurance covering bodily injury, property damage, and certain personal injury claims arising from ordinary business operations. The foundation of business insurance planning.

Grantor The person who creates and funds a trust. Also called settlor or trustor. In asset protection trusts, grantors often retain some beneficial interest while transferring legal control.

Grantor Trust A trust where the grantor retains certain powers, causing income to be taxed to the grantor rather than the trust. Many DAPTs are grantor trusts for tax purposes while still providing creditor protection.

H

Homestead Exemption A state-law protection that shields some or all equity in a primary residence from certain creditor claims. Ranges from unlimited (Florida, Texas) to minimal (some states cap at $5,000 to $25,000).

I

Indemnification A contractual obligation to cover another party's losses or liabilities, which can create exposure beyond insurance coverage. Personal guarantees are a form of indemnification that pierce entity protection.

Independent Trustee A trustee with no personal interest in trust assets, required in many asset protection structures. Critical for offshore trusts and DAPTs to maintain creditor protection.

Insolvency A financial condition where liabilities exceed assets or debts cannot be paid as they come due. Transfers made while insolvent are often deemed fraudulent even without intent to defraud.

Insurance Coverage Limits The maximum amount an insurance policy will pay for a covered claim. Amounts beyond the limit become the insured's personal responsibility. Understanding policy limits is critical because excess verdicts can reach personal assets.

Intent A critical factor courts evaluate when determining whether asset protection planning is legitimate or designed to evade creditors. Timing and circumstances surrounding transfers reveal intent.

International Business Company (IBC) A foreign company often used for holding assets or operating internationally. Common in offshore jurisdictions.

IRA (Individual Retirement Account) Tax-advantaged retirement account with varying levels of creditor protection depending on state law. Generally strong protection but not as absolute as ERISA-qualified plans.

Irrevocable Trust A trust that generally cannot be changed or revoked once created. Most asset protection trusts must be irrevocable because creditors can reach assets in revocable trusts.

J

Judgment A court's final determination of liability and damages, creating enforceable collection rights for the prevailing party. Once entered, judgment creditors can use various collection tools including garnishment, liens, and asset seizure.

Judgment Creditor A creditor who has obtained a court judgment against a debtor. Has enhanced collection powers compared to creditors without judgments.

Jurisdiction The legal authority under which laws apply, often determined by geography. In asset protection, determines which state's or country's laws govern your structures and what power courts have over assets.

Jurisdiction Shopping Selecting the jurisdiction whose laws will govern legal structures based on favorable provisions. Common and legal when done for legitimate purposes before claims arise.

L

Landlord Insurance Specialized property insurance for rental properties, covering liability, property damage, and loss of rental income. Different from standard homeowners insurance.

Layering Using multiple asset protection strategies together so that failure of one does not expose all assets. The foundation of effective asset protection planning.

Liability Legal responsibility for harm, loss, or damage suffered by another party. The risk that asset protection planning seeks to manage and contain.

Liability Shield The protection afforded by entity structures preventing business liabilities from reaching personal assets. Works in one direction: business debts can't reach personal assets, but personal debts may reach business interests.

Lien A legal claim against property to secure payment of a debt. Types include mortgage liens, tax liens, mechanic's liens, and judgment liens.

Limited Liability The legal principle that owners of certain entities are not personally responsible for the entity's debts or liabilities, subject to exceptions like personal guarantees, veil piercing, and personal wrongdoing.

Limited Liability Company (LLC) A flexible business entity that can separate personal assets from business liabilities when properly formed and maintained. The most popular entity for small businesses and real estate due to flexibility and pass-through taxation.

Lookback Period The timeframe during which transfers can be challenged as fraudulent. Varies by jurisdiction: typically 2 years in bankruptcy for intentional fraud, 4 to 6 years under state fraudulent transfer statutes.

M

Malpractice / Malpractice Insurance Professional negligence that falls below the accepted standard of care, often giving rise to high-value claims. Malpractice insurance covers such claims for doctors, lawyers, accountants, and other licensed professionals.

Management Company An entity used to manage operations while separating assets from risk. Can employ professionals and provide services to operating entities.

Member An owner of a limited liability company. The LLC equivalent of a shareholder in a corporation.

Multi-Member LLC An LLC with two or more owners. Generally receives stronger charging order protection than single-member LLCs because creditors cannot harm innocent co-owners.

N

Nominee A person or entity listed as owner in name only; often risky and legally problematic if misused. Using nominees to hide ownership is illegal and considered fraudulent.

Non-Recourse Debt A loan where the lender can only take the collateral upon default and cannot pursue the borrower personally for any deficiency. Contrast with recourse debt where borrowers remain personally liable.

O

Offshore Asset Protection Trust (OAPT) A trust established under foreign law (Cook Islands, Nevis, Belize) designed to provide enhanced creditor protection through jurisdictional resistance.

Operating Agreement A governing document outlining ownership, management, and financial rules of an LLC. Critical for credibility, demonstrating the LLC is legitimate and properly operated.

P

Pass-Through Taxation Tax treatment where business income "passes through" to owners' personal tax returns rather than being taxed at the entity level. Applies to LLCs, S-corporations, and partnerships.

Personal Guarantee An agreement making an individual personally responsible for business debts, often negating entity-level protection. Should be minimized or avoided when possible.

Phantom Income Income attributed to a taxpayer without actual cash distribution. Relevant with charging orders: creditors may owe taxes on LLC income without receiving distributions, creating settlement pressure.

Piercing the Corporate Veil (Veil Piercing) A court's decision to hold owners personally liable because the entity was misused, undercapitalized, or treated as an alter ego. Destroys the liability shield that entities are designed to provide.

Plaintiff The party who initiates a lawsuit seeking damages or other relief. In asset protection contexts, the person or entity making claims against you.

Premises Liability Liability arising from injuries occurring on property due to unsafe conditions or failure to warn. Common source of landlord and business owner liability.

Professional Liability Legal exposure arising from licensed or fiduciary services, often exceeding general insurance coverage. Includes malpractice, errors and omissions, and breach of professional duties.

Protective Jurisdiction A jurisdiction with laws favorable to asset protection, such as states with strong charging order protection or offshore jurisdictions with debtor-friendly trust laws.

Q

QDRO (Qualified Domestic Relations Order) A court order in divorce proceedings dividing retirement plan benefits between spouses. One of the few ways retirement accounts can be accessed despite creditor protections.

R

Registered Agent A person or business designated to receive legal documents and official correspondence on behalf of an LLC or corporation. Required in the state where the entity is formed.

Remedy Legal means of enforcing a right or correcting a wrong. Creditor remedies include charging orders, foreclosure, garnishment, and liens, varying by asset type and jurisdiction.

Reporting Requirements Mandatory disclosures to tax or regulatory authorities regarding assets, entities, or accounts. Critical for offshore planning (FBAR, FATCA) and domestic entities (tax returns, information returns).

Retirement Account Tax-advantaged savings vehicle such as a 401(k) or IRA, often protected by statute from creditors. One of the strongest asset protection tools available.

Revocable Trust A trust that can be modified or terminated by the grantor during lifetime. Offers no asset protection because grantor retains complete control. Used primarily for estate planning and probate avoidance.

Risk Profile The combination of activities, assets, income, and exposure that determines how vulnerable a person is to legal claims. Drives asset protection strategy selection more than net worth alone.

S

S-Corporation A corporation electing pass-through taxation under Subchapter S of the Internal Revenue Code. Avoids double taxation while maintaining corporate structure. Has restrictions on number and type of shareholders.

Self-Settled Trust A trust where the creator (grantor) is also a beneficiary. Traditionally provided no creditor protection, but DAPT states now allow self-settled trusts with protection under specific conditions.

Series LLC A specialized LLC structure where one parent LLC establishes multiple legally separate "series," each holding different assets. Useful for multiple properties while limiting cross-liability. Allowed in some states.

Settlor Another term for grantor or trustor, the person who creates and funds a trust.

Single-Member LLC An LLC with only one owner. Often receives weaker charging order protection than multi-member LLCs in many states.

Sole Proprietorship A business owned by one person with no legal separation between business and personal assets, maximum exposure. Offers no liability protection whatsoever.

Spendthrift Clause A trust provision restricting a beneficiary's creditors from reaching trust assets and preventing beneficiaries from transferring their interests. Standard in most trusts.

Statute of Limitations The time period within which a lawsuit must be filed or a legal right exercised. Expiration bars legal claims. Offshore jurisdictions often have shorter statutes of limitation than the U.S., creating additional creditor barriers.

Statutory Protection Asset protection created by law rather than contract or structure. Examples include homestead exemptions, retirement account protections, and wage garnishment limits.

Structure The legal arrangement of ownership, entities, insurance, and asset placement that determines how liability flows and which assets are exposed to which risks.

T

Tail Coverage Insurance covering claims made after a policy expires for incidents occurring during the policy period. Critical for professionals who may face claims years after providing services.

Tenancy by the Entirety A form of property ownership available only to married couples in some states. Each spouse owns the entire property. Creditors of only one spouse generally cannot reach property held this way.

Trust A legal arrangement where one person (trustee) holds legal title to property for the benefit of others (beneficiaries). Serves many purposes including estate planning, asset protection, and wealth management.

Trust Protector An individual with limited oversight authority over a trust, such as replacing trustees. Common in asset protection trusts to provide oversight without grantor retaining control that would compromise protection.

Trustee The person or entity holding legal title to trust property and managing it according to trust terms for beneficiaries. In asset protection trusts, must be independent from the grantor.

U

Umbrella Liability Insurance / Umbrella Liability Policy Insurance providing excess liability coverage above standard home, auto, or rental policies. Relatively inexpensive way to add $1 to 5 million or more in liability protection.

Undercapitalization Failure to provide an entity with sufficient funds to operate realistically, often cited in veil-piercing cases. Shows the entity was created as a shell rather than for legitimate business purposes.

V

Veil Piercing / Veil Piercing Factors See Piercing the Corporate Veil. Common indicators courts consider include commingling, lack of records, personal use of business funds, inadequate capitalization, and failure to observe formalities.

W

Wage Garnishment See Garnishment.

Wildcard Exemption A statutory exemption that can be applied to any type of property chosen by the debtor. Not available in all states. Useful for protecting assets that don't fit other exemption categories.

Workers' Compensation Insurance Insurance covering medical costs and lost wages for employees injured on the job. Generally required by law for businesses with employees. Protects employers from most employee injury lawsuits.

Worst-Case Planning Planning based on low-probability but high-impact events. Asset protection balances worst-case planning with proportionality to avoid excessive cost and complexity.

Final Note

Terms in asset protection often sound intimidating. Most represent simple ideas: separation, timing, jurisdiction, and discipline. Understanding the language removes fear, worry or stress, and allows you to plan clearly and responsibly.

Key Principles Across All Terms:

- **Timing matters more than sophistication.** Early planning beats complex late planning.
- **Structure requires maintenance.** Entities and trusts only work when properly operated.
- **Transparency is required.** Legal asset protection works within the law, not around it.
- **Layering provides resilience.** Multiple tools working together are stronger than any single strategy.
- **Proportionality is essential.** Protection should match your actual risks and resources.
- **Intent is scrutinized.** Courts look beyond paperwork to determine whether planning was done in good faith.

This glossary provides the vocabulary for informed asset protection planning. Use these terms with confidence when speaking with advisors, but always remember that understanding concepts matters more than memorizing any terminology. The goal is not to sound sophisticated. It's to think clearly about risk, structure, and protection.

About the Author

Ngozi E. Bolin, Esq. brings more than three decades of extensive legal and litigation experience to this comprehensive guide on consumer rights and protection. With a distinguished career spanning multiple jurisdictions and legal disciplines, Ms. Bolin offers readers the benefit of deep legal knowledge, strategic insight, and practical courtroom wisdom grounded in real-world practice.

Educated under the British Commonwealth legal system and having studied at the Harvard Extension School, Ms. Bolin brings a uniquely global perspective to the law. Her international legal career began with her admission as a Barrister and Solicitor of the Supreme Court of Nigeria in 1989. She later relocated to the United States, where she was admitted to the New York State Bar in 1991, the United States Court of Appeals for the Second Circuit, and the California State Bar in 2013.

Throughout her career as a seasoned trial attorney, Ms. Bolin has been committed to making legal knowledge more accessible and affordable. She has been a strong advocate of unbundled legal services, empowering consumers to better understand the legal system and assert their rights with confidence. Her practice has encompassed a broad range of areas, including consumer protection, personal injury, employment law, unfair business practices, real estate, bankruptcy, probate, and insurance disputes.

Ms. Bolin has successfully negotiated and litigated numerous cases, consistently emphasizing fair settlements and practical outcomes for her clients. Her professional record includes participation in significant cases such as *Louis Capital Markets, LP v. Refco Group Ltd., LLC, et al.* (9 Misc.3d 283, 801 N.Y.S.2d 490, N.Y. Co. 2005), addressing issues of corporate misconduct and fiduciary duties; *Giordano v. Thomson, et al.* (438 F. Supp. 2d 35, E.D.N.Y. 2005); and *Davis v. Commercial Bank of New York* (275 F. Supp. 2d 418, S.D.N.Y. 2003), involving employee benefits and unjust enrichment.

Through her writing and legal work, Ms. Bolin continues to bridge the gap between complex legal principles and the everyday concerns of consumers, offering guidance that is both authoritative and practical.

Made in United States
Orlando, FL
04 November 2026

90209056R00212